SUSTAINING THE REGIME

North Korea's Quest for Financial Support

I0027909

Robert Daniel Wallace

University Press of America,® Inc.
Lanham · Boulder · New York · Toronto · Plymouth, UK

Copyright © 2007 by
University Press of America,® Inc.
4501 Forbes Boulevard
Suite 200
Lanham, Maryland 20706
UPA Acquisitions Department (301) 459-3366

Estover Road
Plymouth PL6 7PY
United Kingdom

Library of Congress Control Number: 2006933308
ISBN-13: 978-0-7618-3614-8 (paperback : alk. paper)
ISBN-10: 0-7618-3614-4 (paperback : alk. paper)

The views expressed in this book are those of the author and
do not reflect the official policy or position of the
Department of Defense or the US Government.

♾™The paper used in this publication meets the minimum
requirements of American National Standard for Information
Sciences—Permanence of Paper for Printed Library Materials,
ANSI Z39.48—1984

To my wife and daughters for providing
love, perspective, and purpose.

Contents

List of Graphics

Figures

Map

Tables

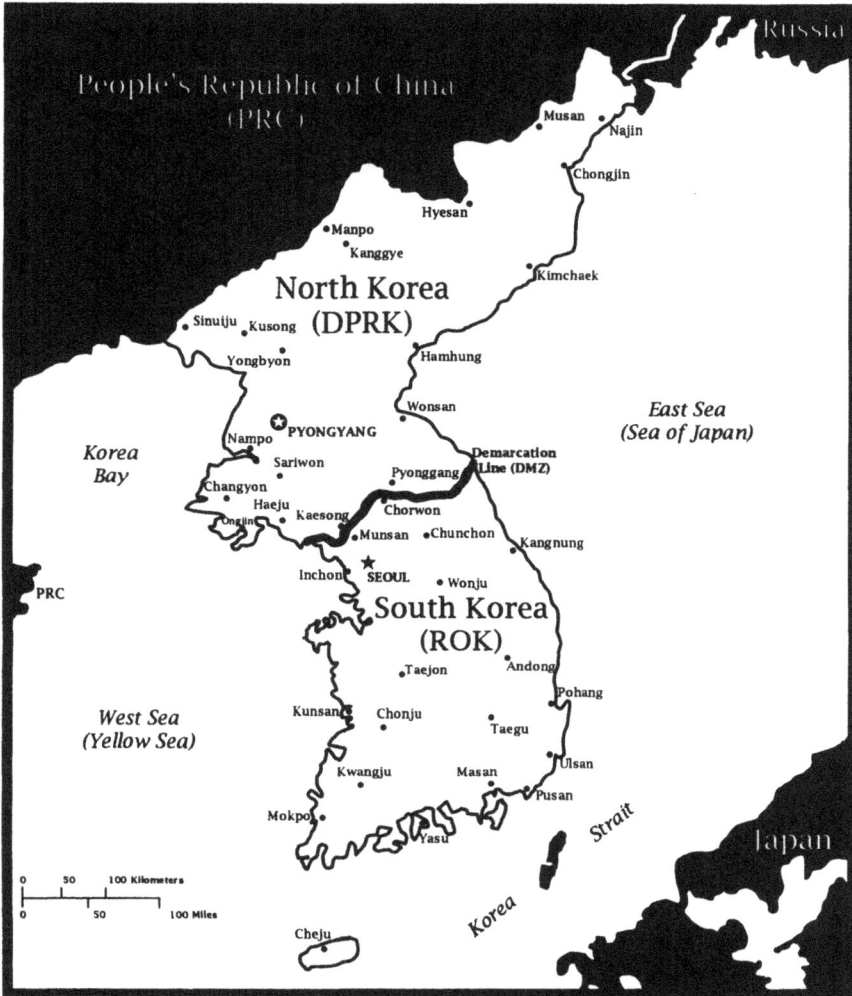

Map 1. Korean Peninsula

Adapted from Central Intelligence Agency, "Korea Peninsula Map,"
University of Texas Libraries Online, 1993,
www.lib.utexas.edu/maps/middle_east_and_asia/korean_peninsula.gif,
accessed 20 January 2005

Preface

My interest in the Korean peninsula began with an assignment to the 2nd Infantry Division in Uijongbu, Republic of Korea (ROK) as an intelligence officer with the US Army. I arrived in 1995 and began work while the first Korean nuclear crisis was ending. After spending almost three years on the peninsula, I began to understand and appreciate the uniqueness of the area and its people who live in the constant and unpredictable shadow of the North Korea.

In 1997, I solidified my ties to the ROK by marrying the former Yonghui Yi, whose family, like almost all others in South Korea, had personally experienced both the Japanese occupation and war with the North. After introducing her to my home in Kansas, we returned to South Korea in 2002 and I worked as an intelligence analyst in Seoul. This second adventure on the peninsula gave me unique insight into the predictably cyclic nature of North Korea's political and military activities, leadership decisionmaking attributes, and uncompromising efforts to remain intact. During this tour in South Korea, I was nominated for and accepted to the Joint Military Intelligence College (JMIC) in Washington, DC.

The resulting yearlong adventure at DIA allowed me to reflect on my time in South Korea and conduct research on intelligence-related issues worthy of attention. The inspirations for this text are these cumulative experiences in South Korea and at JMIC and this effort could not have been possible without the support of my family, colleagues, and friends. These include my supervisors and peers while stationed in South Korea, Dr. Perry Pickert and Lieutenant Colonel Peter Read at JMIC, Dr. Katy Oh from the Brookings Institution, and the patient help of many others at the Joint Military Intelligence College and the Defense Intelligence Agency.

Robert Daniel Wallace

July 1, 2006
Seoul

Chapter 1

North Korea and the Quest for Support

> We never asked questions. . . . We thought we were showing our loyalty to
> Kim Jong-il. We thought he would use the money to improve our lives.
> —*North Korean defector, quoted by*
> *Anthony Spaeth in "Kim's Rackets."*

As one of the only remaining communist nations, North Korea stands apart in
the world as a truly unique and dangerous country. Over the past 30 years, North
Korea has endured a significant downturn in its economy, a countrywide famine,
and continued hostilities with South Korea, Japan, and the United States. The
economic failure of North Korea's government has continued and despite internal changes and massive external assistance, Pyongyang is currently ex-
periencing its tenth straight year of food shortages. While the future of Democratic People's Republic of Korea (DPRK)[1] remains bleak, Kim Jong-il retains
firm control over the nation and the elite of the nation continue to live well. To
compensate for its market failures, resistance to change, and focus on national
defense, the Kim regime's bizarre "cult of personality" government[2] has resorted
to extreme efforts to obtain hard currency cash flows. These cash flows help
Kim retain his key supporters, the North Korean elite class and military, who
enjoy an infinitely higher standard of living than the common citizens.

North Korea's methods of obtaining hard currency fall into two categories:
overt and covert activities. The overt efforts include cash obtained through conventional weapons sales and arms technology transfers, remittances from overseas Koreans, humanitarian aid diversion, and overseas trade and banking activities. The covert activities include illegal actions such as narcotics production and
trafficking and counterfeit money operations. North Korea's efforts to raise hard
currency in this manner indicate its willingness to use any method, regardless of
legality, to maintain cash inflows to support the regime. Pyongyang's efforts in
these areas date back to the very beginnings of North Korea as a state and have
become both institutionalized and increasingly sophisticated, making detection
and interdiction by affected nations extremely difficult.

While these fundraising efforts pose a limited direct threat to other states,
the most important aspect of these overt and covert funding activities is that *they
provide essential support for the survival of North Korea as a sovereign state*. A
number of analysts have attempted to explain parts of this funding puzzle, but an
all-encompassing review of these sources and an analysis of the relative impor-

tance of these activities has yet to be published. Identifying the characteristics of these funding sources and relative value to the regime will help provide clearer outlines of this key aspect of support for the North Korean government.

This book will describe the background, sources, and methods of North Korean hard currency fundraising, assess the role of illegal components of the effort in supporting the regime, and discuss the overall implications for the United States. The text is divided into five chapters and relies solely on unclassified information available from US and international sources.

This first chapter introduces the issue by examining the historical background of the peninsula to include the domestic and international forces and events that influenced the founding of North Korea and their contribution to its current economic crisis. Additionally, this chapter reviews available open source literature on the role of hard currency support to the regime.

The second chapter provides an overview of the evolution of North Korea's economic deterioration resulting in hard currency shortfalls and the development of overt activities to compensate for cash deficits including preferential trade and aid from the Soviet Union and China, weapons and technology transfers, and diversion of humanitarian aid from the West.

Chapter three examines North Korea's clandestine activities to raise funds to include support from Koreans living overseas, drug production, smuggling, and counterfeiting operations. The fourth chapter discusses Bureau 39, the organization which controls most of the DPRK's clandestine fundraising efforts. The last chapter discusses the research findings, implications for the United States, and suggests issues for further research.

Shaped By Conflict

North Korea presents itself to the world in a constant state of volatility: current crises include the ongoing nuclear issue, widespread famine and hunger, political prisoners, defectors, and the cult of personality surrounding Kim Jong-il and his modern Asian dynasty. On the surface, these aspects of North Korean society seem disjointed, incongruent, and inexplicable. How can a society over 3,000 years old develop into the first "communist dynasty" in the history of the world, and manage to retain that title through every imaginable catastrophe? The answer lies in the stalwart nature of the Korean people who have developed the ability to weather invasions, occupations, and catastrophic actions, sometimes of their own making.

Considering the terrain, climate, size, and location of Korea in relation to its neighbors is helpful in any discussion of conflicts in the region. Modern day North and South Korea have the combined area of almost 84,000 square miles, which equates roughly to the size of the US state of Utah. Compared to its immediate neighbors, unified Korea has historically stood as the smallest nation in

East Asia and sits juxtaposed between China (over 9 million square miles total area) and Russia (17 million square miles) to the north, and Japan (375,000 square miles) to the east.[3]

By examining these issues, we can begin to grasp the environment that has both surrounded and shaped the development of both North and South Korea. Although the modern state of North Korea was the result of civil war during the 1950s, its societal characteristics, government, and even its foreign policy have been influenced by the turbulence on the peninsula since 400 B.C. To understand North Korea, analysts must consider the development of Korea throughout the ages, the influence of its neighbors and the West, and the constant disorder that helped make this oppressive but extremely hardy nation what it is today.

Ancient Korea

Korea's modern civilization can be traced to the formation of clan societies on the peninsula between 4000 and 2000 B.C. with strong links to developments in China. The advent of Korea's Bronze Age, around 800 B.C., saw the emergence of a distinctly Korean culture characterized by rice farming, a defined social order, territoriality, and ritualistic tombs and burials.[4] By 400 B.C., Korean society had become populated with city-states that provided protection while demanding fealty from the local peasant population. The nearby Chinese states interacted with the Koreans both in commerce and in competition, often resulting in conflicts between these groups.

The first true unification of the peninsula occurred in A.D. 930, when armies from the Korean state of Koguryo defeated the rival Silla and Paekche kingdoms. The name of this new dynasty was shortened to Koryo with its capital situated in the middle of the country at Kaesong.[5] This era saw the rise of trade with China and the peaceful coexistence of Buddhism and Confucianism. Nearly 300 years later, the rising Mongols in Manchuria launched their first invasion of Korea in 1231, resulting in the eventual downfall of the Koryo dynasty. In 1254, the Mongols captured over 200,000 Koreans and forced the Koryo government to adhere to Mongol rule. Although the dynasty lasted for another 100 years, it was ruled effectively under the watchful eye of the Mongol leadership.[6]

During the next century, Korea's Choson Dynasty drove out the Mongol rulers by forming an alliance with the Ming Dynasty in China. The new state was reminiscent of the old Choson kingdom that existed over 1,500 years before and chose Seoul as its capital.[7] In 1636, the Manchus invaded from the north as part of their bid to overthrow the Ming Dynasty. Koryo surrendered, but retained its sovereignty under the system of tribute of the new Manchu Qing Dynasty (1644–1911).[8]

During this period, Korea developed as a sovereign nation and experienced an era of relative peace and cultural transformation. The next 250 years saw "a new self-confidence that manifested itself in philosophy, politics, history, and the arts and in an increased openness to new and foreign ideas and technologies."[9] Economic progress was characterized by new methods of planting rice that increased harvests and the development of commercial crops to include tobacco, cotton, and ginseng resulted in a new class of Korean entrepreneurs.[10] Yet the progress of this period soon gave way to gradual change in Korean society, due to corruption and negative influences from the West and Japan; these factors resulting in the eventual decline of the Choson Dynasty.

Modern Influences and Decline

In the early 1800s, Korea experienced decreases in agricultural production resulting in large numbers of peasants taking to the mountains to conduct "slash and burn" farming.[11] Additionally, the entire century was filled with war throughout the East Asia region. After witnessing China's experience during the Opium Wars from 1839–1842, Korea attempted to close its borders to the outside world and remained militarily unprepared to deal with conflict either from domestic uprisings or outside attack.[12] But the peninsula did experience some contact with the West and this period included encounters and small-scale armed conflicts with both the French in 1866 and United States in 1871. The Koreans repelled both incursions deterring further contact; in fact, the limited nature of the French and US attacks "left the Koreans with the illusion that they had defeated the West."[13]

This period also saw the rise of anti-Westernism and the advent of the Tonghak or "Eastern Learning" religion. Tonghak included elements of Confucianism, Buddhism, Taoism, Catholicism, and Korean Shamanism and advocated equality for all humans and reform of corrupt government officials.[14] In the 1860s, the Tonghak Movement began to spread throughout Korea in response to worsening conditions for the commoners, to include rising prices and increasing taxes. Several droughts exacerbated the situation and through the 1890s, demonstrations and rebellions were common throughout the land.[15]

Occupation and Division

In 1876, while most of the world was oblivious to activities on the Korean peninsula, Japan began to consider options for expansion and, through military and diplomatic pressure, forced Korea to sign the Treaty of Kanghwa opening three domestic ports to Japanese merchant ships. After the treaty was signed, Korea began to see an influx of Western traders, merchants, and diplomats. In the 1890s, Japan's influence over the peninsula grew and, in reaction, the Tonghak Movement spurred popular rebellion throughout Korea in 1894. In reaction to the uprisings, both China and Japan sent troops to the peninsula and the conflict soon erupted into the Sino-Japanese War of 1894–1895.

Japan defeated both the Tonghak and the Chinese armies and declared Korea independent, ending the centuries old Korean-Chinese relationship. Tokyo used this pretext to send troops into Seoul, taking control of the royal palace and forcing Korea's King Kojong to appoint many pro-Japanese officials. These officials enacted over 200 new laws based on the Japanese system of government and included provisions for "Japanese advisors in every ministry."[16]

Japan's New Colony

Beginning in 1905, Japan laid the groundwork for its complete "colonization" of the peninsula. One of the recently signed decrees, the Korea Protectorate Treaty of 1905, effectively allowed for Japan's control over the peninsula and provided for a "Japanese resident-general who would be de facto ruler of the country."[17] In 1910, Japan used anti-occupation guerilla incidents to tighten its grip on the country by suspending newspaper publication, dissolving Korean patriotic organizations, and arresting dissident leaders.[18] At that time, Japan officially annexed Korea, ending the rule of the 500-year-old Choson dynasty. This marked the beginning of an era that witnessed deliberate Japanese efforts to eradicate Korean's historic social, political, and cultural characteristics from the peninsula.

Cultural Assimilation

The Japanese chose to replace Korea's ancient societal and government systems and culture with their own, which caused both resentment and conflict among the Koreans. In fact,

> The Japanese engaged not in creation but in substitution after 1910: substituting a Japanese ruling elite for the Korean yangban scholar-officials, colonial imperative coordination for the old central state administration, Japanese modern education for Confucian classics, Japanese capital and expertise for the budding Korean version, Japanese talent for Korean talent, and eventually, the Japanese language for Korea. Koreans never thanked the Japanese. . . . Koreans never saw Japanese rule as anything but illegitimate and humiliating.[19]

During this same time, Korean-language newspaper publications all but disappeared, public assembly without a permit was forbidden, and the police carefully watched individuals or groups considered threatening to Japanese rule.[20] Changes were made to the education system to help Koreans be "good citizens of the Japanese empire" and included government control of school materials and lessons on Japanese culture, society, and language.[21]

For ordinary Koreans, the situation continued to deteriorate as Tokyo continued to demand more social and political acquiescence from the Koreans and the late 1930s saw heightened efforts to destroy the indigenous Korean society and local culture. The following timeline illustrates the "progressive" changes levied on the Koreans by the Japanese authorities:

1937	Mandatory periodic worshiping at Shinto shrines
1937	Loyalty pledges to the Japanese emperor required at public gatherings
1938	Korean language eliminated and use of Japanese in all public places
1938	Korean youth volunteers allowed into the Japanese army
1939	Koreans pressured to adopt Japanese family and personal names
1940	Remaining Korean language newspapers ceased publication
1943	Koreans conscripted into the Japanese Army[22]

Hopes for Self-Determination

Even before the Japanese surrender in 1945, the world powers expressed interest in the fate of the Korean peninsula. Although during two international conferences (Cairo in 1943 and Yalta in 1945) the United States pledged to guard the sovereign nature of Korea, there were no actual agreements among the great powers on the future of the peninsula. Sensing their inevitable defeat at the end of World War II, Japanese authorities in Korea began to institute a caretaker government staffed by pro-Japanese Koreans.[23] Near the end of the war, the Soviets invaded Manchuria and liberated much of the Korean peninsula, which caused immediate concern for American leaders who were wary of communist post-war annexations. In light of the Soviet's hasty advance, American planners in Washington hurriedly decided on the 38th parallel as the dividing line between US and Soviet spheres of control. Although no Korean experts were consulted, this plan was quickly presented to the USSR.[24] The Soviets agreed and occupied the northern half of the peninsula; nearly three weeks later, American troops arrived from Okinawa. Within a few weeks, over 25,000 US troops occupied the southern part of the peninsula.[25]

This period held high expectations for the Koreans. They saw the defeat of the Japanese as an end to the repressive period of occupation and their civilian leadership quickly formed an interim government. Unfortunately, both the Soviets and United States saw Korea as a "trustee state" and, after taking control of separate geographic areas, began to shape Korea according to their own political ideologies. There were intense disagreements among the Koreans themselves on how to proceed after the lengthy Japanese occupation. Stuek observed that "Koreans in 1945 were deeply split among themselves – between close collaborators with the Japanese and underground dissenters; between landowner and peasants; between businessmen and factory workers; between police and civilians."[26]

At this same time, most of the nearly 2.4 million ethnic Koreans in Japan began returning home and by 1947, only 600,000 remained.[27] Those Koreans who elected to remain in Japan continued to be treated as resident aliens. Organizations in Japan were established to promote the culture and rights of the resident Koreans. The most significant of which was the *Choren*, established in

1945 by ethnic Koreans living in Japan to provide and administrative body to deal with "repatriation and economic aid for needy Koreans."[28]

Two Koreas Declare Independence

Although the US and Soviet Union met in 1946 and 1947 to set up a national interim Korean government, as agreed to at the Yalta Conference, both sides failed to agree how to proceed.[29] In August 1948, the US-backed Republic of Korea (ROK) declared itself a sovereign nation and was followed by the Soviet-supported Democratic People's Republic of Korea's (DPRK) announcement of its independence in September of the same year.[30] A United Nations-sponsored commission was established in 1947 to hold peninsula-wide elections but after Pyongyang's refusal to participate and American insistence to move forward, elections were only held in the ROK during the following year.[31] South Korea held "peninsula-wide" elections in May 1948 and chose long-time expatriate Syngman Rhee, 70 years old at the time of his election, as its leader. In the North, 34-year-old Kim Il-sung was named premier. Soviet troops left the peninsula at the end of 1948 and after American troops were removed in 1949, the Korean peninsula became host to two separate countries.

Reunification of the two Koreas became the stated goal of both governments. There is considerable evidence that President Rhee would have invaded the DPRK in 1949 if he had gained US backing, but neither the US nor Soviet Union were interested in war on the Korean peninsula.[32] During the same period, the DPRK's Kim Il-sung began actively lobbying both the Soviets and China for assistance to invade the South, first broaching the idea to Stalin in 1949 and then later to China's Mao Zedong in 1950. Without Soviet and Chinese backing, Kim knew he could not effectively unify the peninsula.[33]

The Making of North Korea

Kim Il-sung's plan to reunite the peninsula by military means was dependent on Soviet support in terms of weapons and training, and he was confident of Chinese support if things went poorly.[34] The offensive was conducted with extensive knowledge of Southern defenses and weak points along routes, which continue, to this day, to be the assumed avenues of North Korean invasion.[35] Although the DPRK forces quickly swept down the peninsula past Seoul, Kim was surprised by the rapid commitment of American forces and UN support to South Korea. North Korea failed to drive United Nations forces from the peninsula and its attack was stalled near the southeastern port of Pusan by ROK and US troops.[36]

The allied forces, led by General Douglas MacArthur, responded with a brilliant amphibious landing led by US marines near the center of the peninsula, split the North Korean army in half, and quickly drove north towards China. In

October 1950, Mao Zedong committed over 200,000 Chinese "volunteer" troops across the Yalu River to drive back US and ROK advancing forces. After two years of static warfare along the 38th parallel, the original dividing line between the two countries, a cease-fire was signed at the border village of Panmunjom in July, 1953. After three years of war, casualties were horrendous and included 520,000 North Koreans, 900,000 Chinese, 400,000 United Nations (mostly ROK) troops, and an estimated 2 million civilians.[37]

The (un) Democratic People's Republic

After the end of the Korean War, Pyongyang struggled to recover from the destruction wrought by ground and air attacks including devastation caused by three years of aerial bombing that "reduced cities like Pyongyang to ashes and rubble."[38] Kim Il-sung quickly moved to consolidate power, and with substantial aid from both China and the Soviet Union, he developed the infrastructure of North Korea through massive internal modernization programs and pushed its economy forward at an accelerated rate. North Korea's centrally controlled economy prospered for the first 20 years, benefiting from significant amounts of Chinese and Soviet aid; in fact, North Korea's economy grew at a phenomenal rate during the 1950s and 1960s and outperformed the fledgling South.[39]

Throughout the 1970s, North Korea's economy began to show signs of fatigue as growth rates slipped. Pyongyang initially responded by increasing trade with the West and by attempting to introduce limited capitalistic reforms.

Western-style factories, production plants, and technologies were imported and more debt was incurred. This period also included the beginnings of significant dealings by North Korea in international criminal operations. Efforts to sell drugs and weapons and counterfeit money by the North Korean government and its diplomats were beginning to make headlines as Pyongyang increased its efforts to gain hard currency at all levels.[40] Kim Jong-il, the elder Kim's son destined to be the future leader of North Korea, was also beginning to make his mark, was officially appointed to his first political office in 1973, and was designated "the leader of the party and of the people" by the North Korean press.[41]

Ironically, the rise of Kim Jong-il coincided with the fall of the North Korean economy. The 1980s included a fundamental change in the Soviet-North Korean relationship. The arrival of the Perestroika era saw the Soviets begin to scale back their ideological and material commitments, including Pyongyang-Moscow ties. In 1989, Moscow officially ended its economic aid to the North and in 1990, the Soviets demanded hard currency for all future oil purchases. In 1991, Pyongyang's oil imports fell by 75 percent and North Korea looked to China to assist in obtaining needed energy resources. China's economic relationship with the DPRK changed in the same manner as the Soviet Union's. In 1992, Beijing also started demanding cash payments for oil and North Korea's total consumption fell considerably with negative effects on its agricultural sector.[42] During this same period, North Korea began to actively market domestically produced ballistic missiles to a number of nations to include Egypt, Iran, Iraq, Libya, Pakistan, Vietnam, and Syria.[43]

North Korea's Struggle to Survive

Beginning in the 1980s, US intelligence sources began to detect North Korean efforts to develop nuclear technology at its complex at Yongbyong.[44] The DPRK had obtained nuclear technology from the Soviet Union and China beginning in the 1960s[45] and these efforts coincided with economic retraction and famine and desperate measures by North Korea to alleviate these issues. The lack of Soviet aid and demands by China for hard cash payments for goods and services served to cripple the already unsteady North Korean economy. The world feared an unstable North Korea and was shocked in 1993 when Pyongyang announced that it was withdrawing from the Nonproliferation Treaty and working towards production of nuclear weapons.[46] Former President Jimmy Carter's intervention and promise of US and ROK aid averted a full-scale crisis. Negotiations between the US, South Korea, and the DPRK resulted in the 1994 Agreed Framework under which the US provided energy assistance to North Korea in return for the cessation of Pyongyang's development of dangerous nuclear technology.[47] During this same time, North Korea's economic downturn continued and the DPRK began to experience the beginnings of a full-scale food crisis.

Although North Korea had been previously able to feed itself, significant imports of grains began in 1988 and by the mid-1990s, North Korea became dependent on international food aid to nourish its people. Kim Jong-il inherited the leadership of North Korea after his father's death in 1994 and took the helm of a state-controlled society with a ruined economy, famine-stricken population, and adversarial relationship with all of its neighbors with the exception of China. During the summer of 1995, heavy rains caused significant crop damage, followed by more flooding in 1996 and drought in 1997. Along with inefficient and outdated farming and distribution practices, these weather factors served to cause a humanitarian food crisis. From 1995–1998, North Korea experienced a severe famine which killed one to two million people.[48]

Illicit Activities to Support the Regime

One of Pyongyang's answers to the severe economic problems it has experienced has been to conduct and condone any actions that support its "greater struggle" of revolution and professed goal of unification of the Korean peninsula. Kim Il-sung and his successor-son have supported "alternative" methods of obtaining resources and cash to maintain the regime including drug trafficking, counterfeiting, aid diversion, weapons proliferation, and support from Koreans abroad. This system of providing support the regime is a critical source of needed income to ensure Kim Jong-il's grip on power. Funds and goods obtained through these types of transactions have provided Pyongyang's communist leaders, military, and elite significant amounts of cash and goods, which help to maintain the core of Kim's support.

Pyongyang's Fundraising Efforts

One of the most significant aspects of research into this subject is the *lack of an all-encompassing analysis* on the topic of Pyongyang's illicit activity. With few exceptions, this subject is seen as a peripheral issue and an interesting "sub-topic" scattered throughout works on the Kim Jong-il regime and North Korean society. Yet there has been some valuable data and research published on the components of this issue, to include government research, Congressional testimony, master's theses, journal papers, magazine articles, and press reports. These critical sources of information form the research basis for this study.

Drug Trafficking and Counterfeiting Sources

Among the most alarming of North Korea's illicit activities is the alleged government sponsorship and planning of programs to grow and market illegal narcotics. North Korea's efforts to smuggle drugs dates back to the 1970s. North Korean diplomats in Scandinavia were accused of using their status to sell alcohol, cigarettes, and drugs on the black market to provide economic support for their embassies as early as 1976. Several authors have mentioned North Korea's relationship with narcotics production and sales to include former Swedish Charge d'Affaires in North Korea Eric Cornell, who described Pyongyang's attempts at government-sponsored black marketing and observed that North Korean diplomatic culture was vastly different from any other country in the world. Marcus Noland also provides a partial analysis of North Korea's illicit activities in *Avoiding the Apocalypse: The Future of the Two Koreas* and described the Kim Jong-il regime as "a continuing criminal enterprise, and illicit activities – smuggling, drug trafficking, and counterfeiting for example – offer other possibilities for financing the trade gap."

Other relevant sources include a host of US government research to include analysis and published reports by Congressional Research Service (CRS)[49] staffer Raphael Perl and at least one government-sponsored master's thesis by Kenneth Strong, a US Navy officer.[50] Congressional testimony continues to provide credible evidence of North Korea's drug program counterfeiting efforts. In a hearing before the US Senate in 2003, economist Nicholas Eberstadt also stated that North Korea's "drug and counterfeiting trade is entirely consistent with the official DPRK view of its legal and treaty obligations . . . part of the strategy for state survival."[51]

Additional sources of information on drug and counterfeiting activity include US and UN reports on these issues. The *United Nations World Drug Report* is another valuable resource and notes while North Korea does produce opium, global opium production continues to be dominated by Afghanistan with over 85 percent of the market, followed by Myanmar and Laos.[52] Similarly, the US State Department's annual *International Narcotics Control Strategy Report* provides detailed descriptions of DPRK trafficking efforts. The report provides convincing evidence of state-sponsored trafficking and states that "there is also strong reason to believe that methamphetamine and heroin are manufactured in North Korea as a result of the same state directed trafficking, but we lack reliable information on the scale of such manufacturing."[53]

The CIA's *World Factbook Online*, a recognized and easily available source, describes North Korea as "emerging as an important regional source of illicit drugs targeting markets in Japan, Taiwan, the Russian Far East, and China."[54] Additionally, the CIA's declassified "International Crime Threat Assessment," describes the problem of US currency counterfeiting throughout the world and notes that "internationally isolated states of concern, like North Korea and Iran, that have in the past resorted to illegal means to finance their operations may be involved in printing or distributing counterfeit US currency."[55]

Humanitarian Aid Diversion Literature

North Korea's well-known famine during the mid-1990s changed its internal dynamics and the nature of its interactions with the outside world. For the first time in its history, North Korea publicly requested food aid support in 1995 from the United Nations and the entire world. Although the analysis of North Korea's famine is ongoing, there has been some notable research on its causes and resulting effects on the Kim Jong-il regime from non-governmental organizations (NGOs) associated with humanitarian relief. Andrew Natsios provides an excellent commentary on the famine from the late 1980s through the worst phases from 1995 to 1999.[56] NGO operations are discussed in detail by Michael Schloms, who described North Korea as a "country in permanent crisis" and by Gordon Flake and Scott Snyder, whose collaborative work provides a European view of the North Korean crisis.[57]

Additionally, several CRS analysts to include Mark Manyin and Larry Niksch discuss aid issues. Manyin observed that the US has provided over $1 billion in foreign assistance to Pyongyang since 1995.[58] Also, Manyin commented that improved harvests and increased direct donations from South Korea and China served to cover the yearly food shortfalls, which were between one and two megatons of food per year.[59] Niksch noted that, in June 2002, the US stated that future food aid would depend on "North Korea's willingness to allow access to all areas of the country," a proposal which was immediately rejected by Pyongyang.[60] Finally, investigations and hearings by the US Congress also provide unique insight into the issue of North Korea. One example is Representative Brad Sherman's (D-CA) statement in 2000 that due to the "fungible nature" of aid, any humanitarian donations to North Korea contribute to the military and Pyongyang's elite, regardless of whether or not they are diverted.[61]

Weapons Sales and Arms Technology Export Information[62]

North Korea's weapons sales are habitually considered among the most important sources of direct financial support for the Kim Jong-il regime, yet credible estimates of their value remain difficult to obtain. The most comprehensive look at the development of North Korea's ballistic missile program can be found in Joseph S. Bermudez' *A History of Missile Development in the DPRK*.[63] Bermudez traces 30 years of research and development of North Korea's program beginning in the 1960s and provides detailed information on the customer base Pyongyang has been able to establish over the years. Congressional Research Service analysts also provide credible data on the development of the DPRK's program, ballistic missile threats, and sales to foreign countries. Andrew Feickert published three CRS reports in 2003 and 2004, which detail North Korea's efforts to develop and market ballistic missiles and the threats these pose to the United States.[64] Additionally, Congressional testimony helps support the contention that North Korea actively sells missile technology to the highest bidder. In a 1997 hearing, Senator Thad Cochran commented:

> In addition to the missiles themselves, North Korea has made a practice of selling the technology needed to produce these weapons. In doing so, it has created a missile trade among other states, creating a bootstrap effect in which other states are becoming self-sufficient with respect to ballistic missile technology.[65]

During US Senate testimony in 2003, Dr. Larry Wortzel commented that North Korea earned about $560 million in missile sales and notes that China often used North Korea as a "close partner" when sales involved areas of North Korean expertise.[66] In 2003, CRS researcher Sharon A. Squassoni examined the relationship between North Korea and Pakistan and identified North Korea as both a nuclear weapons and missile technology trader.[67] Additionally, in a 2002 report to Congress on weapons proliferation the CIA noted, "exports of ballistic missiles and related technology are one of the North's major sources of hard currency."[68] Most analysts agree that North Korea's ballistic missile program remains one of its few ways of earning currency for the regime. The US Congress-appointed North Korean Advisory Group described ballistic missiles as "one of North Korea's few exportable goods with international appeal."[69]

Chosen Soren Support

Remittances from ethnic Koreans living in Japan provide another source of revenue for the Kim Jong-il regime and one that has provided significant support over the years. The *Chosen Soren*, or General Association of Korean Residents in Japan, is a pro-Pyongyang group of ethnic Koreans that run schools, a daily newspaper, sports teams, credit institutions, and an import-export company and has membership estimated at 60,000–180,000 ethnic Koreans living in Japan.[70] Oh and Hassig provide an excellent synopsis of the Chosen Soren's development in Japan and noted that in the 1950s, North Korea provided "more political and financial support to ethnic Koreans in Japan than did the South Korean government." North Korea began requesting money from the Chosen Soren beginning in the mid-1970s and as its economy began to decline, requests for aid increased.[71] William Triplett also provides an overview of Chosen Soren activities in his book *Rogue State*, and describes the group as an "island of Korean identity in a sea of Japanese culture. . . . North Korea's unofficial embassy in Japan."[72] He also pointed out the role of the Chosen Soren as a conduit for Japanese technology for the North Korean military using an established ferry system that openly runs between the two countries.[73]

Dewayne Creamer's 2003 thesis, *The Rise and Fall of Chosen Soren*, provides a comprehensive review of the development of the organization from its beginnings during the Japanese colonial era to its current state of decline.[74] He notes that Kim Jong-il's 2002 admission of North Korea's kidnapping of Japanese citizens in the 1970s and 1980s was the "final nail into Chosen Soren's coffin, prompting Japanese authorities to crack down on the organization's ability to provide aid to the DPRK."[75] Another relevant master's thesis is Alice Lee's *Koreans in Japan: Their Influence on Korean-Japanese Relations,* which provides a comprehensive survey of the history of Koreans in Japan, the hardships faced, and ongoing assimilation of Koreans into Japanese society.[76]

Background material on Koreans living in Japan include texts by Sonia Ryang, an ethnic Korean who grew up in a Chosen Soren community in Japan, and George Hicks, who provides personal testimonies of what it feels like to grow up as a North Korean in Japan.[77] Older references are also useful and include two works, with the same title: *The Korean Minority in Japan*, published as a monograph by Edward Wagner in 1951 and as a book by Richard Mitchell in 1967.[78] Both of these provide detailed statistics on Koreans in Japan during the Japanese occupation of Korea, the interwar period, and in the aftermath of the Korean War. Finally, CRS analyst Emma Chanlett-Avery's report entitled *North Korean Supporters in Japan: Issues for US Policy* is frequently referred to as an "official" source document for Chosen Soren activities. In this document, analyst Chanlett-Avery observes, "the Chosen Soren organization has long supported North Korea by facilitating trade, remitting cash donations, establishing personal contacts, and possibly coordinating illicit transfers of narcotics and weapon parts."[79]

Illicit Activities and Global Implications

These sources provide an excellent basis for research into the issues surrounding Pyongyang's efforts at questionable and often criminal activities to support the Kim regime. Understanding the background of the region and of the development of North Korea is helpful in comprehending the eccentric, stubborn, and often schizophrenic nature of the DPRK, its leaders' goals and the means used to remain in power. These state-sponsored criminal practices present a difficult problem for North Korea's neighbors and others who have a vested interested in the stability of East Asia. Japan, China, Russia, and the United States continue to publicly stress the need for gradual and coherent change in North Korea to ensure peace in the region. At the same time, some observers call for increased interdiction of the sources of support for the regime. These are difficult choices entailing both risk and costs if pursued as policy objectives.

To provide a better understanding of the DPRK's fundraising activities and their actual threat to the US, a review of North Korea's economic situation is necessary, along with an introduction to the history and current status of Pyongyang's overt sources of income. The next chapter presents the specific mechanics of how North Korea generates additional funds to support both its government and society.

Notes and references

1. *North Korea, the DPRK, the North* and *Pyongyang* are used interchangeably throughout the text to refer to North Korea.

2. This "cult" phenomenon remains a unique aspect of North Korea's communist government, which systematically enforces government-sanctioned idolizing of both the "Great Leader" (Kim Il-sung) and "Dear Leader" (Kim Jong-il) as infallible rulers. See Kongdan Oh and Ralph Hassig, *North Korea Through the Looking Glass* (Washington, DC: The Brookings Institution, 2000), 81–104.

3. North Korea is roughly the size of Pennsylvania (46,500 square miles) and South Korea is almost the size of Indiana (38,000 square miles). Central Intelligence Agency, *The World Factbook Online 2004: North Korea,* www.cia.gov/cia/publications/factbook/geos/kn.html, accessed 28 February 2005.

4. These included the establishment of walled city-states, signifying the emergence of political structures on the peninsula. Carter J. Eckert and others, *Korea Old and New: A History* (Cambridge, MA: Harvard University Press, 1990), 9–10.

5. *Koryo* is the basis for the modern name of Korea. *North Korea: A Country Study,* ed. Andre Matles Savada, Federal Research Division, Library of Congress (Washington, DC: Library of Congress, 1994), 11–12; Eckert, *Korea Old and New,* 60–61.

6. Eckert, *Korea Old and New,* 86, 91; *North Korea: A Country Study,* 12–13.

7. This dynasty endured the longest of any of the dynasties on the peninsula and remained mostly intact until modern-day Japan annexed Korea in 1910. *North Korea: A Country Study,* 13; Eckert, *Korea Old and New,* 99.

8. *North Korea: A Country Study,* 18, 20; Eckert, *Korea Old and New,* 147–148; Warren I. Cohen, *East Asia at the Center* (New York: Columbia University Press, 2000), 213.

9. *Sources of Korean Tradition, Volume II,* eds. Yongho Choe and others (New York: Columbia University Press, 2000), 4.

10. *North Korea: A Country Study,* 22.

11. Bruce Cumings, *Korea's Place in the Sun: A Modern History* (New York: W.W.

Norton and Company, 1997), 83.

12. *North Korea: A Country Study*, 22. Korea's unpreparedness was due partially to the two and a half centuries of relative peace it experienced through 1800. Neither China nor Japan was a threat at that time and there were no significant domestic uprisings. As a result, Korea's focus was not on defense, but the other necessities of the time. *Sources of Korean Tradition Vol. II*, 5.

13. Eckert, *Korea Old and New*, 195; Donald S. Macdonald, *The Koreans: Contemporary Politics and Society*, 3rd ed. (Boulder, CO: Westview Press, 1996), 37.

14. Eckert, *Korea Old and New*, 187.

15. Cumings, *Korea's Place in the Sun*, 116–117.

16. Eckert, *Korea Old and New*, 218–222; Cumings, *Korea's Place in the Sun*, 120.

17. Japan forced this treaty on Korea after the end of the Russo-Japanese War. *Sources of Korean Tradition Vol. II*, 289.

18. Eckert, *Korea Old and New*, 241.

19. *North Korea: A Country Study*, 26.

20. Eckert, *Korea Old and New*, 260–261.

21. Eckert, *Korea Old and New*, 262.

22. *Sources of Korean Tradition, Vol. II.*, 315.

23. Eckert, *Korea Old and New*, 329.

24. Don Oberdorfer, *The Two Koreas: A Contemporary History* (Indianapolis: Basic Books, 1997), 5–6.

25. Cumings, *Korea's Place in the Sun*, 189.

26. William Stuek, *Rethinking the Korean War: A New Diplomatic and Strategic History* (Princeton, NJ: Princeton University Press, 2002), 67.

27. Richard H. Mitchell, *The Korean Minority in Japan* (Berkeley, CA: University of California Press, 1967), 103–104.

28. Captain Dewayne J. Creamer, USAF, *The Rise and Fall of Chosen Soren: Its Effect on Japan's Relations on the Korean Peninsula*, Master's Thesis chaired by Edward A. Olsen (Monterey, CA: Naval Postgraduate School, 2003), 13–16; Mitchell, *The Korean Minority in Japan*, 104.

29. *Sources of Korean Tradition Vol. II*, 368.

30. Oberdorfer, *The Two Koreas*, 7.

31. Eckert, *Korea Old and New*, 343.

32. Cumings, *Korea's Place in the Sun*, 252–254.

33. Stuek, *Rethinking the Korean War*, 69–73; Cumings, *Korea's Place in the Sun*, 247.

34. *North Korea: A Country Study*, 39.

35. T.R. Fehrenbach, *This Kind of War: A Study in Unpreparedness* (New York: The Macmillan Company, 1963), 55–57.

36. By August 1950, US and ROK troops had formed a tight perimeter in the extreme southeastern portion of the peninsula. Retaining this area and the seaport at Pusan allowed reinforcements to arrive and by September 1950 UN coalition forces had retaken Seoul. Cohen, *East Asia at the Center*, 385–386; Eckert, *Korea Old and New*, 344–345.

37. Cumings, *Korea's Place in the Sun*, 288; Fehrenbach, *This Kind of War*, 649; Eckert, *Korea Old and New*, 345; Oberdorfer, *The Two Koreas*, 9–10.

38. Eckert, *Korea Old and New*, 345.

39. Cumings, *Korea's Place in the Sun*, 423; MacDonald, *The Koreans*, 21; Marcus Noland, *Avoiding the Apocalypse: The Future of the Two Koreas* (Washington, DC: Institute for International Economics, 2000), 3–4.

40. William C. Triplett III, *Rogue State: How a Nuclear North Korea Threatens America* (Washington, DC: Regnery Publishing, 2004), 93, 102.

41. Oh and Hassig, *North Korea Through the Looking Glass*, 89.

42. Seongji Woo, *The Politics of Asymmetrical Triangles: Cooperation and Conflict in Northeast Asia*, Doctoral Thesis (Indiana University, May 2001), 129–130; David Reese, *The Prospects for North Korea's Survival*, Adelphi Paper 323, International Institute for Strategic Studies (New York: Oxford University Press, 1998), 27–28.

43. "North Korea's Ballistic Missile Exports," *Center for Nonproliferation Studies Nuclear Threat Initiative Online*, www.nti.org/e_research/profiles/NK/Missile/66_1279.html, accessed 1 March 2005.

44. Noland, *Avoiding the Apocalypse*, 145.

45. Cumings contends that North Korea, like Israel, decided to publicly display the *plausibility* of nuclear weapons technology without an announcement of actual capability. Thus, the activities at Yongbyong were, and continue to be, easily monitored by intelligence collectors. Cumings, *Korea's Place in the Sun*, 467.

46. Pyongyang had entered into the Nonproliferation Treaty in 1985 as a condition for Soviet-supplied nuclear reactors. Cohen, *East Asia at the Center*, 461.

47. Oh and Hassig, *North Korea Through the Looking Glass*, 168–170.

48. This estimate is from Michael Schloms' *North Korea and the Timeless Dilemma of Aid* (Piscataway, NJ: Transaction Publishers, 2004), 120. Although some estimates state that up to 3 million people died, most analysts support a slightly lower figure; all agree that between 3–10 percent of the North Korean population died and the entire population of 22 million suffered because of this crisis. Marcus Noland, "Famine and Reform in North Korea, Working Paper 03-5," *Institute for International Economics Website*, July 2003, www.iie.com/publications/wp/2003/03-5.pdf, accessed 30 April 2005; Andrew S. Natsios, *The Great North Korean Famine: Famine, Politics, and Foreign Policy* (Washington, DC: United Stated Institute of Peace, 2001), 13; Reese, *The Prospects for North Korea's Survival*, 28–31.

49. The CRS conducts "nonpartisan, objective analysis and research on all legislative issues" according to its mission statement. Congressional Research Service, "What is the Congressional Research Service?" *CRS Website*, www.loc.gov/crsinfo/whatscrs.html, accessed 28 February 2005.

50. Raphael F. Perl, "Drug Trafficking and North Korea: Issues for US Policy," *CRS Report for Congress* RL32167 (Washington, DC: Congressional Research Service, Library of Congress, 5 December 2003); Lieutenant Commander Kenneth A Strong, USN, *North Korea: The Transnational Criminal State,* Research Report chaired by Paul R. Kan (Maxwell Air Force Base, AL: Air Command and Staff College Air University. April 2003).

51. US Congress, Senate, Financial Management, The Budget, and International Security Subcommittee of the Committee on Governmental Affairs, *Drugs, Counterfeiting, and Weapons Proliferation: The North Korean Connection,* 108th Cong., 1st sess., 20 May 2003, S. Hrg. 108-157 (Washington, DC: US Government Printing Office, 2003), 5, 16.

52. United Nations, "World Drug Report 2004, Volume 1: Executive Summary," *United Nations Office on Drugs and Crime Website,* www.unodc.org/unodc/world_drug_report.html, accessed 28 February 2005, 14.

53. US Department of State, Bureau for International Narcotics and Law Enforcement Affairs, "International Narcotics Control Strategy Report 2003, Vol. 1: Southeast Asia," *US Department of State Website* (March 2004), www.state.gov/g/inl/rls/nrcrpt/2003/vol1/html/29837.htm, accessed 28 February 2005.

54. CIA, *The World Factbook Online 2004: North Korea.*

55. Central Intelligence Agency, "International Crime Threat Assessment," *CIA Electronic Reading Room,* December 2000, www.foia.cia.gov/search.asp, keyword search International Crime Threat Assessment, accessed 28 February 2005.

56. Natsios, *The Great North Korean Famine.*

57. Schloms, *North Korea and the Timeless Dilemma of Aid,* 100; *Paved with Good Intentions: The NGO Experience in North Korea,* eds. L. Gordon Flake and Scott Snyder (Westport, CT: Praeger Publishers, 2003).

58. Mark E. Manyin, "US Assistance to North Korea: Fact Sheet," *CRS Report for Congress* RS21834 (Washington, DC: Congressional Research Service, Library of Congress, 11 February 2005), 1.

59. Manyin, "US Assistance to North Korea: Fact Sheet," 3.

60. Larry A. Niksch, "Korea: US-Korea Relations – Issues for Congress," *CRS Report for Congress* IB98045 (Washington, DC: Congressional Research Service, Library of Congress, 27 August 2003), 10.

61. Comments by Representative Brad Sherman, US Congress, House, Committee on International Relations, *US Policy Toward North Korea II: Misuse of US Aid to North Korea,* 106th Cong., 1st sess., 27 October 1999, Hrg. 106-01, (Washington, DC: US Government Printing Office, 1999), 32–33.

62. Weapons sales are often associated with North Korea's quest for nuclear technology. While these issues are often intertwined, this text focuses on conventional arms and technology transfers by North Korea to other nations.

63. Joseph S. Bermudez Jr., *A History of Ballistic Missile Development in the DPRK,* Center for Nonproliferation Studies Occasional Papers: #2 (Monterey, CA: Cen-

ter for Nonproliferation Studies, Monterey Institute of International Studies, November 1999).

64. See Andrew Feickert, "North Korean Ballistic Missile Threat to the United States," *CRS Report for Congress* RL21473 (Washington, DC: Congressional Research Service, Library of Congress, 25 March 2003); Andrew Feickert, "Missile Survey: Ballistic and Cruise Missiles of Foreign Countries," *CRS Report for Congress* RL30427 (Washington, DC: Congressional Research Service, Library of Congress, 5 March 2004); and Andrew Feickert and K. Alan Kronstadt, "Missile Proliferation and the Strategic Balance in South Asia," *CRS Report for Congress* RL32115 (Washington, DC: Congressional Research Service, Library of Congress, 17 October 2003).

65. US Congress, Senate, International Security, Proliferation and Federal Services Subcommittee of the Committee on Governmental Affairs, *North Korean Missile Proliferation.* 105th Cong., 1st sess., 21 October 1997, S. Hrg. 105-241 (Washington, DC: US Government Printing Office, 1997), 1–2.

66. US Congress, *Drugs, Counterfeiting, and Weapons Proliferation: The NK Connection,* 51, 57.

67. Sharon A. Squassoni, "Weapons of Mass Destruction: Trade Between North Korea and Pakistan," *CRS Report for Congress* RL31900 (Washington, DC: Congressional Research Service, Library of Congress, 7 May 2003), 1.

68. Central Intelligence Agency, "Unclassified Report to Congress on the Acquisition of Technology Relating to Weapons of Mass Destruction and Advanced Conventional Munitions, 1 January Through 30 June 2002," *CIA Website,* www.odci.gov/cia/reports/721_reports/jan_jun2002html, accessed 1 March 2005.

69. US Congress, House, *Final Report of the North Korean Advisory Group,* 29 October 1999, *Federation of American Scientists Website,* www.fas.org/nuke/guide/dprk/nkag-report.htm, accessed 28 February 2005.

70. This group is also referred to as the *Chongryun* in Korean. Bertil Lintner, "It's Hard to Help Kim Jong-il," *Far Eastern Economic Review* 166, no. 12 (27 March 2003): 20–22; Doug Struck, "Murder Shines a Light on the Lives of Koreans in Japan," *The Washington Post,* 1 June 2000, A21.

71. Oh and Hassig, *North Korea Through the Looking Glass,* 179–180.

72. Triplett, *Rogue State,* 108.

73. Triplett, *Rogue State,* 110–111.

74. Creamer, *The Rise and Fall of Chosen Soren.*

75. Creamer, *The Rise and Fall of Chosen Soren,* 39; Mitchell, *The Korean Minority in Japan,* 39.

76. Alice K. Lee, *Koreans in Japan: Their Influence on Korean-Japanese Relations,* Master's Thesis chaired by Claude A. Buss (Monterey, CA: Naval Postgraduate School, 1979).

77. Sonia Ryang, *North Koreans in Japan: Language, Ideology and Identity* (Boulder, CO: Westview Press, 1997); George Hicks, *Japan's Hidden Apartheid: The Korean Minority and the Japanese* (Brookfield, VT: Ashgate, 1997).

78. Edward W. Wagner, *The Korean Minority in Japan, 1904–1950* (New York: International Secretariat, Institute of Pacific Relations, 1951); Richard H. Mitchell, *The Korean Minority in Japan* (Berkeley, CA: University of California Press, 1967).

79. Emma Chanlett-Avery, "North Korean Supporters in Japan: Issues for US Policy," *CRS Report for Congress* RL32137 (Washington, DC: Congressional Research Service, Library of Congress, 17 November 2003).

Chapter 2

Balance Sheet and Overt Funding

> It gradually became clear that most of the international aid was being diverted
> by the army, the secret services, and the Government.
> —*Jean Ziegler,*
> *UN Commission on Human Rights*

When examining the issue of Pyongyang's quest for funds, the first question is
why does North Korea need hard currency? The answer lies in the extreme failure of its command economy and the risk of loss of elite support to Kim Jong-il.
North Korea's economic collapse was initially mitigated by Soviet and Chinese
assistance, but eventually resulted in Pyongyang's quest for hard currency by
any means available. The next section will examine the reasons for this activity,
how North Korea evolved from a "model" communist economy to one of the
poorest nations in the world, and the covert methods it has developed to raise
additional money.

With one quarter of the world's gross domestic product (GDP), the economic health of Asia now directly influences the international economy.[1] Yet,
Asian communist nations historically have failed to deliver the promise of socialist societies: all citizens sharing equally in a nation's wealth. States with centrally planned economies lack the market advantages of capitalist societies and
are often characterized by poor performance.

As one of the newest members of the World Trade Organization (WTO),
China is moving on a path towards economic prosperity. Vietnam is a latecomer
to the world marketplace, but through its own internal reforms begun in the
1990s and a recent trade agreement with the US, its future also looks bright.
Predictably, North Korea stands in stark contrast to its Asian neighbors and its
problematic economy is a direct reflection of its static and outdated communist
government. Pyongyang remains the "problem child" of Asia and the success or
failure of its economy directly affects the stability of the region.

Financial Data and Performance

North Korea's recent economic performance measured against other nations
provides a clear indication of the problems its economy continues to face. When
comparing these national economies, using simple benchmarks like gross domestic product (GDP)[2] helps to provide a basic means of overall comparison.

The Central Intelligence Agency's *World Factbook* provides income statistics, which allow an evaluation of the levels of a country's wealth weighted for comparison on an international level. Gross domestic product levels for several nations compared to the DPRK follow:

Nation	GDP (billions)	Population (millions)	GDP per capita
United States	$10,990	293	$37,800
Japan	$ 3,580	127	$28,200
South Korea	$ 857	48	$17,800
Thailand	$ 477	64	$ 7,400
China	$ 6,490	1,298	$ 5,000
Vietnam	$ 203	82	$ 2,500
North Korea	**$ 29**	**22**	**$ 1,300**

Table 1. GDP Comparisons

Source: CIA, *The World Factbook Online 2004: North Korea.*

Comparing the total amount of output (GDP) per capita provides a measure of the relative size of each economy and provides a method of comparison with other countries. The overwhelming output of China's economy compared to Vietnam and North Korea reveals its size relative to other nations in Asia. Additionally, the GDP data provides a basis for comparison with other countries in a global perspective. As expected, the US and Japan rate among the most productive while China's large population offsets the relatively high levels of national production; nevertheless, it leads the Third World in GDP per capita.

However, this type of basic comparison fails to tell the entire story. While there is no argument that North Korea's economic system is an utter failure, there is much debate on the magnitude and extent of Pyongyang's ability to manage its domestic economy. North Korea has not published official statistics for over 30 years[3] and the obscure nature of the DPRK makes economic data gathering fall in the realm of "art" rather than "science." The most widely used information on North Korea's economy comes from the South's Bank of Korea (BOK), Korea Trade-Investment Promotion Agency (KOTRA), and the South Korean Ministry of Unification. This data compromises the "official" South Korean estimate of the DPRK economy. Yet there is some debate on the validity of the information provided, as Marcus Noland commented:

These figures are apparently derived by taking classified data on physical output generated by South Korean intelligence agencies and then applying South Korean prices and value-added weights to indices of physical production . . . there is little opportunity to check their plausibility. . . . Moreover, the ultimate growth rate figure is reportedly subject to interagency bargaining within the

South Korean government.[4]

Despite the questionable nature of this data, it remains one of the only use-ful sources of information available on North Korea's economic performance and analysts agree that the North's performance over the past 25 years has been appalling by any standard. The factors leading up to the failure of North Korea's economy and the need for alternate sources of income are fairly straightforward and have their roots in the changes the world experienced at the end of the Cold War.

North Korea's Economic History

North Korea's state controlled economy traces its roots to the programs im-plemented by Kim Il-sung and carried on by his son Kim Jong-il. In stark con-trast to Western economies, North Korea's government has maintained control of all real estate, directed allocation of food, and guided economy policy through the lens of its political ideology rather than market factors.[5] The development of its economy began in the immediate aftermath of World War II, the North en-gaged in "nation-building" activities to include land reform, nationalization of industries, and the initial preparations for a state-run economy. During this time light industry and agriculture were stressed to solve shortages of food and neces-sary items.[6] The Korean War had devastating effects on the North's economy and its production infrastructure. As a result, Pyongyang's focus during that period was reconstruction followed by an emphasis on growth in the late 1950s.[7] Although North Korea's reported growth during the 1950s and early 1960s was up to 25 percent per year, it slowly began to experience "sectoral imbalances" resulting from its military first policy, decreases in product quality, and growing dissatisfaction of the population with the consumer goods rationing system.[8] Despite these simmering issues, this era saw significant economic advances and recovery from the effects of civil war.

The 1970s: Stagnation

North Korea's over-reliance on nationalized enterprises and lack of ad-vanced technology resulted in economic stagnation in the 1970s.[9] The goal of DPRK economic planners during this decade was to place "more emphasis on technological advance, self-sufficiency in industrial raw materials, improving product quality, correcting imbalances among different sectors, and developing the power and extractive industries."[10] During that same period, North Korea began importing goods from capitalist nations, financed by hard currency bor-rowing, to support industrial development. In an attempt to modernize produc-tion and cater to consumer needs, purchases consisted of turnkey plants, to in-clude a petrochemical plant, cement factory, and a complete panty hose factory.[11] By the mid-1970s, the DPRK began defaulting on its debt obligations, the only communist nation to do so at that time, and suffered significant damage to its credit rating and ability to conduct business with foreign partners.[12]

The 1980s: Loss of China and Soviet Support

The 1980s saw declining trade and subsidies from both China and the Soviet Union, and North Korea was left with significant shortages of many products, most importantly, oil.[13] Pyongyang has no domestic source of petroleum and when its main supplier, the Soviet Union, significantly reduced its oil supply, the effects were felt throughout all of North Korea.[14]

Other factors that affected the economic slowdown during this period include the heavy burden of defense spending, which accounted for 15–20 percent of the national budget, and the outdated economic practices pursued by the regime.[15] In response to this decline, North Korea implemented limited economic reforms by attempting to modify its system without sound economic "market-style" changes. Pyongyang's adjustments included an increased emphasis on worker participation in production decisions, accountability of state enterprises, and attempts to attract foreign investment.[16] These reforms had little effect and the end of the decade marked the beginning of North Korea's economic crisis. Although the causes of North Korea's economic decline continue to stir debate, the inflexible nature of its system and changes in the relationships between North Korea and its communist allies were among the most significant factors.

Throughout the 1980s, the Soviet Union still provided oil at two-thirds of market price but officially ended its economic aid to the North by the end of the decade. This change occurred due to the advent of Gorbechev's Perestroika Era and improved Soviet-South Korean relations.[17] In 1990, the Soviets demanded hard currency for all future DPRK oil purchases and by 1991, North Korea oil imports fell by 75 percent.[18] As a result, Pyongyang turned to China as its major supplier of fuel.[19] As North Korea looked to China to assist in obtaining needed energy resources, Beijing's economic relationship with North Korea followed the same downturn as the Soviet Union. In 1992, Beijing also started demanding cash payments for oil and North Korea's total consumption fell considerably with negative effects on its agricultural sector.[20]

The 1990s: Economic Crisis

For the DPRK, the 1990s were an unprecedented decade of poor economic performance that contributed to its nation-wide famine.[21] Although North Korea blamed seasonal flooding for causing the crisis, these weather factors were actually the "final straw," arriving after reserve food stocks had been used and production was unable to make up for food shortages.[22] Economic growth from 1990–1998 included contracted growth rates at between *negative* 3 and 4 percent per year.[23] This downturn was exacerbated by Kim Il-sung's continued adherence to the *juche*, or "self-reliance," policy coupled with an emphasis on "military first," a state policy of emphasizing national defense needs above most other economic priorities. Although North Korea attempted to gain further independence from external trading partners, the overall shortages of food and fuel were overwhelming and threatened to destabilize the government. During this time, US oil shipments began in 1994 and an infusion of large amounts of food aid helped Pyongyang survive the crisis.[24] Despite these inputs, North Korea's foreign trade also plummeted throughout the decade and did not begin to recover until the year 2000. The following figure shows the fluxuation in national output that began in 1989:

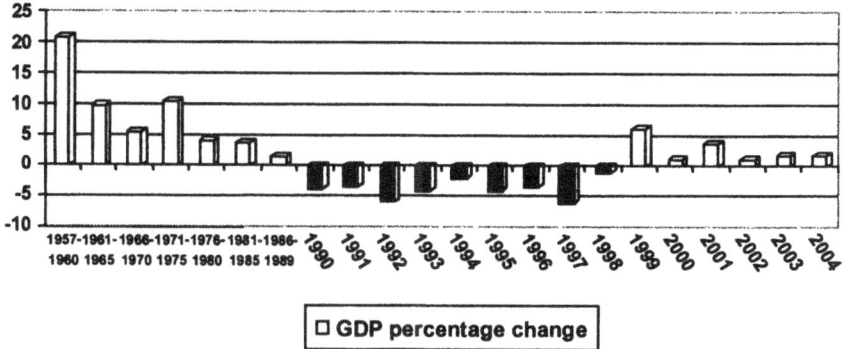

Figure 1. DPRK Gross National Product Fluctuation

Source: "GDP of North Korea," *Bank of Korea Online*,
www.bok.or.kr/index.jsp, keyword search
North Korea, accessed 6 February 2005.

The Millennium: Desperate Attempts to Change

In response to continued discouraging performance, Pyongyang initiated significant economic reforms in July 2002. These changes included devaluating the won, raising wages, increasing the size of land allowed for private citizens to cultivate, allowing farmers to keep produce in excess of quotas, and the initial groundwork for a phased withdrawal of the national distribution system.[25] These adjustments along with an official recognition of farmer's markets in June 2003[26] give rise to speculation that North Korea is making efforts at limited changes to its system. Regardless of the status of these initiatives, North Korea's economy remains one of the worst in the world. Nicolas Eberstadt commented that North Korea's poor long-term performance was "a direct consequence of official DPRK policy and doctrine."[27]

China remains North Korea's staunchest ally and biggest trading partner with $738 million in total imports and exports in 2003. South Korea runs a close second with $642 million in total trade during the same period.[28] North Korea's total trade during 2003 was just over $3 billion, which is far below its peers in the region and a clear indication of the absolute poverty its citizens live in due to its economic policies.[29] Nevertheless, North Korea has shown tremendous resilience in dealing with significant economic problems and its state control was so effective that governmental collapse did not occur even during the one of the worst famines ever experienced in the region.

Asian Wildcard

North Korea's ongoing pursuit of a "three-track policy" – threatening the West to obtain aid, illicit activities, and collaborating economically with South Korea – indicates the regime is willing to attempt anything to ensure continued flows of cash and required goods. Pyongyang remains the *wild card* in East Asia, both in terms of economic stability and regional security. Only by moving away from its established communist infrastructure will Pyongyang ever begin to reshape its economy to achieve even modest growth.

The Trade Gap

Pyongyang's economy remains stagnant and requires yearly international injects of both food aid and supplies to stave off widespread famine. As shown below, North Korea continues to experience a significant gap between imports and exports. Financing this gap through alternate means has been the only way North Korea has been able to forestall total economic collapse, and Pyongyang has been able to generate support and stabilizing income through "nonmarket transactions."[30] These transactions have included the variety of activities mentioned, to include illegal drug smuggling, counterfeiting, aid diversion, and a host of "gray area" pursuits.

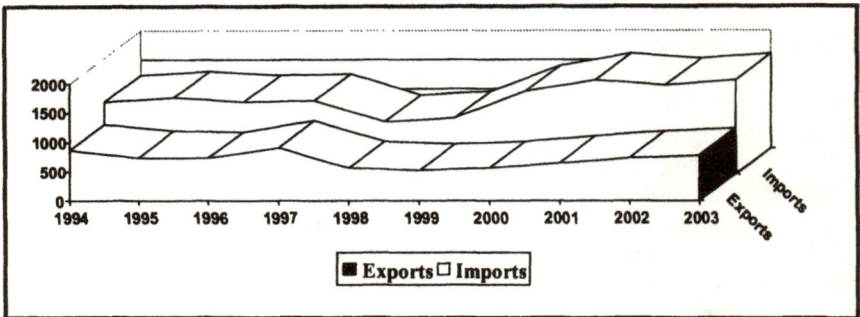

Figure 2. North Korea's Trade Gap ($ millions)

Source: "GDP of North Korea."

Marcus Noland described the Kim Jong-il regime as "a continuing criminal enterprise, and illicit activities – smuggling, drug trafficking, and counterfeiting for example – offer other possibilities for financing the trade gap."[31] Continued governance by Kim Jong-il relies heavily on ensuring Pyongyang's elite does not directly experience the effects of North Korea's economic failures. By maintaining financial inflows through fundraising activities, the DPRK strives to maintain its current governance structure by providing the means for the elite leadership core to live well in this impoverished nation.

Public Fundraising Efforts

North Korea needs hard currency due to numerous issues directly tied to its own internal requirements and Pyongyang's need to interact with the world. The DPRK's strict control over its monetary policy and volatile economy has resulted in a series of official or "pegged" rates for the won ranging from 150 to 1,000 won per US dollar.[32] Fixing these rates serves to hide significant problems within a monetary system and many North Koreans have turned to hoarding US dollars, Japanese yen, Chinese yuan, or euros.[33]

Since Pyongyang's monetary policies have rendered its own won relatively useless as a medium for exchange abroad, North Korea requires viable currency to conduct overseas trade and business dealings. As a result, hard currency in the form of dollars, yuan, and yen are required to interact with the outside world. These interactions range from legitimate business operations to the purchase of luxury items for Kim Jong-il and his inner circle. Given the current state of North Korea's economy, the need for hard currency to maintain business interests and keep the core of Kim Jong-il's support satisfied has never been greater. The following sections examine the overt methods the Kim regime uses to gain hard currency and how these contribute to the overall scheme of support for North Korea.

Weapons and Arms Technology Exports

For North Korea, one of the "fringe benefits" of maintaining a large, and fairly dynamic military force has been the development of an export market in arms and technology. During a US congressional hearing on North Korean missile proliferation in 1997, Senator Thad Cochran noted that "North Korea acquired 300-kilometer-range Scud-B missiles in 1981, taught itself in a few short years how to produce them, and then sold them to Egypt, Iran and Syria . . . an estimated 30 percent of North Korea's export income is generated by arms sales."[34]

Pyongyang has established a reputation for conventional arms and technical defense-related expertise among nations throughout the Middle East, Africa, and Southeast Asia earning as much as $500 million per year in sales of ballistic missiles alone.[35] While ballistic missiles are its principal weapons export, Pyongyang also deals in small arms, technology transfers, military advising, and various other types of defense-related products and services as shown in following table:

System or Technology	Buyers
Hwasong-5 (Scud-B)	Iran, Syria, Libya, Pakistan, Yemen Vietnam, Former USSR, Egypt
Hwasong-6 (Scud-C)	Iran, Syria, Libya, Pakistan, Yemen, Vietnam, Egypt
No Dong (Scud-D)	Libya, Iraq, Pakistan, Egypt, Iran, Russia, Ukraine
Taepo Dong-1 and 2	Iran and Pakistan / Iran
Anti-ship missiles	Burma, China
Anti-aircraft missiles	Egypt, Cuba, China, Vietnam
Tanks/artillery systems	Iran, Cuba, Burma, Egypt
Small arms	Burma, The Moro Islamic Liberation Front, Iran
Submarines	Vietnam
Turnkey factories	Iran, Sudan
Tunnel tech agreements	Iraq, Iran, Congo, Ethiopia
Other technical cooperation	Egypt, Iran, and Pakistan, Burma
Training agreements/ support	Over 62 nations[36]
Nuclear cooperation	Iran, China, Pakistan, Russia, Libya

Table 2. Weapons Sales and Cooperation[37]

Beginning in the 1970s, North Korea became a major exporter of arms within Asia and to third world nations across the globe. As the DPRK's prosperity waned, arms exports became an additional source of hard currency for the regime and essential to support continued weapons research and development. Throughout the 1980s and during the famine and economic crisis of the 1990s, arms exports represented an increasingly significant portion of total exports. In fact, during the height of the economic crisis between 1996 and 1998, arms sales represented between 10 and 17 percent of total exports.[38] Of these exports, missile sales constitute the most lucrative product associated with North Korea and these remain the most successful component of Pyongyang's overseas arms export program.

Ballistic Missile Production and Sales

Over the past 30 years, North Korea has established itself as a low-cost provider of missiles and related technology to any nation who has the funds. Arms sale analysts have asserted that North Korea "has become the most prolific exporter of ballistic missiles and related equipment, materials and technology" and that Pyongyang has sold hundreds of Scud and No Dong ballistic missiles to countries in the Middle East, Asia, and Africa.[39] North Korea has exported missile technology to a host of nations to include Egypt, Iran, Iraq, Libya, Pakistan, Vietnam, and Syria.[40] In a 2002 report to Congress on weapons proliferation, the CIA noted that "exports of ballistic missiles and related technology are one of the North's major sources of hard currency."[41] Ballistic missiles provide the optimal platform for employment of nuclear weapons, and some argue that North Korea's full-scale production of ballistic missiles in the 1980s occurred in concert with its development of nuclear weapons.[42] Most analysts agree that North Korea's ballistic missile program remains one of its few venues for earning currency for the regime. The US Congress-appointed North Korean Advisory Group described ballistic missiles as "one of North Korea's few exportable goods with international appeal."[43] The following sections provide details on the development of North Korea's ballistic missile program.

Soviet Origins

In 1968, North Korea obtained its first ballistic missiles when it received Free Rocket Over Ground (FROG-5/7) systems from the USSR. Although the Soviets provided the missiles, they declined to provide production technology.[44] Pyongyang's missile export program is "based primarily on Soviet Scud missile technology," and presently includes the production of short range Hwasong-5/6 missiles (copies of Scud-B and -C-type missiles), medium range No Dong systems (Scud-D equivalents), and the longer range Taepo Dong missiles.[45]

Domestic Production and Middle East Sales

In 1975, North Korea decided to decrease it reliance on imported equipment and to begin its own ballistic missile program in hopes of eventually producing its own systems.[46] Between 1979 and 1981, North Korea and Egypt signed an agreement on missile cooperation and Egypt transferred a "small number" of Soviet R-17E Scud-type (Scud-B) missile systems and MAZ-543 mobile launchers (also known as transporter-erector-launchers or TELs) to the DPRK.[47] By reverse-engineering these systems, the DPRK was able to begin indigenous production of these Scud missiles, called the Hwasong-5 systems, and to conduct its first test launch into the East Sea (also known as the Sea of Japan) in 1984.[48] This marked the beginning of Pyongyang's missile production efforts.

North Korea conducted five test launches of Hwasong-6 missiles between 1990 and 1993; both Syria and Iran also conducted four similar tests between 1991 and 1994.[49] The success of North Korea's ballistic weapons program spurred investment and purchases by other nations to include Syria, Egypt, Libya, and Vietnam. These nations obtained either missile technology or Hwasong-5/6 missiles, with a purchase price of $1.5 to $2 million each.[50] By the end of 1999, North Korea had produced between 600 and 1000 Hwasong-5/6 missiles and exported 300 to 500 of these to foreign nations.[51] Currently, North Korea is assessed to have the ability to produce four to eight Scud missiles each month.[52]

Longer Range Missile Development

During the same time North Korea was developing the Hwasong-6, it began work on a longer-range missile system, the No Dong (also referred to as the Scud-D). The DPRK intended to develop a nuclear-capable missile that could deliver a 1000-1500 kg warhead on targets as far away as 1000-1500 km and able to serve as a "first stage" for a more advanced system.[53] Pyongyang recruited Russian engineers to assist in the technical aspects of missile development and test fired its first No Dong missile into the East Sea in 1993.[54]

Since 1993, there have been no detected No Dong tests by North Korea, although there were launch preparations observed in 1994 and 1996.[55] Additionally, if Iranian and Pakistani tests were counted, there have been six No Dong test launches.[56] North Korea continues to use these types of missile tests or the threat thereof for both developmental purposes and for "political and military leverage."[57]

The Taepo Dong

North Korea's Taepo Dong missile development has gained international attention over the past few years: this weapons program includes missile research and development to produce a nuclear-capable missile able to range up to 8,000 km.[58] Missile development for the Taepo Dong dates back to the 1980s and included significant assistance from Russia, China, Pakistan, and Iran throughout its evolution.[59] The project includes the shorter range Taepo Dong-1 (1,500-2,500 km) and the longer Taepo Dong-2 (4,000–8,000 km). Prototype models were initially produced in the mid-1990s, and in 1998 the Taepo Dong-1 was used in a failed attempt to put North Korea's first satellite, the Kwangmyong-song-1, into orbit for "peaceful space exploration."[60] The 3-stage Taepo Dong-1 was launched from northeastern North Korea, crossed over Japan and fell into the Pacific Ocean.[61] This incident caused an international uproar, resulting in widespread condemnation of continued North Korean missile development efforts. South Korean government officials stated in 1999 that North Korea planned to export its Taepo Dong-1 missiles at a price of $6 million each.[62]

North Korea's next generation Taepo Dong-2 missile is also intended as delivery means for nuclear weapons.[63] The Taepo Dong-2 system is considered to be completely original with a new airframe and engine, but also might face significant technical developmental challenges.[64] In 1999, North Korea prepared to launch a Taepo Dong-2, but agreed to cease missile tests in return for US lifting of economic sanctions. Yet Pyongyang has effectively subverted this agreement by using Pakistan and Iran to test these missiles.[65] In fact, some analysts contend that test launches of Shalab-6 missiles by Iran or Ghauri-3 missiles by Pakistan were "substitute" for tests of the Taepo Dong and possibly had North Korean experts in attendance.[66] With North Korea cooperating with Iran and possibly other countries to develop this missile,[67] the Taepo Dong-2 could potentially be the most dangerous system Pyongyang has fielded to date. While North Korea will often fire lesser missiles for "political and military leverage," as it did in 2003, North Korea has not conducted any ballistic missile launch tests since the Taepo Dong incident in 1998.[68]

Missile Production and Sales Continue

Middle Eastern and African nations remain ardent customers for North Korean missile technology. In 2002, Iraq reportedly made a $10 million down payment on delivery of a single No Dong missile.[69] North Korea did not deliver the system, citing pressure from the US, and failed to provide a refund.[70] In 2002, media reports commented that North Korea had sold $60 million in missile technology to Iran, Syria and Yemen and predicted 2003 sales would be at the same or higher levels due to increased cooperation with Iran.[71] A US Defense Department report concluded that the effect of these North Korean sales and technology sharing has been significant. The sales to Iran have increased tensions in the Middle East and other missile sales have affected the "strategic balance" in both the Middle East and South Asia.[72]

Pakistan's missile programs have made significant advances in recent years due in part to North Korea assistance and in return, it is likely that Pakistan has been providing missile test flight data to Pyongyang to assist in continued missile improvements.[73] Pakistan remains a significant customer for North Korean missiles and in 2002 reportedly purchased "a number" of No Dong missiles from North Korea, which were transported in American-made Pakistani C-130 cargo aircraft.[74] China also continues to be substantially involved in North Korea's development of missiles and has used Pyongyang as a "close partner" when sales involved areas of North Korean expertise.[75] Overseas Koreans have facilitated development through direct support as many of the electronic components for missile systems were of Japanese origin and reportedly smuggled through *Chosen Soren* channels.[76] While missile sales have been historically projected at over $500 million annually, a more accurate estimate is that North Korea continues to earn from $50 to $100 million from missile technology exports.[77] Pyongyang has remained a key player in the development and exportation of ballistic missiles and continues to market its weapons to a variety of buyers throughout the world.

Other Weapons and Technology Sharing Programs

Although most press coverage of North Korean weapons proliferation relates to ballistic missile sales, there are reports of North Korean transactions involving other conventional weapons to include small arms deals throughout the world to countries like Burma and to Philippine rebel groups.[78] Compared to ballistic missiles, this issue seems insignificant, but possible transactions with terrorist organizations have resulted in renewed international interest in all aspects of North Korea's weapons export activities. Sales do occur and at notable levels: in fact, between 2000 and 2003, North Korea delivered approximately $600 million in military weaponry to developing nations.[79]

Supplier of Small Arms and Training

North Korea has been a supplier of weapons and military expertise to Third World countries since the 1960s, including "equipment transfers, in-country training, and advisory groups."[80] For North Korea, much of its military assistance initially was considered "an instrument of foreign policy," and included military training to groups in 62 countries, support to North Vietnam in the 1960s, financial aid to Sri Lanka rebels, training for the Thai communist party in the 1970s, and training support to Central American, South American, Middle Eastern, and African nations beginning in the 1980s.[81]

In 1982, the Iran-Iraq War provided an opportunity for North Korea to gain hard currency as Pyongyang sold a total of $800 million in weapons and provided 300 military instructors to Tehran.[82] Arms included a large amount of small arms and ammunition North Korea obtained from the Soviet Union, China or produced domestically and included 150 Soviet T-62 tanks, 1,000 mortars, and 1,000 anti-aircraft guns; Iran paid for these purchases using both cash and oil.[83] In 1991, North Korean weapons were fielded in the western hemisphere as it reportedly provided 203mm artillery systems to Cuba.[84] As of 1993, over 5,000 foreign military personnel had been trained in North Korea and the DPRK had reportedly sent as many as 7,000 military advisors to 47 countries.[85]

North Korea has found a "niche" in arms markets traditionally dominated by Soviet-produced equipment by providing low-cost, albeit low-tech equipment.[86] A more recent example was the revelation that between 1999 and 2002, North Korea reportedly sold 10,000 rifles and other equipment worth $2.2 million to the Moro Islamic Liberation Front, a pro-Al-Qaida rebel group in the Philippines.[87] While North Korea's small arms sales might seem insignificant compared to US and Russian sales,[88] they do represent a willingness to sell arms and provide training, regardless of the buyer, and are an indication of the extensive international ties North Korea retains throughout the world.

Nuclear Technology Provider

At the same time, evidence of North Korea's efforts to sell nuclear technology remains hard to prove. Yet there is evidence of cooperation between North Korea and Iran, China, Pakistan, Russia, and Libya.[89] North Korea and Iran have been conducting cooperative efforts to develop weapons technology for several years. The most alarming activity is recent alleged joint DPRK-Iranian attempts to develop nuclear warheads in conjunction with Taepo Dong-2 missiles. One report stated that the "number of North Korean weapons experts in Iran is now so large . . . the North Koreans have a seaside community in Iran of their own."[90]

Additional press reports in 2005 charged that Libya acquired enriched uranium from North Korea via Pakistan.[91] While these instances are shrouded in secrecy, they assuredly involved payments to North Korea for nuclear material or technology, with nations like Libya and Iran possibly paying with a mixture of cash and oil. But no clear picture exists on the amount of money or material North Korea received for these types of transactions. Since these are direct dealings between sovereign states, they involve a mix of both foreign policy and attempts at economic gain and the hard currency earned is difficult to quantify. Nevertheless, North Korea's efforts to market nuclear technology most likely falls in line with other attempts to sell its weapons technology and only occurs when profit for the regime or political advantages can be gained in exchange.

Weapons and Technology Transfers Support the Regime

North Korea's weapons sales remain among the most important sources of direct financial support for the Kim Jong-il regime. While estimates of sales remain somewhat speculative and include "analytical judgments, based on evaluations and estimations of capabilities and motivations, rather than hard conclusions based on conclusive evidence,"[92] there have been attempts to quantify the amount of arms sales by US, South Korean, and international arms trade analysts. Data does exist, as shown in Appendix C, which estimates yearly income from these transactions.

Weapons sales have historically accounted for a significant portion of North Korea's export market and have ranged as high as 40 percent in the 1980s.[93] Considering the limited capacity of the North Korean economy, these figures are remarkable and indicate that during the 1980s, legal and illegal transfers of weapons constituted a significant portion of overall exports. While total arms exports were at their peak in the 1980s, they have decreased to sales from $50–$100 million annually.[94] Some analysts contend that up to 40 percent of arms export revenue is reinvested into its missile program and the remaining balance flows to the central government with Pyongyang gaining approximately $30 to $60 million in hard currency.[95] While ballistic missiles make up the majority of overseas sales, North Korea has gone to considerable effort to establish markets in other areas of arms sales and continues to provide some of the lowest priced weapons and technical assistance available in the world.

Exports continue to occur, as evidenced by the 2003 Spanish seizure of a North Korean shipment of Scud missiles to Yemen. Although the vessel and its cargo were later released, this is clear evidence that North Korea intends to continue to market and deliver weapons technology.[96] These types of ventures by North Korea have been profitable, although estimates on actual income produced remain varied. The revenues from these sales support future weapons development efforts and these transactions provide direct support to Pyongyang in the form of hard currency.[97] In the end, weapons and technology transfers continue to be an essential part of Pyongyang's both legitimate and illicit efforts to stay afloat.

Aid Diversion

North Korea has been often accused of diverting aid intended for its people to Pyongyang's elite class and military forces. Some analysts contend that North Korea continues to use foreign assistance to support its regime through this diversion of humanitarian aid from the common citizens to the military and elite class. In support of these claims, there have been documented reports of donated goods being moved from distribution points directly into the hands of the military or government leaders. Additionally, personal observations of aid workers in North Korea, refugees in China, and defectors to South Korea substantiate these accusations. While some critics argue that the progress in North Korea's overall humanitarian situation is enough proof that food and medicine is being received by those who need it most, others contend that aid only serves to help support the continued rule of Kim Jong-il. The following paragraphs will discuss North Korea's food production and economic crisis, the issues surrounding humanitarian aid and conflicts with North Korea and its *juche* ideology, and evidence of illegal diversion efforts.

Food Production and Economic Crisis

With only 20 percent of its land able to support food production, most of North Korea is not suitable for intense agricultural production.[98] Despite this limitation, the DPRK's food production through the 1980s was notable: in fact, grain production doubled between 1961 and 1988 and was sufficient to cover domestic demands through the late 1980s.[99] During the late 1980s, the North's economy had stalled and had reached the limits of growth as a socialist economic nation.[100] The sweeping changes that occurred in the Soviet Union in the late 1980s had a negative effect on its relations with North Korea and significantly lowered trade levels between the countries. China also significantly decreased its subsidized support to the DPRK during the same time.

In 1990, after the loss of the Soviet Union as a fuel supplier, trading partner, and provider of "energy infrastructure support" and changes in the Sino-North Korean trade relationship, North Korea pursued a policy of conservation of resources and limiting trade with foreign nations.[101] When fuel imports dropped significantly in the early 1990s, devastating impacts on coal production resulted, which affected all aspects of the economy and in part caused the economic crisis.[102] The floods in the mid-1990s helped plunge North Korea into its food crisis following the failure of its economy to provide enough income to compensate for increasing food deficits.[103]

The confluence of these three factors – economic decline, loss of energy support, and natural disasters – led to the economic crisis that plagued the DPRK during the 1990s, leading to a significant decline in North Korean food production.[104] These losses in production were felt throughout the DPRK and its attempts to adhere to the *juche* doctrine of self-sufficiency and rejection of external aid did not improve the situation.

North Korea Asks for Help

North Korea's 1995 appeal for help from the World Food Program (WFP) was seen as a "radical departure from the governing philosophy of self-reliance . . . to accept international charity was an ideological heresy from the start – an admission of failure."[105] On the other hand, medical support provided by South Koreans was not deemed in violation of the *juche* principle due to their focus on solutions to "fundamental long-term problems" and North Korea's critical need for assistance in this area.[106]

After this appeal, North Korea began accepting significant amounts of external aid to alleviate its economic problems and total inability to feed its people. Aid organizations see North Korea as a unique problem due to its ideological and political characteristics, and describe this famine as "one of the most devastating of the 20th century."[107] North Korea had to make the choice between the *juche* national ideological philosophy and survival as an independent state and chose the latter, accepting aid from the international community.

The Famine

Beginning in 1988, North Korea began to experience food shortages and with a failing economy, could not produce or buy enough food to feed its people. As mentioned previously, these failings were caused both by changes in Pyongyang's relationship with its communist peers and economic difficulties. Between 1996 and 2003, North Korea was only able to cover between 55 and 80 percent of its total need for grain through domestic production.[108] In 1995 and 1996, North Korea experienced severe flooding followed by a drought in 1997 that resulted in 50 percent decrease in corn harvests.[109] While North Korea blames weather factors as the primary causes of the famine, food shortages were at significant levels *before* the floods occurred in July 1995 and these natural disasters only affected 15 percent of the tillable land.[110] There is no doubt that the floods made the famine more acute, but the extent of damage does not fully explain the food and critical supply shortages: the North Korean government itself was to blame for the crisis. One of the most vocal critics of North Korea, German physician Norbert Vollertsen, traveled with few restrictions throughout the North and observed:

> It became clear to me that Kim Jong-il and his Stalinist regime had made little effort to distribute medical supplies and food to the people who needed it most. I soon realized that North Korea's starvation is not the result of natural disasters or even lack of natural resources. Like the Holocaust in Europe, the horror is man-made.[111]

Additionally, the North Korean Public Distribution System (PDS) was an utter failure in providing adequate food during the crisis.[112] When asked about people who depended on the PDS as their sole source of food, a refugee who left North Korea in 1998 commented simply: "they died."[113] North Korea's appeal to the United Nations World Food Program in 1995 for aid caught many by surprise, but came after the crisis was well underway. Appendix A provides a timeline for the events surrounding the famine.

The Human Toll

Schloms provides a realistic estimate based on the wide range of observations and available evidence: between 1–2 million North Koreans, equating to 5 to 10 percent of the population, died as a result of the famine.[114] While the numbers of casualties vary widely and will most likely never be verified, the famine North Korea experienced in the 1990s was certainly its own worst internal catastrophe experienced to date.[115]

> In contrast with other famines and food crises around the world, the North Korean government remained in full control and continues, to this day, to retain a "deep suspicion of the outside world and a heavily institutionalized inclination toward state secrecy."[116] Critics of aid to North Korea contend that providing assistance to Pyongyang has led to only "marginal changes in the DPRK's behavior at best" and allowed for the misuse and diversion of aid to the military and elite.[117]

North Korea's Humanitarian Aid Diversion Efforts

Most analysts agree that North Korea gives priority for food aid distribution to two primary groups: the communist leaders and elite class in Pyongyang and the military.[118] Aid provided by the US and other nations does serve the function of allowing North Korea to sustain itself by reducing the government's requirement to feed its people (and thus provide more staples to government leaders and the military). Reports of diversion of food are largely based on defector testimonies. In a survey conducted by a South Korean NGO in 1999, over 90 percent of defectors stated they had not received food aid from international sources.[119] One former DPRK army officer provided the following example of aid diversion:

> My superior gave the order to take two trucks loaded with cereals from our barracks to the PDS distribution center in the dong [urban district] administration. He told me that a foreign organization wanted to take pictures of the food distribution. I carried out the order with my subordinates. Some food was distributed to civilians, and the foreigners took pictures of that. After that, we brought the food back to our barracks. No more than four bags were distributed.[120]

In 1999, the US General Accounting Office (GAO) commented that food tracking was a consistent problem: while food was monitored from the port of entry to storage facilities, the actual deliveries to distribution centers were not tracked.[121] Aid organizations simply cannot monitor the distribution of food and determine if aid is actually getting to those in need.[122] None of the agencies providing aid in North Korea has "random access" to monitor the distribution of food to institutions or households, although there have been reports, in rare instances, of North Korean officials allowing unscheduled visits.[123] Additionally, the GAO reported that between 1995 and 1999, $11 million (75,000 metric tons) of fuel provided by the United States was diverted for use by the North Korean government.[124] International assistance in terms of food, fuel, fertilizer, and other items has had a direct effect on North Korea's economic bottom line: any assistance North Korea receives allows it to divert some of these or other resources to government officials and military activities at its own discretion.[125]

Evidence of Diversion

The experience of the NGO Medecins Sans Frontieres (MSF), also referred to as Doctors Without Borders, conflict with claims by the WFP that intended recipients are receiving aid. In 1998, after four years of work in North Korea, MSF withdrew its staff because, "despite the best efforts of our field teams, our aid was not reaching those most in need." The vast majority of interviews conducted by the MSF of North Korean refugees support this conclusion, as people in the targeted groups of pregnant women, children, and older people reported never receiving aid.[126] A retired North Korean couple interviewed in 2001 commented:

> When you're over 61 years old you're unable to work because of the age limit. But right now in North Korea, they write the [retirement] annuity on a piece of paper. With that you can get 600 grams of rice for one day but it is only a piece of paper, and I never receive anything, and I cannot eat the paper, we are not goats. I never get any distribution nor any grant and I never receive a wage.[127]

Refugees report that when international aid arrives in North Korea, it is initially loaded onto trucks and then sent to army warehouses with drivers being changed at regular intervals, the final one "always a loyal member of the party."[128] Many also state that in the warehouses, war supplies are stored along with the international aid and only the party leaders still receive adequate distributions and goods, to include grain, clothing, and sometimes alcohol, are delivered directly to their homes.[129]

North Koreans interviewed by MSF commented that that the North Korean population knows government officials are diverting food aid to the military, selling it through the black market, or keeping it for themselves.[130] Medicins Sans Frontieres also observed that the Public Distribution System (PDS) distributed food based on class labels and publicly argued that "any assistance channeled through the PDS was discriminatory by nature; by using the PDS as the distribution channel for assistance, organizations are collaborating in organized government discrimination of its own citizens based on politics instead of needs."[131]

Medicines were also scarce and, despite efforts by aid organizations to provide, were never available; yet medicine was readily available on the black market. One defector commented that "it was always the same thing in the hospitals: no medicine. You could find great quantities of medicine on the market, however. Some of them came from Japan or China—you could see where from the labels [sic.] Others had labels in foreign languages."[132]

Other defectors observed that drugs were sold on the black market by doctors and observed that "they, too, have to live."[133] There have also been reports that Pyongyang embarked on a propaganda campaign to justify why aid being delivered was not distributed to the population. One technique used by North Korea to decrease foreign aid consumption was to issue false information on the safety and reliability of the products donated by other nations. One North Korean refugee reported that "propaganda is rife. We are told that we'll have to tighten our belts . . . that clothing from China spreads viruses, that food from international aid projects causes weight loss and that the foreign medicine causes sickness!"[134]

There are some accusations of diversion that might be explained by the characteristics of North Korean society. An example of this involves grain bags marked "World Food Program" in markets and other places. When observed, the presence of these bags implies that food provided by the WFP is being sold on the open market. World Food Program officials contend that this does not provide credible evidence that food aid is being diverted; rather they argue that these bags are "valuable items" and are used repeatedly.[135] The culture of North Korea, which has evolved to fully utilize items often discarded by more advanced nations, supports the contention that some of these bags have been re-used for other purposes.

Regardless of these claims, the outside world does not know whether WFP grain is being sold on the market, but the presence of the bags being openly displayed may indicate that the practice might be occurring. One aid official commented that during a 2005 trip to the DPRK, he personally observed a bag that stated, "Wheat – Gift of Russia to the people of North Korea." This bag was filled with locally produced beans.[136] Unfortunately, his trip, like all other aid-monitoring trips, was scheduled with North Korean authorities and his personal observation might have been staged to lend credence to the "bag re-use" argment.

UN Attempts to Boost Monitoring Efforts

Significant obstacles to NGO operations in North Korea include lack of appropriate counterparts because no North Korean non-governmental organizations exist, access problems, and the difficulty of measuring impact because opportunities for post-aid evaluations are few.[137] In a 2001 report to the UN,

Jean Ziegler, a special rapporteur for the Commission on Human Rights, commented that UN food aid had been provided since 1995, "but it gradually became clear that most of the international aid was being diverted by the army, the secret services and the Government."[138]

While the report itself was disputed by the WFP, the UN decreased the proportion of rice in the food aid and increased the corn and wheat in response. The intent was to decrease the possibility of aid diversion because corn and wheat are "less favored" in North Korea.[139] Additionally, the GAO issued a report in 1999 stating that WFP monitors had not visited 90 percent of the North Korean institutions, to include hospitals, orphanages, and schools.[140] The GAO report concluded that the WFP could not adequately monitor food aid and that humanitarian aid might not be reaching those in need and was possibly being sent to government officials or the military.[141] The WFP reacted to the issue of limited access to certain areas in North Korea by instituting a "no access, no food aid" policy.[142]

In 2002, World Food Program official John Powell commented on the military's role in food distribution and stated that "the army takes what it wants from the national harvest up front, in full. It takes it in the form of food Koreans prefer—Korean rice."[143] Additionally, North Korea has shown a willingness to resell aid, as was the case with Thai grain sold at subsidized prices to Pyongyang in 2002. That year, North Korea obtained 300,000 tons of rice originally from Thailand on a concessionary basis for humanitarian purposes. Later that year, the Thai rice was diverted by North Korean officials and resold.[144]

The Famine Continues

Reports persist concerning food aid diversion and North Korea continues to face problems feeding its population. In 2003, the South Korean government denied food aid was being used by the North Korean military, but did admit that imported food was being sold at "minimal price" at 46 won (US 35 cents) per kilogram.[145] Amid continuing reports of aid diversion, the WFP chief asserted that all humanitarian assistance to North Korea was going to the needy free of charge and any reports of diversion and sales in open markets probably involved food provided in bilateral aid from nations like South Korea.[146] But North Koreans remain hungry and in 2004, the WFP observed that over 70 percent of all households were dependent on their daily rice rations and that 6.5 million people in North Korea were considered "at risk" for starvation.[147] A World Food Program regional director visited North Korea in March 2005 and observed:

> The Public Distribution System has just recently cut its ration size for the average North Korean from 300 grams a day to 250 grams a day. This glass here [holds up small glass containing rice] has 250 grams of rice. That is what people are living on in North Korea, day after day. Without any meat, proteins, vegetables—except perhaps what they're able to hunt in the forests or get from relatives in the countryside.

They are obviously suffering from, in many cases, severe malnutrition. The statistics from the nutrition survey are quite clear in that respect. More than a third of the population is chronically malnourished. About a third of the mothers in North Korea are malnourished and anemic. So there is a continuing, very serious food crisis in the country. That's clear from the statistics, and its very clear based on observations. And it's hard to imagine anyone visiting the country would conclude differently.[148]

Currently, the major areas of frustration cited by the United Nations in continuing attempts to provide food aid to North Korea include incomplete access to over 40 counties, no access to local farmers' markets, the inability to conduct random spot checks of food distribution, and that the UN must use North Korean interpreters.[149] Access has improved for the WFP, but still remains incomplete. In 1998, the UN was not allowed to visit 61 of 206 counties, although by 2004, that number had been reduced to 42.[150] NGOs continue to report difficulties in operating in North Korea to include movement limitations, donor concerns over aid diversion, limited access to DPRK government agencies, limited understanding by North Korea of the difference between humanitarian aid and development assistance, and lack of transparency in program implementation.[151] One official commented that the UN conducted over 300 monitoring visits every month, but observed, "They don't mean anything, because there are no random visits."[152]

The UN estimated that aid needed for North Korea for 2005 was at $171 million for emergency aid.[153] In the stated WFP objectives for North Korea the same year, there were no plans for "developmental aid" and aid efforts were referred to as "emergency assistance."[154] But food aid from international sources can be described as "implicit balance of payments support" which relieves North Korea of the burden of purchasing or producing the amount of donated food and allows Pyongyang to commit those funds to other items.[155]

All Aid Supports the Regime

In the end, the human impact of the North Korean famine can be directly tied to factors that could not be controlled by international food agencies, and are the direct result of the economic failures of the Kim regime. The economic and political factors that caused this crisis can only be corrected through "massive financial, technical, and structural inputs."[156] North Korea's inherent isolationist and paranoid view of the world make these types of essential changes almost impossible. The DPRK economy remains in trouble as of this writing as one South Korea official observed that North Korea "doesn't produce any manufactured goods, the government doesn't have any money. They don't pay wages for labor, and they don't have raw materials."[157]

Two facts are certain: first, North Korea experienced the worst famine in its history, and second, given the overwhelming evidence provided by North Koreans and aid workers, Pyongyang diverted a portion of the international aid received to alternate uses. This diversion has resulted in a denial of intended aid to those in need with adverse effects on North Korean society. Yet the overall impacts are not easily determined and, given the closed nature of North Korean society, observers are dependent on refugee and defector reporting to assess the damaged caused by this activity. While estimates on aid diversion vary widely, economist Marcus Noland, citing a South Korean NGO, stated that approximately half of all aid to North Korea is diverted for sale on the black market or used by other than the intended recipients. Noland's own estimate is that between 10 and 30 percent is actually diverted.[158] Additionally, the United Nations estimated that in 2005, North Korea would require at least $200 million in emergency food aid.[159] Thus, if 10–50 percent of food aid is possibly diverted according to these sources, then we can estimate that North Korea annually diverts humanitarian aid worth $20–100 million. In view of the characteristics and past performance of the DPRK, diversion of donated food, medicine, and other supplies will most likely continue as long as foreign nations provide humanitarian aid.

Through selling weapons and arms technology and by diverting food aid, North Korea continues to siphon funds from legitimate transactions to support the regime. Weapons sales continue to be an integral part of North Korea's moneymaking machine, but one that does entail production and transportation costs. On the other hand, humanitarian aid requires little expense on North Korea's part and constitutes a significant resource for the regime. In effect, the US, South Korea, Japan, and the European Union contribute to Kim Jong-il's coffers by continuing to provide aid, which ultimately sustains the regime.

Notes and references

1. Anthony Smith, "Asia Pacific Security: Dilemmas of Dominance, Challenges to Community," *East-West Center Senior Policy Seminar 2003*, www.eastwestcenter.org/stored/pdfs/SeniorPolicySeminar2003.pdf, accessed 4 February 2004.

2. Gross Domestic Product (GDP) generally refers to the overall domestic output, usually in terms of US dollars, of a nation. Economists often provide comparisons between nations of total GDP or GDP per person.

3. "North Korea Country Profile 2005," *Economist Intelligence Unit Online*, db.eiu.com/report_dl.asp?mode=pdf&eiu_issue_id=618020461, accessed 22 February 2005.

4. Noland, *Avoiding the Apocalypse*, 81.

5. Noland, *Avoiding the Apocalypse*, 61.

6. Chul Yang Sung, *The North and South Korean Political Systems: A Comparative Analysis* (Elizabeth, NJ: Hollym International, 1999), 590–591.

7. Donald M. Rodgers, *Taiwan and North Korea: Division, Legitimacy, Competition, and Nation-State Identity*, Doctoral Dissertation (Athens, GA: University of Georgia,

2000), 170.

8. Joseph Chung, "North Korea's Economic Development and Capabilities," *Asian Perspective* 11, no. 1 (Spring–Summer 1987): 45–74; Sung, *The North and South Korean Political Systems*, 590.

9 Doowon Lee, "North Korean Economic Reform: Past Efforts and Future Prospects," in *Reforming Asian Socialism: The Growth of Market Institutions*, eds. John McMillan and Barry Naughton (Ann Arbor, MI: University of Michigan Press, 1996), 321.

10. *North Korea: A Country Study*, 114–115.

11. Nicholas Eberstadt, *Policy and Economic Performance in Divided Korea, 1945–1995*, Doctoral Dissertation (Cambridge, MA: Harvard University, December 1995), 97–98; Cumings, *Korea's Place in the Sun*, 424.

12. "Deadbeat Debtor," *Financial Times*, 29 April 1995, accessed via LexisNexis Research Database, 19 April 2005.

13. Lee, "North Korean Economic Reform," 328.

14. Lee, "North Korean Economic Reform," 328.

15. During the same period, South Korea dedicated 5 percent of its GDP to the military; more recent estimates indicate South Korea spends just under 3 percent of GDP on defense while Pyongyang dedicates 7 percent to its military operations. Oberdorfer, *The Two Koreas*, 98; *The Military Balance: 2003–2004*, ed. Christopher Langton, International Institute for Strategic Studies (London: Oxford University Press, 2003), 299; Woo, *The Politics of Asymmetrical Triangles*, 130.

16. Lee, "North Korean Economic Reform," 322, 324, 328.

17. Noland, *Avoiding the Apocalypse*, 97.

18. Reese, *The Prospects for North Korea's Survival*, 27.

19. China provided more than two-thirds of its imported energy support at this time. Reese, *The Prospects for North Korea's Survival*, 27.

20. *North Korea: A Country Study*, 154.

21. The causes and effects of the famine are discussed later in this chapter.

22. Erich Weingartner, "NGO Contributions to the Transition from Humanitarian to Development Assistance in DPRK," in *North Korea in the World Economy*, eds. E. Kwan Choi and others (New York: RoutledgeCurzon, 2003), 210.

23. "GDP of North Korea," *Bank of Korea Online*, www.bok.or.kr/index.jsp, keyword search North Korea, accessed 6 February 2005.

24. The US provided heavy fuel oil to North Korea as part of the "Agreed Framework" in exchange for North Korea's agreement to cease its nuclear research and development program.

25. Cumings, *North Korea: Another Country*, 183.

26. "North Korea Country Profile 2005."

27. Nicolas Eberstadt, "The Persistence of North Korea," *Policy Review Online* (Oc-

tober 2004), www.policyreivew.org/oct04/eberstadt.html, accessed 15 March 2005.

28. "North Korea Country Profile 2005."

29. In comparison, during 2003 Vietnam's total trade was $40 billion, Thailand had $141 billion in trade, and South Korea's total imports and exports stood at $376 billion. Korean Overseas Trade Association (KOTRA), *KOTRA Website,* www.crm.kotra.or.kor/main, accessed 18 March 2005; South Korean Ministry of Unification, *Ministry of Unification Website,* www.unikorea.go.kr/en/northkorea, accessed 18 March 2005; "North Korea Country Profile 2005"; CIA, *The World Factbook Online 2004: North Korea.*

30. Eberstadt, "The Persistence of North Korea."

31. Noland, *Avoiding the Apocalypse,* 119.

32. "North Korea Country Profile 2005."

33. In 2002, North Korea announced that its official currency was the euro and forbid the use of US dollars. Whether or not this remains in practice is unclear. "North Korea Country Profile 2005."

34. US Congress, *North Korean Missile Proliferation,* 1.

35. Noland, *Avoiding Apocalypse,* 117–118.

36. For a more thorough review of North Korea's smaller-scale weapons transactions and support provided, see *North Korea: A Country Study,* 258–261.

37. *North Korea's Weapons Programmes: A Net Assessment,* International Institute for Strategic Studies, ed. Gary Samore (New York: Palgrave Macmillan, 2004), 63–82; Robert Karniol, "Vietnam Stocking up 'SCUDs,'" *Jane's Defence Weekly,* 14 April 1999, 63; "North Korea's Ballistic Missile Exports"; Duk-Min Yun, "Long-range Missiles," in *North Korea's Weapons of Mass Destruction: Problems and Prospects,* ed. Kim Kyoung Soo (Elizabeth, NJ: Hollym, 2004), 124; Bermudez, *History of DPRK Missile Development,* 10–32; Triplett, *Rogue State,* 157 (No Dong), 171 (nuclear), 172 (Taepo Dong 1 and 2), 170 (China); Ronald H. Siegel, "The Missile Programs of North Korea, Iraq, and Iran," *Institute for Defense & Disarmament Studies Working Paper 3,* September 2001, www.nautilus.org/VietnamFOIA/archives/DPRKbriefingbook/missiles/IDDS-SeigelReport.html, accessed 21 December 2005; Bertil Lintner and Shawn W. Crispin, "Dangerous Bedfellows: Evidence of a blossoming military relationship between Rangoon and Pyongyang," *Far Eastern Economic Review* 166, no. 46 (20 November 2003): 22–23; *North Korea Country Study,* 258–261; Richard Halloran, "Iran Is Said To Get North Korean Arms," *The New York Times,* 19 December 1982, accessed via LexisNexis Research Database, 25 April 2005; Bill Gertz, "Cuba, North Korea Getting Cozy, US fears," *The Washington Times,* 29 November 1991, accessed via LexisNexis Research Database, 25 April 2005; *The Military Balance: 2003–2004,* 174; Noland, *Avoiding the Apocalypse,* 117; Il-Young Kim and Lakhvinder Singh, "The North Korean Nuclear Program and External Connections," *The Korean Journal of Defense Analysis* 16, no. 1 (Spring 2004): 81; "US Ties N Korea to Nuclear Deal," *BBC News Online,* 5 February 2005, www.news.bbc.co.uk/1/hi/world/asia-pacific/4228713.stm, accessed 10 February 2005.

38. M.A. Cho, "North Korea's 2003 Foreign Trade," *KOTRA Website,* 13 August 2004, www.crm.kotra.or.kr/main/info/nk/new2003/, accessed 22 March 2005.

39. *North Korea's Weapons Programmes: A Net Assessment,* 81–83.

40. "North Korea's Ballistic Missile Exports."

41. CIA, "Acquisition of Technology Related to Weapons of Mass Destruction."

42. Yun, "Long-range Missiles," 122.

43. US Congress, *Final Report of the North Korean Advisory Group.*

44. Yun, "Long-range Missiles," 123.

45. These surface-to-surface missiles can carry conventional and chemical munitions and have the following ranges: Scud-B – 300km, Scud-C – 500km, and No Dong – 1300km. *North Korea's Weapons Programmes: A Net Assessment,* 63, 72.

46. Bermudez, *A History of Ballistic Missile Development in the DPRK,* 4.

47. Bermudez, *A History of Ballistic Missile Development in the DPRK,* 10; Yun, "Long-range Missiles," 124.

48. Yun, "Long-range Missiles," 124–125.

49. The Syrian and Iranian tests were conducted with North Korean assistance Bermudez, *A History of Ballistic Missile Development in the DPRK,* 17–19.

50. Syria received an estimated 60 missiles and 12 mobile launchers from North Korea between 1991 and 1995; Egypt's President Hosni Mubarak visited Pyongyang in 1990 and subsequently obtained Hwasong-6 technology from North Korea; Libya purchased DPRK technical components to maintain its own Scud systems; and Vietnam also possibly obtained a few Hwasong-6 missiles from North Korea in 1998 or 1999. Bermudez, *A History of Ballistic Missile Development in the DPRK,* 18–19; Karniol, "Vietnam Stocking up 'SCUDs,'" 63.

51. Bermudez, *A History of Ballistic Missile Development in the DPRK,* 16.

52. US Congress, *North Korean Missile Proliferation,* 33.

53. *Bermudez, A History of Ballistic Missile Development in the DPRK,* 20.

54. Yun, "Long-range Missiles," 127.

55. Bermudez, *A History of Ballistic Missile Development in the DPRK,* 22; "NSP Issues Press Release on Hwang's Comments," (text), Seoul *Agency for National Security Planning* (9 May 1997), FBIS Document ID FTS199705122001202, accessed 14 June 2005.

56. Ronald H. Siegel, *The Missile Programs of North Korea, Iraq, and Iran,* Working Paper 3, Institute for Defense & Disarmament Studies, September 2001, www.idds.org/iddswkp3.html, accessed 15 May 2005.

57. Feickert, "Missile Survey: Ballistic and Cruise Missiles of Foreign Countries," 9.

58. With this capability, the Taepo Dong could range much of the western United States. There is a significant amount of debate on the actual range and delivery ability of the Taepo Dong-2, with reports of ranges up to 10,000 km. See Robert Wapole's testimony in US Congress, *CIA National Intelligence Estimate of Foreign Missile Developments,* 6. The ability of the missile to deliver a nuclear payload over that distance due to technical and reentry constraints remains slim. Feickert, "Missile Survey: Ballistic and

Cruise Missiles of Foreign Countries," 4–6.

59. Joseph S. Bermudez, "North Korea's Long Range Missiles," in *Ballistic Missile Proliferation: Jane's Special Report* (Coulsdon, United Kingdom: Jane's Information Group, 2000), 5.

60. Bermudez, *A History of Ballistic Missile Development in the DPRK,* 29; Nick Nanto, "North Korea: Chronology of Provocations, 1950–2003," *CRS Report for Congress* RL30427 (Washington, DC: Congressional Research Service, Library of Congress, 2003), 17; "North Korea Fires Missile Across Northern Japan Into Pacific," *Korea Times,* 1 September 1998, accessed via LexisNexis Research Database, 15 May 2005.

61. Bermudez, *A History of Ballistic Missile Development in the DPRK,* 29.

62. "North Korea's Taepo Dong I Missile Priced at $6 Million," *Korea Times,* 29 October 1999, accessed via LexisNexis Research Database, 16 May 2005.

63. Feickert, "North Korean Ballistic Missile Threat to the United States," 5.

64. Christopher Torchia, "North Korea's Missiles: A Source of Cash, Prestige and Bargaining Power," *The Associated Press,* 21 February 2002, accessed via LexisNexis Research Database, 15 March 2005.

65. Larry A. Niksch, "North Korea's Nuclear Weapons Program," *CRS Report for Congress* IB91141 (Washington, DC: Congressional Research Service, Library of Congress, 28 September 2004), 9; Yun, "Long-range Missiles," 129.

66. For more information on how ballistic missiles work and a description of the links between the development of North Korean and other missile programs, see Siegel, "The Missile Programs of North Korea, Iraq, and Iran"; "US Official Worried North Korea May Be Receiving Missile Test Data From Iran," *Financial Times Information,* 27 May 2004, accessed via LexisNexis Research Database, 13 March 2005.

67. Niksch, "North Korea's Nuclear Weapons Program," 10.

68. These "lesser missiles" have most likely been North Korean "Seersucker" HY-2 anti-ship missiles. Feickert, "Missile Survey: Ballistic and Cruise Missiles of Foreign Countries," 12–13.

69. Fredrick Kempe and David S. Cloud, "Baghdad Records Show Hussein Sought Missiles, Other Aid Abroad," *The Wall Street Journal,* 3 November 2003, 1.

70. Kempe and Cloud, "Baghdad Records Show Hussein Sought Missiles," 1.

71. Nicholas Kralev, "Pakistan Purchases N. Korean Missiles," *Washington Times,* 31 March 2003, 1.

72. Hon. William S. Cohen, Secretary of Defense, *Proliferation: Threat and Response,* January 2001, Office of the Secretary of Defense (Washington, DC: US Government Printing Office, 2001), 13.

73. Feickert and Kronstadt, "Missile Proliferation and the Strategic Balance in South Asia," 20.

74. Kralev, "Pakistan Purchases N. Korean Missiles," 1.

75. US Congress, *Drugs, Counterfeiting, and Weapons Proliferation: The NK Connection,* 51, 57.

76. The *Chosen Soren* is an association of ethnic Koreans living in Japan that retains significant ties to the North. Testimony of Ju-hwal Choi, US Congress, *North Korean Missile Proliferation*, 27.

77. During US Senate testimony in 2003, Dr. Larry Wortzel commented that North Korea earned about $560 million annually in missile sales, US Congress, *Drugs, Counterfeiting, and Weapons Proliferation: The NK Connection*, 51, 57; Noland provides more realistic figures of between $50–100 million per year in *Avoiding the Apocalypse*, 118.

78. Lintner Crispin, "Dangerous Bedfellows," 22–23; "North Korea armed Islamic group in Philippines," *World Tribune*, online ed., 5 January 2005, www.worldtribune.com/worldtribune/05/breaking2453376.1868055556.html, accessed 2 March 2005.

79. Richard F. Grimmett, "Conventional Arms Transfers to Developing Nations," *CRS Report for Congress* RL32547 (Library of Congress, Washington, DC: Government Printing Office, 2003), 59.

80. *North Korea: A Country Study*, 258.

81. For a review of previous military assistance provided by North Korea, see *North Korea: A Country Study*, 258–261.

82. Halloran, "Iran To Get North Korean Arms."

83. Halloran, "Iran To Get North Korean Arms."

84. Gertz, "Cuba, North Korea Getting Cozy."

85. The military advisors were primarily North Korea special operations personnel from its Reconnaissance Bureau. *North Korea: A Country Study*, 258.

86. *North Korea: A Country Study*, 261.

87. Yoshinari Kurose, "North Korea reportedly sold arms to group linked to al-Qaida," *The Yomiuri Shimbun*, 4 January 2005, accessed via LexisNexis Research Database, 25 April 2005.

88. In 2003, the US accounted for 56.7 percent of all weapons transfers to developing nations with $14.5 billion in sales; Russia was second with 16.8 percent and $4.3 billion in sales. Grimmett, "Conventional Arms Transfers," 3.

89. Triplett, *Rogue State*, 171; Kim and Singh, "The North Korean Nuclear Program and External Connections," 81; "US Ties N Korea to Nuclear Deal."

90. Henry Sokolski, "Axis of Proliferators," *The Wall Street Journal*, 19 August 2003, accessed via Proquest Research Database, 15 March 2005.

91. "US Ties N Korea to Nuclear Deal."

92. *North Korea's Weapons Programmes: A Net Assessment*, 3.

93. US Arms Control and Disarmament Agency, *World Military Expenditures and Arms Transfers 1995* (Washington, DC: US Government Printing Office, 1996), 131.

94. Marcus Noland citing South Korea's defense ministry, the Stockholm International Peace Institute and US government officials in *Avoiding Apocalypse*, 118; also see "NK Earns $100 Million annually from Missile Exports" and "Scud missile sales 'earned North Korea 60 million dollars in 2002,'" *Deutsche Presse-Agentur*, 23 October 2003,

accessed via LexisNexis Research Database, 28 March 2005.

95. Marcus Noland citing several sources to include South Korea's defense ministry, the Stockholm International Peace Institute, and US government officials in *Avoiding Apocalypse*, 118; "NK Earns $100 Million Annually from Missile Exports"; and "Scud missile sales 'earned North Korea 60 million dollars in 2002.'"

96. Between 12 and 15 Scuds were found, based on a variety of sources. North Korea was found to be conducting a "legitimate transaction" and the vessel proceeded to Yemen after inspection. Jay Solomon, "A Global Journal Report: Some Speak of Pyongyang Blockade – Bush Administration Hawks Consider Ways to Stop Exporting of Arms, Drugs," *The Wall Street Journal*, 5 May 2003, accessed via ProQuest Research Database, 2 April 2005; David Sanger and Thom Shanker, "Reluctant US Gives Assent for Missiles to Go to Yemen," *The New York Times*, 12 December 2002, 1.

97. Noland, *Avoiding the Apocalypse*, 118.

98. Both North and South Korea are mostly mountainous nations (over 65 percent) with limited land suitable for food production. CIA, *The World Factbook Online 2004: North Korea.*

99. Schloms, *North Korea and the Timeless Dilemma of Aid*, 96.

100. Eberstadt, *The End of North Korea*, 46.

101. Schloms also notes that North Korea's options for obtaining fuel have been limited due to US economic sanctions. Schloms, *North Korea and the Timeless Dilemma of Aid*, 98.

102. Schloms, *North Korea and the Timeless Dilemma of Aid*, 98.

103. Weingartner, "NGO Contributions," 209.

104. Schloms, *North Korea and the Timeless Dilemma of Aid*, 100–101.

105. Natsios, *The Great North Korean Famine*, 5–6.

106. Chung Oknim, "The Role of South Korea's NGOs: The Political Context," in *Paved With Good Intention*, 99.

107. Schloms, *North Korea and the Timeless Dilemma of Aid*, 92.

108. The total amount of grain required included food for the North Korean people, grain for animals, and seed for planting. Schloms, *North Korea and the Timeless Dilemma of Aid*, 103.

109. Hi Kim Suk, *North Korea at a Crossroads* (Jefferson, NC: McFarland Publishers, 2003), 80.

110. Noland, *Avoiding the Apocalypse*, 275.

111. Michael Judge, "North Korea's Dr. Evil," *The Wall Street Journal*, 15 October 2002, A20.

112. North Korea's Public Distribution System is based on the Soviet system of the same name and provides subsidized food staples to citizens as compensation for work. Food distribution historically depended on both occupation and party loyalty. Natsios, *The Great North Korean Famine*, 92–93.

113. Schloms, *North Korea and the Timeless Dilemma of Aid*, 121.

114. Schloms, *North Korea and the Timeless Dilemma of Aid*, 120.

115. Marcus Noland argues that only around 600,000 people died during the famine but comments that regardless of the figure it was "a bad experience" for North Korea. Testimony of Marcus Noland in US Congress, Senate, Subcommittee on East Asian and Pacific Affairs of the Committee on Foreign Relations, *Life Inside North Korea*, 108th Cong., 1st sess., 5 June 2003, S. Hrg. 108-131 (Washington, DC: US Government Printing Office, 2003), 39.

116. L. Gordon Flake, "Testimony Before the Subcommittee on Asia and the Pacific, House Committee on International Relations," US House of Representatives Committee on International Relations Website Committee on International Relations Website, 28 April 2004, wwwc.house.gov/international_relations/108/fla042804.htm, accessed 30 April 2005.

117. Manyin and Jun, "US Assistance to North Korea," 3.

118. Niksch, "Korea: US-Korea Relations – Issues for Congress," 10–11.

119. Out of 1544 individuals interviewed, 1402 stated they received no aid. Christine Y. Chang, "A Field Survey Report of North Korean Refugees in China," *The Commission to Help North Korean Refugees*, 1999, www.cnkr.org/, accessed 30 April 2005; Schloms, *North Korea and the Timeless Dilemma of Aid*, 176.

120. Schloms, *North Korea and the Timeless Dilemma of Aid*, 177.

121. Testimony of Benjamin Nelson in US Congress, *Misuse of US Aid to North Korea*, 21.

122. Schloms, *North Korea and the Timeless Dilemma of Aid*, 170; US GAO, "Foreign Assistance: North Korea Restricts Food Aid Monitoring," 11–13.

123. The tracking system established by the WFP only monitors the aid from the seaport to country warehouses, but there is no provision for spot checks on the transportation routes or final storage sites. Schloms, *North Korea and the Timeless Dilemma of Aid*, 170; US General Accounting Office, "Foreign Assistance: North Korea Restricts Food Aid Monitoring," Report to the Chairman, Committee on International Relations, House of Representatives, *GAO Archive*, GAO/NSIAD-00-35, October 1999, www.gao.gov/archive/2000/ns00035.pdf, 11–13.

124. US Congress, *Misuse of US Aid to North Korea*, 1; Gary L. Jones, "Nuclear Nonproliferation: Heavy Fuel Oil Delivered to North Korea Under the Agreed Framework," Testimony before the House of Representatives Committee on International Relations, *US General Accounting Office Website*, 27 October 1999, www.gao.gov/archive/2000/rc00020t.pdf, accessed 30 April 2005, 1.

125. Chaiki Seong, "A Decade of Economic Crisis in North Korea: Impacts on the Military," *Korea Institute for Defense Analyses*, KIDA Paper No. 3 (October 2003), www.kida.re.kr/eng/publications/publications02.htm, accessed 14 March 2005.

126. Between 1995 and 1998, MSF attempted to provide assistance to approximately 1100 health care centers and ran 60 feeding centers for malnourished children. Testimony of Sophie Delaunay in US Congress, House, International Relations Subcommittee on East Asia and the Pacific, "North Korea: The Humanitarian Situation and

Refugees," *Doctors Without Borders Website*, 2 May 2002, www.doctorswithoutborders. org/publications/speeches/2002/sd_nkorea.shtml, accessed 29 April 2005.

127. US Congress, "North Korea: The Humanitarian Situation and Refugees. *"*

128. "North Korea: Testimonies of Famine - Refugee Interviews from the Sino-Korean Border, August 1998," August 1998, *Doctors Without Borders Website*, www.doctorswithoutborders.org/publications/reports/before1999/korea_1998.shtml, accessed 29 April 2005.

129. "North Korea: Testimonies of Famine."

130. From several defector statements cited in Delaunay, "North Korea: The Humanitarian Situation and Refugees."

131. Delaunay, "North Korea: The Humanitarian Situation and Refugees"; Kongdan Oh provides a more detailed description of this societal discrimination in US Congress, *Life Inside North Korea*, 22.

132. "North Korea: Testimonies of Famine."

133. "North Korea: Testimonies of Famine."

134. "North Korea: Testimonies of Famine."

135. Tony Banbury, "Food Programme Press Conference on the DPRK," *The Nautilus Institute's NAPSNet Daily Report*, 31 March 2005, www.nautilus.org/napsnet/sr/ 2005/0528A_Banbury.html, accessed 29 April 2005.

136. Banbury, "Food Programme Press Conference on the DPRK."

137. Weingartner, "NGO Contributions," 210.

138. Jean Ziegler, Special Rapporteur on the Right to Food, "The Right to Food, *"* *United Nations Economic and Social Council Commission on Human Rights*, E/CN.4/ 2001/53, 7 February 2001, 11.

139. "Food Program Official Suspects 'Diversion' of Food Aid in North Korea," *Yonhap News*, 28 February 2002, accessed via InfoTrac OneFile Research Database, 10 February 2005.

140. Barbara Crossette, "US Study Finds Lack of Control in UN Food Aid to North Korea," *New York Times*, 12 October 1999, A8.

141. Crossette, "US Study Finds Lack of Control in UN Food Aid."

142. Banbury, "Food Programme Press Conference on the DPRK."

143. John Powell testimony in US Congress, House, Subcommittee on East Asia and the Pacific of the Committee on International Relations, *North Korea: Humanitarian and Human Rights Concerns*, 107th Cong., 2nd sess., 2 May 2002, H. Rept. 107–95 (Washington, DC: US Government Printing Office, 2002), 52.

144. The rice was diverted and resold to West Africa. "Thai Senate raises suspicions on rice exports to North," *Joongang Daily Online*, 22 May 2002, www.joogangdaily.joins.com/200205/22/200205221602254659900090209021.html, accessed 30 April 2005.

145. All food distributed in North Korea (including the staples available through the PDS) is sold at subsidized prices. The average North Korea earns between 1,500–6,000

won per month (US $10–$40). "No Diversion of Food Aid to N.K.'s Military: S. Korean Officials," (text), Seoul *Yonhap News*, 9 October 2003, FBIS Document ID KPP20031009000107, accessed 5 January 2005.

146. Sarah Suk, "WFP Chief Confident Food for N. Korea Reaching Intended Recipients," (text), Tokyo *Kyodo World Service*, 26 October 2004, FBIS Document ID JPP20041026000087, accessed 5 January 2005.

147. This source also mentioned that not all North Koreans suffer equally: in Pyongyang, civil servants receive twice the amount of rice ration of those in the countryside. "Asia: Through a glass, darkly; North Korea," *The Economist* 370, no. 8366 (13 March 2004): 64.

148. Banbury, "Food Programme Press Conference on the DPRK."

149. Manyin and Jun, "US Assistance to North Korea," 12–15.

150. Manyin and Jun, "US Assistance to North Korea," 12; World Food Program, "World Hunger - Korea (DPR),"*United Nations Website*, www.wfp.org/country_brief/indexcountry.asp?country=408#, accessed 30 April 2005.

151. Weingartner, "NGO Contributions," 215.

152. Flake, "Subcommittee on Asia and the Pacific Testimony."

153. World Food Program, "World Hunger – Korea (DPR)."

154. World Food Program, "World Hunger – Korea (DPR)."

155. Marcus Noland, "North Korea's External Economic Relations: Working Paper," *Institute for International Economics*, February 2001, www.iie.com/publications/papers/noland0201-1.htm#23, accessed 30 April 2005.

156. Schloms adds that given the nature of North Korea, these types of developmental assistance and significant changes to North Korea's system are unlikely. Schloms, *North Korea and the Timeless Dilemma of Aid*, 121.

157. Comment by Eui Chu Choi of the Korean Institute of National Unification in reference to the assistance North Korea needs and efforts to restart nuclear talks in 2005. Don Kirk, "Despite 'Reforms,' Food Crisis Hits N. Korea," *The Christian Science Monitor*, 28 January 2005, www.csmonitor.com/2005/0128/p06s02-woap.htm, accessed 29 April 2005.

158. Marcus Noland and Stephan Haggard, "The North Korean Human Rights Act of 2004: Issues and Implementation," testimony during a Hearing before the Subcommittee on Africa, Global Human Rights, and International Operations, US House of Representatives, *US House Committee on International Relations Website*, wwwa.house.gov/international_relations/109/nol042805.pdf, accessed 11 July 2005.

159. Manyin, "Foreign Assistance to North Korea," 8, 9, 26.

Chapter 3

Covert Fundraising Operations

Opium gets you 300 times the profits you can get from corn.

—North Korean defector, quoted by
Jay Solomon and Jason Dean in "Drug Money"

Kim Jong-il's efforts to raise hard currency are not an option for the regime; they are a "simple choice of economics and regime survival."[1] As described in the previous chapter, North Korea has few options to close the gap between income and expenditures and these efforts are an attempt to ensure its future. Covert support for the regime comes from a variety of sources, to include Korean residents abroad, state-sponsored cultivation of poppies, and the production of heroin, methamphetamines and other narcotics, and counterfeiting operations that have proliferated bogus American currency throughout the world. These organizations and activities are directly sponsored and coordinated by Pyongyang and provide hard currency to support Kim's regime.

Chosen Soren Support

The Chosen Soren, or Organization of Korean Citizens in Japan, was founded in 1955 primarily to support relief and repatriation efforts for ethnic Koreans residing in Japan in the aftermath of the Korean War.[2] Similar organizations have existed in Japan since the end of World War II and have been both credited with giving valuable support to Korean residents and accused of providing direct assistance to the North Korean government. Emma Chanett-Avery observed that "the Chosen Soren organization has long supported North Korea by facilitating trade, remitting cash donations, establishing personal contacts, and possibly coordinating illicit transfers of narcotics and weapon parts."[3] William Triplett described the group as an "island of Korean identity in a sea of Japanese culture . . . North Korea's unofficial embassy in Japan."[4]

After Japan annexed Korea in 1910 and began exploiting both the people and resources of the peninsula, significant numbers of Korean men began to migrate in hopes of making money to support their families. The numbers of Koreans in Japan rose from 790 just before annexation in 1909 to 3,630 in 1914 and to 419,000 in 1930.[5] By the time Japan surrendered to the Allies in 1945, approximately 2.4 million Koreans were living in Japan, which was about 10 percent of the entire Korean population.[6] The presence of these Koreans in Japan spurred the need for mutual support organizations resulting in the eventual establishment and prominence of the Chosen Soren. To adequately understand the significance of this group, we first have to consider the early relationships between these two nations and the migration that resulted in large numbers of Koreans living in Japan. This section will discuss the origins and activities of the Chosen Soren organization and will focus on the organization's current and future relevance as a viable means of obtaining hard currency for North Korea.

Chosen Soren Beginnings

Japan's annexation of Korea in 1910 was based on both security and economic factors: Korea was seen as a "buffer against foreign encroachment" and as an exploitable resource for Japan's expansion.[7] The lack of jobs in Korea at that time resulted in the migration of unskilled laborers and tenant farmers. This population was primarily uneducated and illiterate and many Japanese felt "Koreans who came to Japan exemplified the backwardness" of Korea.[8] From the very beginning, the Korean minority in Japan or "Zainichi" Koreans were viewed as a subordinate class who took jobs the Japanese refused and planned on staying a short time for work and then returning home.[9]

By the 1920s, this influx of Koreans began to affect Japanese society. Some Koreans became associated with leftist Japanese labor groups while, at the same time, nationalism was on the rise in Korea. Overseas Korean laborers were seen as a key source of support for the Japanese labor movement and as a result, the "Japanese government had come to regard all Koreans in Japan as potentially subversive."[10] The roots of the Chosen Soren can be traced to these types of labor groups.

Beginning in the late 1930s, the Japanese war effort had a profound effect on Korean laborers in Japan as increasing numbers of Japanese workers left for military service and Tokyo "first encouraged and then forced Koreans to come to Japan" to alleviate labor shortages.[11] In 1939, the Japanese government enacted the Labor Mobilization Law, which was the beginning of forced labor migration of Koreans to Japan.[12] Beginning in 1942, Koreans were conscripted for military service, which continued through the end of the war.[13] As it became clear Japan would lose the conflict, tensions between Koreans and the Japanese citizens increased and accusations of conspiracy between Koreans in Japan and the Allies circulated, revealing the deep-seeded Japanese mistrust of Zainichi Koreans.[14] As the war ended, Koreans began to return to their homeland and after the Japanese surrender in August 1945, "this movement swelled to a mass exodus."[15] But despite the large numbers that returned to Korea, a sizable Korean minority stayed in Japan: in fact, one fifth or approximately 600,000 Koreans remained after a repatriation period ended in 1947.[16]

The Association of Korean Citizens in Japan

After the end of the war, groups dedicated to ethnic Korean interests began to appear throughout Japan. The most significant of these was the *Choren*, or League of Koreans in Japan. Choren's main functions included assisting repatriation issues, solving Korean-Japanese conflicts, and providing economic assistance to poor Koreans.[17] Additionally, the organization established over 500 separate schools for Korean children.[18] A diverse group of Koreans originally founded this organization but it quickly fell under the control of Korean communists, who were allied with the resident Japanese Communist Party.[19] Fundraising to support the organization was conducted through black-market operations and direct negotiations with the Japanese government to obtain "back wages" or "separation bonuses" for Korean workers, which were mostly retained by Choren.[20]

The activities of the communist and Choren groups in Japan came under increasing scrutiny and in September 1949, the Japanese government ordered the Choren and three other Korean groups to be disbanded and all affiliated schools closed.[21] Immediately after the invasion of South Korea by North Korean communist forces in June 1950, the Japanese government acted to suppress the domestic Japanese Communist Party and Korean left-wing organizations and "directed the police to keep close watch on the entire Korean population in Japan."[22] Despite these efforts, a new pro-North Korean group emerged during the Korean War called the Minsen. In collaboration with the Japanese Communist Party, the Minsen conducted sabotage operations and spread pro-DPRK propaganda throughout Japan. In the mid-1950s, Pyongyang determined that the activities of the Minsen were not supporting its causes and ordered the group to end its association with the Japanese Communist Party. The Minsen disbanded in 1955 and was replaced by the modern-day Chosen Soren, also known as Chongryun.[23]

The Birth of the Chosen Soren

The Zainichi Chosenjin Sorengokai, or Chosen Soren (General Federation of Korean Residents in Japan) was established in May 1955.[24] By 1957, Chosen Soren and affiliated organizations had a total membership of over 150,000.[25] The Chosen Soren began to branch out into many areas to include newspaper publishing, importing and translating North Korean books, and establishing Korean schools throughout Japan.[26] By 1960, the Chosen Soren had established 280 schools that used Korean as their primary language with significant support from the DPRK.[27] Economically, life was difficult for these groups, as many remained unemployed. Those who did have jobs were unskilled laborers or ran dance halls, gambling parlors, theaters, or restaurants.[28] Others turned to criminal activity to make money to include illegal liquor production or narcotics trafficking.[29]

DPRK Support Begins

This time also saw initial evidence of Chosen Soren being directed to support North Korea, which intensified during the 1980s. On 15 September 1986, Kim Il-sung issued instructions to the Chosen Soren to "conduct business activities in a more lively way," which saw the beginnings of significant business efforts to provide a variety of support to North Korea.[30] This support included financial remittances, technology transfers, and support to North Korean defense and intelligence services. These remittances set the stage for significant support in the future, which is partially credited with helping North Korea survive the economic and social crises it experienced during the 1990s.

Chosen Soren Support to Pyongyang

The Chosen Soren engages in a variety of actions to raise funds to support both its own operations and provide hard currency to North Korea. These activities range from tours for Zainichi Koreans to the DPRK to support for North Korean espionage efforts. This next section discusses these efforts to sustain the Kim regime through legal and illicit activities.

The Mangyongbong-92 and Smuggling Operations

One method of support the Chosen Soren provides to North Korea involves the Mangyongbong-92 ferry, a North Korean-flagged vessel that routinely travels between North Korean and Japan. The Mangyongbong-92 is a 9,600-ton ship that makes between 20 and 30 trips per year carrying up to 350 people and cargo on a 12-hour crossing between Wonsan, North Korea and Niigata, Japan.[31] The vessel has been associated with a variety of illegal and "gray area" activities to include drug smuggling, counterfeit currency transfers, technology smuggling, cash remittances, and support to espionage. The Mangyongbong-92 and Chosen Soren have also been associated with smuggling missile parts to North Korea from Japan. In 2003 testimony before the US Congress, a North Korean missile guidance expert stated that "over 90 percent of these [missile] parts come from North Korea" on the Mangyongbong-92 facilitated by Chosen Soren.[32] Additionally, a relationship between spy activities and the Chosen Soren has been ongoing for decades. In 2003, a former North Korean spy in Japan stated he received orders from Pyongyang via the captain of the Mangyongbong-92 to spread propaganda in South Korea and to recruit new spies for Pyongyang.[33] That same year, Japanese officials stated that the vessel had been equipped with military radar capable of both mapping the seabed along the coast of Japan and communicating with North Korean submarines.[34]

Defectors report that the repatriation ships that ran between Japan and North Korea beginning in 1959 provided transportation for Chosen Soren-associated spies moving between these two nations.[35] The year 2002 saw a significant change in Mangyongbong-92 visits to Japan due to issues surrounding the admission of the abduction of Japanese nationals by North Korea. As a result, the Japanese began to tighten shipping regulations for all vessels arriving from the

DPRK. Beginning in 2003, Japanese authorities began inspecting vessels, to include the Mangyongbong-92, for emergency equipment, to include fire extinguishers and lifeboats.[36]

These additional inspection requirements resulted in a seven-month suspension of Mangyongbong-92 trips to Japan, presumably while repairs were made to comply with the new regulations; also, more than 70 percent of 120 North Korean ships inspected from January to August 2003 failed to meet safety standards and many were ordered to halt operations.[37] In 2002, DPRK-flagged ships visited Japan over 1400 times but by 2004, that number was reduced to just over 1000 port calls per year for North Korean vessels.[38] In 2004, the Mangyongbong-92 made approximately 11 trips between Wonsan and Niigata, which is significantly less than in the past.[39]

Visiting Relatives – North Korean Style

Additional sources of income associated both with Chosen Soren and the Mangyongbong-92 includes heavy fees for those wanting to visit relatives in North Korea or Japan. For North Koreans visiting Japan, they are "requested" to make a significant donation to the Koreans Workers Party.[40] The cost for a five member Zainichi Korean family as being between 200 and 300 million yen ($1.8–2.7 million); for this amount, the family received a trip on the Mangyongbong-92 and a two-week "monitored" stay in North Korea. This small group was part of a larger group participating in similar trips, although this "package" is the most expensive available and was among an average of 15–20 of these types of trips per year.[41] In 2002, over 4,000 Korean residents in Japan visited North Korea via the Mangyongbong-92; in contrast, only 162 North Korean residents visited Japan during the same time with only 26 of these being short-term visits to relatives in Japan.[42]

Links to Drug Activities

The Chosen Soren has also been linked to drug smuggling. One of the most significant incidents was the February 2000 arrest of members of a Chosen Soren-run trading company in connection with collaboration with Japanese criminals to distribute 250 kilograms of North Korean-made methamphetamines.[43] The Mangyongbong-92 has also been associated with smuggling of both drugs and counterfeit currency to Japan.[44] A former Korea Worker's Party employee commented that he arranged for narcotics transport on the Mangyongbong-92 for sale to Japanese gangs during the 1990s. He stated that boxes of narcotics arrived from a factory in North Korea and 200-kilogram shipments were loaded and transported five times per year; additionally, he reported there were significant efforts to smuggle stimulant drugs into the lucrative Japanese markets beginning in 1998.[45]

Pachinko Operations

Another source of income for the Chosen Soren includes money made by ethnic-Korean owned businesses running Japanese gambling pachinko parlors.[46]

Pachinko began in the 1920s in the US and migrated across the ocean, finding a large following in Japan. The games are somewhat like pinball, but use a vertical board and steel ball bearings that ricochet off set pins and land in winning or non-winning slots. The managers of these types of businesses have the ability to change the payout for these machines, which overwhelmingly target Japanese businessmen and students. In Japan, businesses associated with gambling are not considered "reputable" and usually the managers and owners tend to be non-Japanese.[47] Pachinko generates annual revenue of $250 billion within the Japanese economy.[48] Korean-run pachinko businesses began in the late 1980s and early 1990s and there were at least 40 pachinko parlors operated by local Chosen Soren affiliates and 20 operated by its central headquarters; these businesses provide funding for "almost all Ch'ongnyon [Chosen Soren] activities."[49]

Another report noted that up to 30 percent of pachinko operations in Japan were controlled by North Koreans living in Japan.[50] Additionally, money is often remitted directly from pachinko enterprises to North Korea and is reportedly transported via the Mangyongbong-92.[51] As with other businesses in the Japanese economy, profits from pachinko enterprises are influenced by the overall domestic economy. These have decreased significantly during the past few years due to the financial downturn Japan has experienced since the 1990s.[52]

Credit Union Scandals and Remittances

Six Chosen Soren-related credit unions, referred to as *chogin* (or "Korean Bank" in Japanese) financial institutions, reportedly funneled at least 15 billion yen ($140 million) into the Chosen Soren through loans paid to fictitious accounts or false names, and was allegedly sent to North Korea.[53] In 1997, 13 of 32 chogin institutions in Japan went bankrupt causing billions of yen in losses.[54] Chogins were accused of offering "preferential loans" to individuals who donated large amounts of money to North Korea and of providing funding above collateral, which often included facilities or land owned by Chosen Soren affiliates.[55] The credit unions also provided a means for direct donations which were forwarded to Pyongyang. For example, if an individual wanted a loan for 200 million yen, the credit union would supply a loan of 250 million yen and make the individual donate the extra 50 million yen back to the bank.[56]

These credit unions have sent billions of yen to North Korea by approving loans to "ghost accounts" and remitting the money to North Korea.[57] In 2001, the Japanese authorities began arresting participants and covered the losses in a 1.2 trillion yen ($11 billion) bailout.[58] In November 2001, Japanese police raided the Chosen Soren headquarters in Tokyo following the arrest of one of its senior officials in connection with the chogin credit scandal. Japanese authorities charged that between 1994 and 1998, Chogin Tokyo provided fake loans to 23 firms valued at 830 million yen ($7.5 million).[59] In 2002, the Japanese government designated four credit unions to assume operations of the failed chogins and required an infusion of 360 billion yen ($3.3 billion) in public funds to cover the bad debts.[60] As of 2003, only seven of the original 38 chogin credit associations remained in operation.[61]

Technology Transfers

The Chosen Soren has provided a key link between North Korea and Japan and the West for technological acquisition. In the 1960s, an organization within the Chosen Soren was established to obtain technologically advanced equipment from Japan.[62] One of the main transportation means for this is through the Mangyongbong-92 and other shipping vessels that openly run between the DPRK and Japan.[63] Another method for moving technical items to North Korea is through Chosen Soren affiliated trading companies. The Chosen Soren's Donghae Trading Company accounted for approximately $518 million in trade between Japan and North Korea, which was nearly 30 percent of Japan's total trade with the DPRK during 1997.[64]

Examples of these technology transfers demonstrate the interconnections between North Korea, the Chosen Soren and Japanese-based technology firms. In 1994, Seishin Enterprises, a Japanese engineering firm, shipped a machine used to convert solid fuel into fine powder used for missiles via the Mangyongbong-92. An official from a Chongryun-affiliated science and technology firm coordinated the exchange.[65] In 2000, IMRI, a South Korean computer peripheral manufacturer and CGS, a Tokyo-based software company, formed UNIKO-TECH, a company designed to develop and market computer software. The Chosen Soren has direct links to CGS and both companies maintain relationships with North Korean information technology firms.[66] In 2001, Japanese-made radar and other sophisticated equipment were found on board a sunken North Korean spy ship possibly supplied by firms in Japan with help from the Chosen Soren.[67] Meishin, a Tokyo-based trading company run by members of Chosen Soren, provided North Korea with electrical current transformers associated with uranium enrichment. These devices were ordered through North Korea's Daesong General Trading Corporation and transferred via Thailand.[68]

The Chosen Soren has also contributed to efforts by North Korea to acquire night vision goggles, tractors used to transport missiles, and Japanese fishing boats for their GPS systems.[69] Others charge that Japan's economic ties via the Chosen Soren were one of the contributing financial factors in helping North Korea develop its nuclear program in the mid-1990s.[70] The link provided by the Chosen Soren through established ties with the Japanese economy and the West has been invaluable to North Korea in obtaining these types of technologies for military and nuclear-related advances.

Financial Support to North Korea

In 2000, Marcus Noland described the Chosen Soren as an organization that "accounts for 80 percent of the foreign investment in North Korea, and much of Japan's trade with North Korea."[71] This investment and the business relations fostered between Zainichi Koreans and the DPRK has resulted in support in a variety of forms. North Korea began requesting money from the Chosen Soren beginning in the mid-1970s and as its economy began to decline, requests for aid increased. Financial transfers between the Chosen Soren continue on a yearly basis and ranged up to a billion dollars per year, prior to Japan's economic difficulties in the 1990s and the death of Kim Il-sung.[72]

By the mid 1990s, this figure had begun to decrease and in March 1994, Japan's Public Security Investigation Agency (PSIA) stated that the Chosen Soren was sending 60–80 billion yen ($650–850 million dollars) to North Korea each year.[73] Nicholas Eberstadt conducted a study of the issue and observed that after 1989, remittances to North Korea decreased significantly due to the downturn in the Japanese economy and the gradual decline of the Chosen Soren as an organization.[74] Officially documented transfers to North Korea between 2000 and 2002 amounted to a total of $117 million and analysts now estimate transfers, including those not documented, to be under $100 million per year.[75] In 2004, Japanese officials stated that since Japan's economic difficulties in the 1990s, Chosen Soren remittances to North Korea have decreased from over $900 million per year to as little as $90 million; some members of the Chosen Soren state that the actual amount is in the hundreds of thousands of dollars.[76] Although these types of transfers have often been conducted illegally, the Japanese government did not act to stem the flow of money until 2003.[77]

The Present and Future Chosen Soren

The modern day Chosen Soren continues to run schools, a daily newspaper, sports teams, credit institutions, and an import-export company; total current membership is estimated at 50,000–180,000.[78] Marcus Noland estimated the organization held over 300 trillion yen ($277 billion) in total assets.[79]

Both the test launch of a Taepo Dong missile over Japan in 1998 and the abduction revelations in 2002 have significantly changed the Japanese government's attitude towards the Chosen Soren. Japan has been more aggressive in monitoring the interactions between Chosen Soren and Pyongyang and has taken steps to enforce or strengthen existing tax laws on the organization.[80] Dewayne Creamer concluded that Kim Jong-il's admission of North Korea's kidnapping of Japanese citizens in the 1970s and 1980s was the "final nail into Chosen Soren's coffin" and allowed Japanese authorities to quickly hamper the organization's ability to provide aid to the DPRK.[81]

By the late 1990s, the Chosen Soren decided to take action to stem its problems with declining membership and influence. In 1999, Kim Jong-il stated that portraits of himself and Kim Il-sung did not have to be displayed in every Chosen Soren classroom, students were not required to wear distinctive North Korean outfits to school, and the organization was not required to echo DPRK criticisms of the Japanese government.[82] By 2002, many of these changes had begun to occur for students enrolled in the 123 Chosen Soren-run Korean schools in Japan to include both the removal of portraits and curriculum revisions that deemphasize the roles of both DPRK leaders.[83] Enrollment in Chosen Soren schools has dropped significantly in the past few years, decreasing from almost 40,000 in 1983 to around 20,000 today.[84] North Korean funding of these schools has also decreased over the past few years: financial support from North Korea to these schools has decreased to approximately 390 million yen ($3.6 million) each year, which is 25 percent of the amount donated in the late 1980s and early 1990s.[85]

Beginning in 2003, the Japanese government increased its scrutiny of North Korean export operations and took measures to stem the flow of dual use technology from Japan to the DPRK.[86] Additionally, the Chosen Soren and many of its associated organizations paid little or no taxes to the Japanese government since it was recognized as a "de facto diplomatic outpost for Pyongyang" in 1972.[87] Also in 2003, the Japanese government began revising the Chosen Soren's status and began imposing taxes on some of its fixed facilities.[88] Japan continues to increase pressure on the Chosen Soren and in September 2003, the local government in Tokyo seized three of its facilities for non-payment of $515,000 in property taxes. Other cities in Japan are following suit and have demanded taxes on many of the facilities owned by the organization.[89]

Chosen Soren membership numbers are down, the pro-North Korean population in Japan is rapidly aging, and many Zainichi Koreans are gravitating towards the pro-South Korean organization Mindan.[90] As Oh and Hassig observed, the future of this organization remains bleak as a significant contributor to the coffers of Pyongyang.[91] Yet the system of providing support through the Chosen Soren remains intact and North Korea can still rely on many of its staunch allies within the organization, the most significant overseas pro-North Korean faction in the world.

Although contributions were significantly higher in the 1990s, Chosen Soren still manages to send an estimated $90 million per year to support the Kim regime.[92] Considering the size of the overall DPRK economy, support from overseas Koreans continues to remain significant. As an important provider of hard currency for the DPRK, the Chosen Soren's days may be numbered, but it remains one of the many sources of needed income for the regime.

Drug Smuggling Activities

Although there is no direct evidence that Pyongyang's narcotics trafficking efforts have significantly affected the United States, some claim the DPRK is the next largest supplier of opium after Afghanistan and the Golden Triangle.[93] In fact, the US Drug Enforcement Administration (DEA) and other sources have reported that since the 1970s, North Korea has been associated with over 50 drug trafficking incidents in at least 20 countries.[94] The following table lists significant international incidents involving North Korea since the 1970s:

Year	Incident
1976	Scandinavian nations expelled DPRK diplomats selling illegal drugs, cigarettes, and alcohol.
1979	DPRK diplomat arrested for smuggling drugs through a Laotian airport.
1985	East German police deport a DPRK diplomat for heroin and morphine smuggling.
1994	Russian police arrest DPRK intelligence agents in Vladivostok selling heroin.
1995	Chinese police arrest a DPRK intelligence officer for smuggling 500 kg of heroin.
1995	DPRK firm attempted to import 15–20 tons of methamphetamine ingredient from Germany.
1996	Russian authorities detained a North Korean lumberjack with 22 kg of opium.
1996	Russian border police arrested a DPRK diplomat stationed in Russia with 20 kg of illegal drugs.
1997	Japanese customs discovered 60kg of drugs in jars of honey from a DPRK freighter.
1997	Chinese authorities arrested a North Korean businessman in trying to sell 900 kg of illegal drugs.
1997	Russian authorities caught a North Korean lumberjack trying to sell 5 kg of opium.
1997	Japanese police traced 660 lb methamphetamine shipment to a disguised North Korean vessel.
1997	Three South Koreans apprehended trying to sell 7 kg of DPRK methamphetamines.
1997	South Korean police discovered drug ring attempting to smuggle DPRK methamphetamines.
1998	DPRK diplomats arrested for smuggling cocaine from Mexico City to Moscow.
1998	Egyptian police arrest a DPRK diplomat attempting to smuggle date rape drugs.
1998	Thai police stop a DPRK shipment of 2.5 tons of methamphetamine ingredients.
2000	Japanese authorities discover 250 kg of DPRK-produced methamphetamines linked to both Japanese criminals and a Chosen Soren trading company.
2001	ROK port authorities find 91 kg of DPRK methamphetamines in noodle packages.
2002	Japanese authorities seize DPRK amphetamines from a Chinese ship off the coast of Fukuoka.
	Taiwanese police arrest eight people attempting to smuggle North Korean heroin.
2003	South Korean port authorities seize 50 kg of North Korean methamphetamines.
2003	Australians arrest 30 North Koreans for attempting to smuggle $50 million of heroin.
2003	Taiwan authorities seize 79 kg of North Korean heroin.
2003	Japanese officials seize 150 kg of North Korean methamphetamines.
2003	Defector reports smuggling 450 kg of drugs from the DPRK into China beginning in 1998.
2004	Seoul police arrest 17 people attempting to sell 5.4 kg of North Korean methamphetamines.
2004	Two DPRK diplomats deported from Turkey for attempting smuggle 700,000 "narcotic pills."

Table 3. Drug Incidents[95]

International drug-related incidents involving North Korea occurred as early as 1976, but the majority of significant illicit activity has been reported since the onset of severe economic crisis in the 1990s.[96] The DPRK is currently recognized as a regional drug-producing threat and described by the CIA as "emerging as an important regional source of illicit drugs targeting markets in Japan, Taiwan, the Russian Far East, and China."[97] Nicholas Eberstadt observed that North Korea's "drug and counterfeiting trade is entirely consistent with the official DPRK view of its legal and treaty obligations . . . part of the strategy for state survival."[98] Making money through illegal narcotics activities is relatively easy and, considering the "diplomatic immunity" issue, North Korean officials face little actual punishment if caught.[99]

North Korea Becomes a Trafficker

Opium farming in North Korea dates back to the Japanese colonial era and has continued with direction and emphasis from the DPRK government. Although most of North Korea does not contain the optimal climate or soil to produce opium poppies, they have been grown for over 100 years in the extreme northeastern portion of the country. Given the shortage of medicines in the DPRK, poppies have been traditionally used to treat illnesses.[100] Poppy cultivation began in North Korea in the early 1900s under the Japanese occupation in the mountainous Hamgyong and Yanggang provinces, the same areas again used to grow poppies decades later in the 1970s.[101]

North Korea entered the international drug business in the 1970s when Pyongyang initiated a campaign called "Loyalty of Earning Foreign Currency" and issued instructions to organizations both in North Korea and abroad to obtain foreign currency to support the "revolution."[102] As a result of these directives, North Korean diplomats became involved in a variety of activities to include drug smuggling, counterfeiting, and other criminal acts.[103] Funds raised from smuggling and other activities directly support embassy operations and have been used for propaganda efforts to include placing expensive advertisements in foreign newspapers to "extol the achievements" of North Korea.[104] Over the years, North Korean drug production and marketing activities have become institutionalized and incorporated into its farming operations, diplomatic missions, and shipping operations under the direct control of Pyongyang.

In the early 1990s, Kim Il-sung ordered increased opium production and there were press reports that the "Great Leader" personally visited collective farms and directed farmers to produce opium to trade for food, speaking of "how opium could be a crucial means for earning hard currency." There were enforced production quotas and incentives, and one defector commenting on the profits compared to grain production, stated that "opium gets you 300 times the profits you can get from corn."[105] Meetings were reportedly held under Kim Jong-il's supervision to determine which areas were best for growing opium poppies and

Southern and North Hamgyong provinces were subsequently chosen.[106] Despite the onset of food shortages and subsequent famine, there were claims that North Korea limited "food crop production in favor of drug crop production."[107] Opium was shipped to government organizations and the poppies were referred to as "broad bellflowers" to maintain secrecy.[108] In 1997, North Korea's central government ordered all collective farms to begin setting aside 25 acres for poppy farming.[109] After this directive, North Korea increased production to 50 metric tons in 1998, up from three metric tons of opium per year in 1992.[110]

For technical assistance with its programs, North Korea relies on experts from major drug producing nations to include Laos, Burma, and Thailand. One defector reported escorting "Southeast Asian drug lords" around Pyongyang and that he attended meetings in 1996 with Laotian and Burmese drug merchants concerning how to ensure North Korean heroin was pure.[111] The opium produced on the farms was sent to pharmaceutical plants in Chongjin City in northeastern North Korea and possibly to a production plant near Pyongyang. Then the opium was processed into heroin under the supervision of the Thai drug experts and to ensure secrecy and security, all drug-related facilities were heavily guarded by the North Korean State Security Department.[112] Reports also surfaced that the "Communist Party's Foreign Currency Department" transported opium produced in North Korea to port for overseas in 1999.[113]

Testimony has also been published on drug production infiltrating into North Korean society to include incorporation into the daily routine of school-children:

> In Chongju, a farming town in northeastern North Korea, classes ended at 2 p.m.—and then the students got to work. Ju [the teacher] marched the teens into fields blooming with pink and white flowers. Working in pairs, one student cut into the bulb of a waist-high plant and the other scraped the sticky white resin into a cup supplied by the North Korean government. They worked four or five hours each afternoon among those plants that, by North Korean government fiat, are known as white bellflowers. In fact, they were poppy plants—and the students were harvesting that year's heroin crop for Dear Leader Kim Jong-il.[114]

Cough Syrup, Meth and Embassy Operations

North Korea's efforts to produce methamphetamine first became apparent in the mid-1990s. One of the most significant incidents occurred in 1998, when officials from Thailand stopped a North Korean shipment of ephedrine enroute from India to Pyongyang. The North Koreans claimed the ephedrine, the key ingredient used in the manufacture of methamphetamines, was for cough medicine. A former North Korean diplomat commented that if used for medicinal purposes, the amount of ephedrine was "enough to last North Korea for 100 years."[115] The market for these narcotics remains lucrative as Japan's primary drugs of choice are imported methamphetamines and 90 percent of all narcotics arrests involve this substance.[116] Additionally, Japanese authorities estimate trafficking to Japan to be at 10–20 metric tons per year and 30 percent of all methamphetamines in Japan come from North Korea.[117] The following chart provides an overview of North Korea's illegal drug operations:

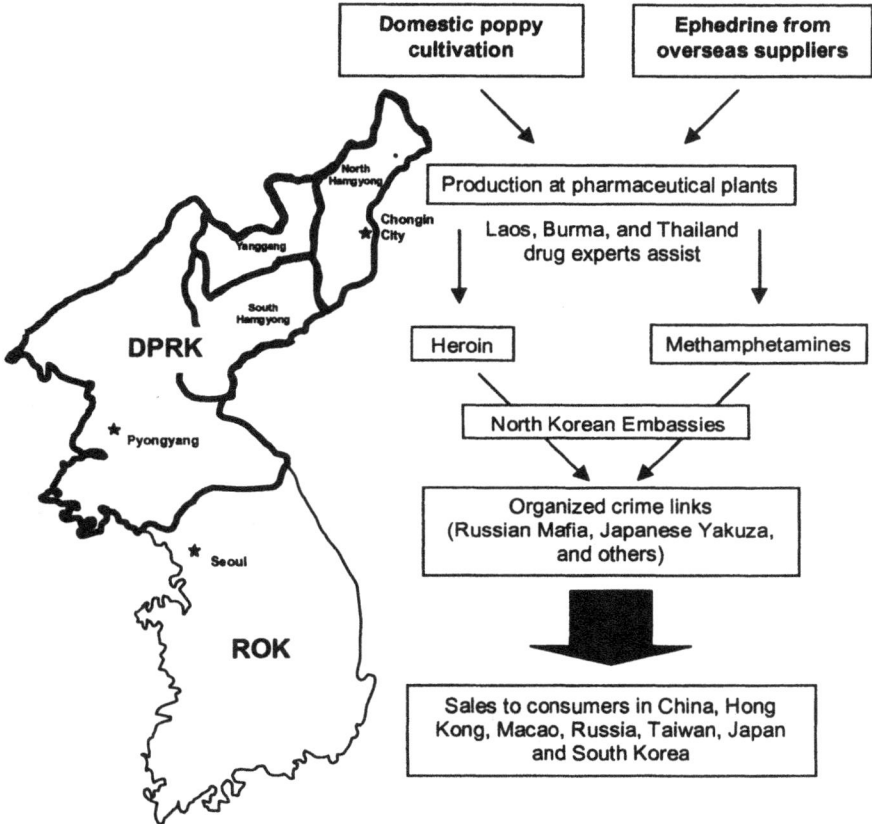

Figure 3. DPRK Drug Operations

Sources: US Congress, *Drugs, Counterfeiting, and Weapons Proliferation: The NK Connection*, 5–26; Solomon and Dean, "Drug Money"; Kim, "North Korea and Narcotics Trafficking," 7; Kaplan, "The Wiseguy Regime"; and Green, "Dealing Drugs: North Korean Narcotics Trafficking," 7.

The late 1990s saw a shift in the scope and intensity of drug smuggling operations and the involvement from North Korean diplomats stationed overseas. In 1998, North Korea closed 14 embassies and instructed its remaining ones to become "self-sufficient."[118]

Drug Production Continues: Regional and Global Impacts

Asian countries continue to provide a lucrative market for North Korean smugglers: Japanese addicts spend approximately $9.3 billion annually on stimulants.[119] The US State Department reports that China and North Korea continue to remain the primary suppliers of illegal narcotics smuggled into Taiwan; traffickers from these two countries provide 95 percent of the methamphetamines and 80 percent of the heroin consumed by the island state.[120]

Regional Supplier of Narcotics

Testimony before the US Congress indicates there is considerable evidence that North Korea continues to remain a key player in the Asian drug market and analysts charge that North Korea sells drugs in China, Hong Kong, Macao, Russia, Japan, and South Korea, with Japan being its biggest market.[121] In 2003, drug shipments may have surged to fund several expensive Pyongyang events to include Kim Jong-il's 60th birthday and the Arirang Festival.[122] Recent reports citing DPRK working relationships with organized crime to include the Russian Mafia and Japanese Yakuza also point to significant Pyongyang involvement in Asian drug smuggling.[123] The 2003 Australian navy seizure of the *Pong Su*, a North Korean cargo ship carrying $50 million in heroin, provided more evidence of entrenched participation by North Korea in drug smuggling operations.[124] In a hearing before the US Senate in 2003, Andre D. Hollis, US Deputy Assistant Secretary of Defense for Counternarcotics, noted:

> The Pong Su seizure heightens concerns that North Korean officials may be using illicit trading activities to provide much needed hard currency to fund its army and weapons of mass destruction programs. . . . It is clear that any illicit trafficking involving North Korea is a potential threat to the security of the US and its friends and allies in Asia.[125]

Production and Returns

Determining the levels of production has been difficult for intelligence agencies and attempts to use satellite imagery failed to identify the presence of substantial numbers of poppy fields in 1996 and 1999.[126] Current opium poppy production levels are estimated at 3,000–4,000 hectares for opium poppies, which would produce 21–28 metric tons of opium annually, although without on-site inspections, it remains difficult to determine actual levels of cultivated land,.[127] Defectors report that drugs which generally sell for approximately $17,000 per kg in the border area with China often are resold for $100,000–$300,000 per kg by organized crime syndicates in Japan and South Korea. In fact, North Korean defectors interviewed in 2004 in China commented that "lately in Pyongyang, quite a number of people lavishly use dollars. They, too, have made fortunes by dealing drugs" and that due to current international restrictions on other illicit sources of income, "virtually nothing but drugs could fetch money."[128] In North Korea, drugs are sold openly at markets and are sometimes used instead of currency for transactions; although Kim Jong-il has increased penalties for narcotics violations, punishments are reportedly not as severe as in China or South Korea.[129]

Accusations and Denial

When confronted by critics, North Korean officials deny any connection to state-sponsored trafficking and contend that individuals are committing these offenses without government involvement.[130] Yet, given the control North Korea retains over its population, there is virtually no way that opium produced for export could go unnoticed.[131] In 2004, US President George W. Bush announced the US position on reports of North Korea's association with narcotics activities. He noted that the US is "deeply concerned about heroin and methamphetamine linked to North Korea being trafficked to East Asian countries. We consider it highly likely that state agents and enterprises in North Korea are involved in the narcotics trade."[132]

The United Nations 2004 World Drug Report commented briefly on heroin seizures in China and Australia that raised the issue of heroin trafficking from North Korea.[133] The statistics section of this report lists estimated retail and wholesale prices for narcotics, which is helpful in determining the dollar value of North Korea's heroin and methamphetamine production efforts.[134] Similarly, the US State Department's Bureau for International Narcotics and Law Enforcement Affairs produces its annual International Narcotics Control Strategy Report which provides detailed descriptions of DPRK trafficking efforts. The 2005 report states:

> The cumulative impact of drug smuggling incidents linked to North Korea . . . support the Department's conclusion that it is likely, though not certain that the DPRK is state trading narcotics. . . . There is also strong reason to believe that methamphetamines and heroin are manufactured in North Korea as a result of the same state-directed conspiracy behind trafficking.[135]

The unpredictable nature of the Kim Jong-il regime and the threat surrounding its nuclear program makes most nations reluctant to act in response to the charges of North Korea's state-sponsored narcotics smuggling. From a diplomatic viewpoint, the nuclear issue overshadows accusations of drug smuggling and economic sanctions based on narcotics remain a contentious issue in United Nations. The international response has been characterized by increased cooperative law enforcement measures in the affected countries to include Japan, Taiwan, and Australia.[136]

These efforts have grown throughout the years and some analysts approximate that North Korea earns between $500 million and $1 billion per year as a result of its illegal narcotics activities.[137] Yet these figures fail to consider the overall effect of increased international scrutiny of DPRK drug operations and historic production levels. Given these issues, Pyongyang probably earns only $50–100 million per year from its drug production and trafficking operations.[138] Production of both opium and methamphetamines continues to this day as illicit means of gaining foreign income and, according to one source, North Korea earns approximately 60 percent of its foreign currency earnings from drug operations.[139] In fact, according to defector testimony, "severe economic depression forced North Korean dictator Kim Jong-il to turn to trafficking as a means of supplanting, rather than simply supplementing, the country's legitimate economy."[140] North Korea remains one of the few countries that provides direct government support to narcotics production and smuggling and is certainly the only one in Asia that relies on this type of illicit income to sustain its own government.

Counterfeiting

North Korea has an extensive, government-supported counterfeit program that was one of the factors in the US Treasury Department's decision to redesign US dollars beginning in 1996.[141] Yet the overall incidence of international counterfeiting is low and in 2002, Federal Reserve researchers estimated that there was only about $125 million in counterfeit notes in circulation.[142]

The United States Secret Service has a unique role in combating counterfeit activities and "investigates violations of laws relating to counterfeiting of obligations and securities of the United States."[143] Within the Secret Service, the International Currency Awareness Program (ICAP) has conducted extensive overseas surveys of the incidence of counterfeit operations and has provided the most credible information on overseas counterfeit operations. The ICAP reported that when it was initially established, there were numerous reports from commercial and other credible sources that "vast quantities of counterfeit dollars were circulating overseas . . . undetected and remained on the marketplace indefinitely."[144]

Counterfeiting 101

Counterfeiting of foreign currency is considered a low-risk and high-payoff "criminal enterprise" throughout the world and generally involves three different types of production: traditional offset printing; digital production; and highly sophisticated intaglio and typographic press methods.[145] The key components of successful counterfeit production involve obtaining the right ink and correct paper. Since 1879, the US Bureau of Engraving and Printing (BEP) has used paper from the same domestic supplier, Crane and Company located in Dalton, Massachusetts, at a cost of $75 million per year.[146] The cloth-like paper is manufactured in large eight foot wide rolls made from a mix of cotton and linen.[147] The materials are boiled in a huge vat, and then cleaned, bleached, and colored with added security features to meet Treasury Department standards.[148] US dollars are printed at BEP plants in Washington, DC and Fort Worth, Texas using Swiss-designed intaglio presses purchased from Britain's De La Rue Giori Corporation, ink from factories in the US run by Swiss-owned Sicpa Company, and high-speed processing machines made in Germany.[149] These same presses are often the "equipment of choice" to reproduce US currency and government-owned De La Rue Giori presses constitute 90 percent of those used to make high quality legitimate currency.[150]

High Production Costs

Despite the attractiveness of counterfeit operations as a criminal activity, costs for production and distribution can often be high. Effective counterfeit operations require access to printing presses, quality inks, and high-grade paper. Credible paper is essential since most bank employees use touch as their primary check against the validity of notes.[151] Additionally, since bogus dollars are produced in large quantities, distribution proves difficult; counterfeit notes often cannot be transferred to an individual or bank more than once and the manufacturer is forced to continually find new markets for his currency.[152] As a result, overhead for producing and distributing forged $100 bills can be as high as $50 per note.[153] Circulation issues also hamper counterfeiting operations. Judson and Porter observed in 2003 that while genuine $100 bills are expected to last an average of eight years, counterfeit ones are expected to be in circulation less than one year due to improved detection methods throughout the world.[154] As a result, counterfeit money usually remains in circulation for a short amount of time, often being detected quickly after its initial use.

Research into the incidence of counterfeiting supports the conclusion that occurrences are not as widespread as anecdotal evidence would suggest. The US Treasury Department estimates the levels of *overseas* counterfeiting fall within the range of 1–2 fake bills per every 10,000 in circulation, which is similar to levels found within the United States.[155] In 2001, the US Secret Service reported $49 million in counterfeit currency was in use throughout the world or about $1 for every $12,400 in circulation.[156] This was based on observations during its own investigations during the same year resulting in 5,241 arrests and the seizure of 651 counterfeiting plants within the US[157] Additionally, when the South Korean government conducted a "no-questions-asked" buyback of US currency in response to the 1997 Asian financial crisis, it found only $264,000 in counterfeit money, roughly equating to 1.8 per 10,000 notes collected, which was consistent with other counterfeit rates throughout the world.[158]

Primary Target: US Currency

The leading target for most counterfeiters of US bills remains the $100 note. Although significant levels of counterfeiting of US currency by "rogue nations" to include Iran and North Korea had occurred since the 1980s, the arrival of more sophisticated copies at the end of the decade presented a new challenge. The new counterfeit dollars, called "Superdollars" or "Superbills," were high-quality, extremely difficult to detect copies of US currency. The first $100 "Superdollars" were detected in the Philippines in 1989 and "to the naked eye they were indistinguishable from the real thing."[159] US currency was a prime target for counterfeiting efforts due to advances in printing technology and the fact that US bills had not been significantly changed since the 1930s, essentially retaining the same features for over 60 years, and with no security measures or watermark.[160] Due to this new high-quality counterfeit threat and the known vulnerability of US currency, the US government redesigned and reissued its currency, beginning in 1996 with the $100 bill.[161] According the Treasury Department, the introduction of the 1996-series $100 bills, also know as the new currency design (NCD), has dramatically lowered the incidence of counterfeiting compared to the older notes.[162] In 2001, the Federal Reserve Bank in New York, which processes the greatest amount of US currency re-entering the states, reported it detected only 35 counterfeit NCDs per million notes compared to a rate of 200 per million for the older $100 bills.[163]

DPRK Counterfeiting Operations

North Korea has been involved in counterfeiting trade operations since the 1970s and possibly purchased a $10 million intaglio-style press, similar to those used by the US mint, from a company in Lausanne, Switzerland in 1974.[164] An alternate theory of the origin of North Korea's printing equipment states North Korea obtained presses from the USSR in the 1980s, which had originally been stolen from the US mint by the KGB sometime after World War II.[165] Regardless of the equipment source, North Korea established itself as a full-scale producer of counterfeit documents during the 1980s at its official state mint, the Pyongyang Printing Corporation, controlled by the North Korea's Ministry of Public Security. The plant is headed by a "colonel-level military officer," employs 700 people from selected families from "high social backgrounds," and has been producing fake US dollars since 1981.[166] This plant was one of at least three locations in North Korea conducting counterfeit operations[167] and these same plants have been used to produce forged labels of well-known liquor and cigarette brands.[168] A North Korean defector and former member of Pyongyang's elite class testified these presses were initially used to make "fake identity documents for espionage" and then were used to produce US $20 and $50 bills in the mid-1980s.[169] He stated that North Korea obtained paper, ink, and equipment from Japan and East Germany, produced counterfeit dollars and shipped the currency using diplomatic pouches to embassies that then put the bills into circulation.

Quality Improves

In 1992, higher quality counterfeit US currency began to appear across the globe.[170] South Korea's National Intelligence Service (NIS) stated that North Korea operated several factories in the Pyongyang area and operations prior to the 1990s gradually evolved from poor quality offset-printed bills to the more recently produced higher-quality bills.[171] During a 2004 BBC interview, another former North Korean who worked in Pyongyang's counterfeit operation stated,

> We bought the best of everything, the best equipment and the best ink, but we also had the very best people, people who had real expertise and knowledge in the field. Then, when government officials or diplomats traveled to South East Asia, they distributed the counterfeit notes mixed in with the real ones at a ratio of about 50–50.[172]

A 19-year veteran of the North Korean Ministry of Public Security commented that the paper was a key component to making the bills passable.[173] He stated that North Korean officials had ordered him to obtain paper used by the US to print its bills and, after failing to secure the material, "obtained many $1 notes and bleached the ink out of them."[174] While initial counterfeit quality was poor, by using bleached US bills and then reprinting them using $100 bill plates or a mixture of paper similar to that used by the US mint, the DPRK increased its counterfeit quality significantly.[175] Another North Korean defector commented that the quality of these notes was so good that they were indistinguishable from genuine currency. When he arrived in South Korea and gave some of the counterfeit $100 bills to South Korea counterfeit experts, "they said, these are not fake notes. They're real."[176] In fact, the copies were so good, they have been detected due to being more artistically correct than actual US bills. When magnified, the copies of $100 bills show Benjamin Franklin's face with a "perfectly formed ear-hole and nostril" and the image of the minute hand of a clock is clearly visible; on genuine bills, both Franklin's face and the clock are blurred and "more clumsily drawn."[177]

Diplomatic Cover

North Korea's state-sponsorship of counterfeit operations has been proven without a doubt through numerous instances of its direct involvement in diplomatic incidents. DPRK officials and well-traveled executives have been arrested or expelled in numerous cases resulting in political damage to the North Korean government.[178] A number of significant counterfeiting efforts have been exposed, many involving North Korean diplomats, since the mid-1990s. The following list provides descriptions of many of the most notable counterfeiting incidents:

Year	Incident
1994	North Koreans arrested depositing counterfeit bills worth $600,000 into Macao bank.
1996	Counterfeit $100 bills worth $90,000 exchanged for Thai baht in Pattaya, Thailand.
1996	Red Army faction terrorist apprehended attempting to use fake US currency valued at $200,000.
1996	DPRK diplomat expelled from Mongolia for attempting to smuggle $90,000 in false bills.
1997	Bogus versions of the new $100 bill ($7,400 total) confiscated in St. Petersburg, Russia.
1997	DPRK diplomat expelled from Mongolia for using over $100,000 in counterfeit $100 bills.
1997	Six Japanese with ties to the DPRK arrested for trying to sell $200,000 in fake US $100.
1998	DPRK diplomat caught attempting to exchange $30,000 in superdollars for rubles.
1998	Several counterfeits (worth $1,000) of the new $100 surface in Great Britain.
2002	British officials conclude an 18-month counterfeiting investigation linking the IRA and Russian mafia to circulation of $27,000,000 in North Korean superdollars.
2003	Kim Jong Il's son, Kim Jong Nam observed using fake dollars in Macao.
2003	$100,000 in counterfeit US dollars worth found in Seoul at a bank and exchange dealer.
2004	Taiwan police find $36,000 in fake US bills possibly originating in North Korea.

Table 4. Counterfeiting Activity[179]

Other reports state that US and British officials have linked former KGB agents in the Russian mafia, North Korean Consulate in Russia, and the Irish Republican Army (IRA) to North Korean counterfeit operations. The British Broadcasting Company (BBC) has claimed millions of dollars in US counterfeit notes had been passed through the North Korean embassy in Moscow, with Russian mafia assistance, into the hands of a high-ranking officer in the IRA beginning in the 1990s. The North Korean embassy in Moscow is Pyongyang's biggest in the world and has been called the "centre for the distribution of superdollars."[180] More recently, DPRK counterfeit bills have surfaced throughout the world to include reports that Kim Jong-il's son, Kim Jong Nam, was spotted using counterfeit dollars while gambling in Macao.[181]

Ongoing State-Sponsored Counterfeit Operations

North Korea probably continues to produce high-quality copies of US currency and most analysts assess Pyongyang still produces and uses $15–20 million counterfeit dollars per year.[182] Unfortunately, as with most information on North Korea, these numbers are based on anecdotal and extrapolated information, rather than hard facts.[183] However, some credible evidence has been revealed to include South Korean NIS reports that between 1994 and 1998, $4.64 million in North-Korean produced "Superdollars" were detected in 13 separate incidents.[184] The NIS estimated in 1999 that North Korea accounted for approximately 10 percent of the total amount of counterfeit US dollars in circulation.[185] Given the cost of counterfeit operations, which can be as high as $50 per note for a $100 bill, North Korea's net earnings for counterfeit operations are approximately 50 percent of its revenue. Thus a realistic estimate is that North Korea earns no more than $7–10 million per year from counterfeit revenues.[186]

The continued development of new technologies has probably contributed to the relatively stable, and not increasing, threat of North Korean counterfeiting operations. There has been considerable progress in combating the continued production of counterfeit US dollars. Aside from the introduction of new US currency, new counterfeit detection machines have been manufactured that promise to detect 99 percent of all counterfeit bills.[187] Yet considering North Korea's dire financial situation, producing money is a viable means of obtaining needed funds, and considering its previous record of continued criminal activity, there is little incentive to cease attempting to copy US and other national currencies to support Pyongyang. While some analysts contend that North Korea's counterfeit efforts are intended partially to destabilize the US economy, the small number of counterfeit bills relative to the amount of US notes in circulation undercuts these assertions' credibility.[188] North Korea produces money for the same reasons as it enters into other criminal enterprises: entirely for its own benefit in order to obtain hard currency to support Pyongyang.

Notes and references

1. Strong, *North Korea: The Transnational Criminal State*, 30.

2. The Chosen Soren is also referred to as the *Chosen Chongryun* or *Chongryun* in Korean. Other variations include *Chongryon, Chongryn, Chongron,* or *Ch'ongnyon.*

3. Chanlett-Avery, "North Korean Supporters in Japan," 1. Strong, *North Korea: The Transnational Criminal State*, 30.

4. Triplett, *Rogue State*, 108.

5. Hee-gwan Chin, "Divided by Fate: The Integration of Overseas Koreans in Japan," *East Asian Review* 13, no. 2 (Summer 2001): 59; *Trans-Pacific*, (Newspaper, Tokyo), 8 August 1929, 11 quoted in Mitchell, *The Korean Minority in Japan*, 41; Kazuichiro Ono, "The Problem of Japanese Emigration," *Kyoto University Economic Review* 28 (April 1958), 47.

6. Koreans were initially encouraged and then forced to move to and work in Japan.

Mitchell, *The Korean Minority in Japan*, 75; Ryang, *North Koreans in Japan: Language, Ideology and Identity*, 80.

7. Creamer, *The Rise and Fall of Chosen Soren*, 7.

8. Lee, *Koreans in Japan: Their Influence on Korean-Japanese Relations*, 11; Creamer, *The Rise and Fall of Chosen Soren*, 9.

9. The Japanese refer to Koreans living in Japan as *Zainichi Kankokujin*, Creamer, *The Rise and Fall of Chosen Soren*, 1. Through the 1920s, most Koreans in Japan were unmarried men who wanted to improve their financial situation and then return home; in the mid-1920s, married couples were encouraged to emigrate to "stabilize the Korean minority." By 1939, 88 percent of Koreans in Japan were living in a "family situation" partly as a result of this emigration policy. Naimucho Keihokyoku, *Showa Hachinen-chu No Okeru Shakai Undo No Jokyo*, 1939, 890, cited by Mitchell in *The Korean Minority in Japan*, 76.

10. Mitchell, *The Korean Minority in Japan*, 48.

11. Mitchell, *The Korean Minority in Japan*, 75.

12. Oh and Hassig, *North Korea Through the Looking Glass*, 178–179; Creamer, *The Rise and Fall of Chosen Soren*, 12.

13. Mitchell, *The Korean Minority in Japan*, 87.

14. Mitchell, *The Korean Minority in Japan*, 88–89.

15. In fact, over 800,000 Koreans returned home between 15 August and 30 November 1945. Mitchell, *The Korean Minority in Japan*, 89 and 102; Edward W. Wagner, *The Korean Minority in Japan, 1904–1950* (New York: International Secretariat, Institute of Pacific Relations, 1951), 43.

16. Mitchell, *The Korean Minority in Japan*, 103–104.

17. Mitchell, *The Korean Minority in Japan*, 104.

18. Mitchell, *The Korean Minority in Japan*, 113.

19. Mitchell, *The Korean Minority in Japan*, 106.

20. Mitchell comments that due to the dire conditions that existed in Japan after the war, many Koreans were involved in the black market. He points out that most Japanese also engaged in this activity and it was "necessary to buy and sell on the black market to obtain food to live." Mitchell, *The Korean Minority in Japan*, 106, 111; Wagner, *The Korean Minority in Japan, 1904–1950*, 52–53.

21. Despite Choren's protests to the American occupation authorities, the Japanese government eventually closed all Choren schools and confiscated its assets. Mitchell, *The Korean Minority in Japan*, 116–117; Wagner, *The Korean Minority in Japan, 1904–1950*, 85.

22. Roger Swearingen and Paul Langer, *Red Flag in Japan: International Communism in Action, 1919–1951* (Cambridge: Harvard University Press, 1952), 243, 251–252.

23. Creamer, *The Rise and Fall of Chosen Soren*, 20.

24. This group is also referred to as *Chosen Chongryun* or *Chongryun* in Korean. Japan refers to this group as the *Chosen Soren* while its members and other Koreans use

Chongryun. Creamer, *The Rise and Fall of Chosen Soren,* 2.

25. Public Security Investigation Agency (Japan), *Current Phases of the Activities of Korean Residents in Japan* (Tokyo: 1957) 7–13 quoted in Mitchell, *The Korean Minority in Japan,* 122.

26. These schools taught in Korean with Japanese as a "secondary language." Mitchell, *The Korean Minority in Japan,* 128.

27 North Korea reportedly sent 1.2 billion yen to support these schools in 1960. S.J. Kim, "In Japan: Educational Plight of Residents Reviewed," *The Korean Republic,* 15 April 1961, 2.

28. Mitchell, *The Korean Minority in Japan,* 131.

29. Mitchell commented that 14 percent of Koreans in 1959 relied on financial support from the Japanese government and the numbers of crimes committed by Koreans were six times the rate of the Japanese. Public Security Investigation Agency (Japan), *Current Phases of the Activities of Korean Residents in Japan* (Tokyo: 1957) 29 quoted in Mitchell, *The Korean Minority in Japan,* 131.

30. "Book Describes Korean Group's Illegal Money Transfers from Japan to DPRK," (text), Tokyo *Waga Chosen Soren no Tsumi to Batsu* (30 April 2002), FBIS Document ID JPP20030403000048, accessed 12 January 2005; "Former Korean University Professor Tells of Bogus Monetary Transfers to North Korea," (text), Tokyo *Shukan Posuto* (2 December 2002), FBIS Document ID JPP20021204000023, accessed 12 January 2005.

31. "Chosen Soren: N. Korean Ship Calls at Niigata as Abduction Issue Stirs Anger," *Asahi News Service,* 26 November 2002, accessed via LexisNexis Research Database, 15 May 2005.

32. US Congress, *Drugs, Counterfeiting, and Weapons Proliferation: The NK Connection,* 30.

33. This ethnic Korean had been in Japan since 1949 and had served as the president of a Chosen Soren associated company. In 1993, he began conducting espionage activities for the Korean Worker's Party and led a group of spies in Japan through 2001. "N. Korean Spy Got Orders on Aid Ship," *Asahi News Service,* 30 January 2003, accessed via LexisNexis Research Database, 15 May 2005.

34. "N. Korean ship to Japan equipped with military sonar," *Kyodo News Service,* 6 June 2003, accessed via LexisNexis Research Database, 15 May 2005.

35. Chang, "Excerpts From Book by North Korean Operative in Japan."

36. "Chosen Soren: North Korean Ferry Back in Niigata Port," *International Herald Tribune,* 27 April 2004, accessed via LexisNexis Research Database, 15 May 2005.

37. Approximately 1,300 North Korean vessels enter Japanese ports each year. Chanlett-Avery, "North Korean Supporters in Japan," 6; "Bar Suspicious Vessels from Port," *Daily Yomiuri,* 5 September 2003, accessed via InfoTrac Onefile Research Database, 15 March 2005; James Brooke, "Japan Frees North Korean Ferry After Holding It For Day In Port," *New York Times,* 27 August 2003, A4.

38. "North Korean ships warned as Japan starts checks on foreign vessels," *Kyodo*

News Service, 1 March 2005, accessed via Infotrac Onefile Research Database, 12 March 2005.

39. "N. Korean ferry arrives at Niigata, inspectors go on board," *Kyodo News Service*, 13 July 2004, accessed via LexisNexis Research Database, 25 March 2005; "SCOPE: Japanese women make trip on N. Korean ferry," *Kyodo News Service*, 21 September 2004, accessed via LexisNexis Research Database, 25 March 2005; "Japanese protesters meet North Korean ferry docking at Niigata port," *BBC Monitoring Asia Pacific*, 20 October 2004, accessed via LexisNexis Research Database, 25 March 2005; "Mangyongbong-92 Expected to Enter Niigata Port on May 18," *Jiji Press*, 11 May 2005, accessed via LexisNexis Research Database, 15 May 2005.

40. "Chosen Soren: One Way Ticket."

41. "Book Describes Korean Group's Illegal Money Transfers."

42. "Chosen Soren: One Way Ticket."

43. Perl, "Drug Trafficking and North Korea," 8.

44. "N. Korean ship to make port call in Japanese port next week," *Yonhap News*, 11 May 2005, accessed via Infotrac Onefile Research Database, 15 May 2005.

45. Suetsugu, "Risky Business Leading North Korea to Ruin."

46. Eric Weiner, "Tokyo Diarist: Pinball Wizards," *The New Republic,* 7 & 14 July 2003, 38.

47. Triplett, *Rogue State*, 110.

48. Weiner, "Tokyo Diarist: Pinball Wizards," 38.

49. Pachinko investment and operations began soon after the "September Instruction" by Kim Jong-il for the Chosen Soren to increase its business operations. "Book Describes Korean Group's Illegal Money Transfers."

50. Mary Jordan and Kevin Sullivan, "Pinball Wizards Fuel North Korea –Japan's Passion Aids Communist State; Pachinko Players Underwrite North Korea," *The Washington Post*, 7 June 1996, A25.

51. "Sailing Across a Sea of Trouble," *Japan Inc*, October 2003, 6.

52. Noland, *Avoiding the Apocalypse*, 103.

53. "Credit Unions Suspected of Sending Money to N. Korea," *Kyodo News Service*, 28 August 1999, accessed via LexisNexis Research Database, 25 March 2005; "Chogins Funneled Money to Group," *Asahi Shimbun*, 8 January 2002, accessed via LexisNexis Research Database, 15 May 2005.

54. The Chogin Tokyo lost approximately 330 billion yen ($3 billion) and the failure of Chogin Osaka resulted in a 310 billion yen ($2.8 billion) public bailout. "Credit Unions Suspected of Sending Money to N. Korea"; "Chogins Funneled Money to Group."

55. "Credit Unions in Japan Suspected of Illegal Remittances to N. Korea," *Agence France Presse*, 29 August 1999, accessed via LexisNexis Research Database, 25 March 2005; "Chogin-Chongryon Ties Said Tight," *Daily Yomiuri*, 30 November 2001, accessed via InfoTrac Onefile Research Database, 26 March 2005; "Chogin Tokyo 'Hid Chongryon Ties' Credit Union Allegedly Granted New Loans to Help Problem Debtors,"

Daily Yomiuri, 20 November 2001, accessed via InfoTrac Onefile Research Database, 26 March 2005.

56. Along with this, many of the Chogins would require employees to donate 10 percent of their yearly bonuses to the same fund. "Book Describes Korean Group's Illegal Money Transfers."

57. This money was sent to North Korea from the Niigata port on the Mangyong-bong-92, Samjiyon, or other "secret" North Korean vessels. Doug Struck, "N. Korea's Closed Society Keeps Trade Routes Open; Flow of Money, Goods Frustrates US Drive to Tighten Isolation," *The Washington Post*, 3 February 2003, accessed via LexisNexis Research Database, 25 March 2005; "Book Describes Korean Group's Illegal Money Transfers."

58. Struck, "N. Korea's Closed Society Keeps Trade Routes Open"; "Book Describes Korean Group's Illegal Money Transfers."

59 ."Police Raid Chongron HQ Over Alleged Embezzlement," *Kyodo News International - Japan Weekly Monitor*, 3 December 2001, accessed via InfoTrac OneFile Research Database, 20 April 2005.

60. "Four Lenders to Take over Chogin Banking Operations," *The Japan Times Online*, 21 March 2002, www.japantimes.co.jp/cgi-bin/getarticle.pl5?nb20020321a7.htm, accessed 1 July 2005; Chanlett-Avery, "North Korean Supporters in Japan," 7.

61. "Hana Credit Union on Notice," *Daily Yomiuri* editorial, 19 December 2002, accessed via InfoTrac Onefile Research Database, 12 April 2005.

62. *Yomiuri Shimbun*, 5 June 2003 quoted in Triplett, *Rogue State*, 111.

63. Triplett, *Rogue State*, 110–111.

64. Jae Hoon Shin, "Koreans Abroad: Shaky Finances," *Far Eastern Economic Review* 160, no. 49 (4 December 1997): 29.

65. "Seishin Sold Jet Mills to China, India," *Daily Yomiuri*, 14 June 2003, accessed via InfoTrac Onefile Research Database, 15 April 2005.

66. US Office of the National Counterintelligence Executive, "North Korea: Channeling Foreign Information Technology to Leverage IT Development," *Archives*, December 2003, www.ncix.gov/archives/docs/north_korea_and_foreign_it.pdf, accessed 18 May 2005.

67. "METI Busts N. Korea Trader," *Daily Yomiuri*, 14 June 2003, accessed via InfoTrac Onefile, 15 April 2005.

68. "Chongron Affiliate Ordered Jet Mill," *The Yomiuri Shimbun*, 15 June 2003, accessed via InfoTrac OneFile, 15 April 2005.

69. *Yomiuri Shimbun*, 5 and 7 June 2003 quoted in Triplett, *Rouge State*, 111.

70. Hicks, *Japan's Hidden Apartheid: The Korean Minority and the Japanese*, 35.

71. Due to the closed and suspicious nature of North Korea's government, legitimate investment by external business organizations was extremely limited up until the late 1990s. Up to that point, the Chosen Soren was one of the only groups that engaged in

substantive business dealings with the DPRK. Noland, *Avoiding the Apocalypse*, 102.

72. George Hicks, *Japan's Hidden Apartheid: The Korean Minority and the Japanese*, 35.

73. Nicholas Eberstadt, "Financial Transfers from Japan to North Korea: Estimating the Unreported Flows," *Asian Survey* 36, no. 5 (May 1996): 523.

74. Eberstadt, "Financial Transfers from Japan to North Korea," 538–539.

75. "12.7 billion yen sent to North Korea over 3-year period," *Yomuiri Shimbun*, 28 June 2003, accessed via LexisNexis Research Database, 25 March 2005; Eberstadt, "Financial Transfers from Japan to North Korea," 524; Kasumi Sato quoted by Noland in *Avoiding the Apocalypse*, 104; Chanlett-Avery, "North Korean Supporters in Japan," 4; Mark E. Manyin, "Japan-North Korea Relations: Selected Issues," *CRS Report for Congress* RL32161 (Washington, DC: Congressional Research Service, Library of Congress, 26 November 2003), 14.

76. Eric Johnston, "The North Korea Abduction Issue and Its Effect on Japanese Domestic Politics," *Japan Policy Research Institute*, JPRI Working Paper 101 (June 2004), www.jpri.org/publications/workingpapers/wp101.html, accessed 18 May 2005.

77. Triplett, *Rogue State*, 109.

78. This group is also referred to as the *Chongryun* in Korean. Lintner, "It's Hard to Help Kim Jong-il," 20–22; Struck, "Murder Shines a Light on the Lives of Koreans in Japan," A21; Masakazu Honda, "Under Fire: Chongrun is Dragged Kicking and Screaming," *Asahi News Service*, 27 September 2002, accessed via LexisNexis Research Database, 15 May 2005.

79. Noland, *Avoiding the Apocalypse*, 102.

80. During a joint summit between Kim Jong-il and Japanese Prime Minister Koizumi in September 2002, the DPRK leader admitted that "overzealous" individuals within North Korea's security services had abducted 13 Japanese citizens between 1977 and 1982. Chanlett-Avery, "North Korean Supporters in Japan," 6.

81. Prior to the 2002 kidnapping admission, the Chosen Soren vehemently denied accusations of abductions of Japanese citizens by North Korea as "purely propaganda intended to poison people's minds about 'the worker's paradise of North Korea'" which later caused the organization severe embarrassment after Kim Jong-il's admission implicating his country in the incidents. Honda, "Under Fire"; Creamer, *The Rise and Fall of Chosen Soren*, 39.

82. Oh and Hassig, *North Korea Through the Looking Glass*, 180.

83. These have been in response to the changing dynamics of the student population, which now consist of third or fourth generation ethnic Koreas who feel much less connected with North Korea than previous generations. "Chosen Soren: Chongryun Schools to Ax Kim Portraits," *Asahi Shimbun*, 10 September 2002, accessed via LexisNexis Research Database, 17 April 2005.

84. Charles Smith, "Cash Lifeline: Koreans in Japan Subsidise Pyongyang," *Far Eastern Economic Review* 156, no. 36 (9 September 1993): 23; Anthony Faiola, "Revolution is Brewing at N. Korean Schools in Japan," *The Washington Post*, 10 October 2003,

A1.

85. Surprisingly, North Korea sent funds annually to support these pro-Pyongyang schools. Faiola, "Revolution is Brewing."

86. Manyin, "Japan-North Korea Relations," 5.

87. Eric Johnston, "Chongryun Tax Breaks Face Hard Scrutiny," *The Japan Times*, 26 July 2003, accessed via LexisNexis Research Database, 17 April 2005.

88. These changes were in response to an overall reevaluation of the status of the Chosen Soren in the aftermath of the abduction admissions; educational institutions were not included and retained their tax-exempt status. "Chongryun Tax Breaks Face Hard Scrutiny."

89. "Tokyo Seizes 3 Chongryn Facilities," *International Herald Tribune*, 10 September 2003, accessed via LexisNexis Research Database, 17 April 2005.

90. Mindan membership is currently about four times that of the Chosen Soren. Chung, "Japan's Korean Community In Transition," 32.

91. Oh and Hassig, *North Korea Through the Looking Glass*, 181.

92. See Johnston, "The North Korea Abduction Issue and Its Effect"; "12.7 billion yen sent to North Korea over 3-year period"; Eberstadt, "Financial Transfers from Japan to North Korea," 524; Kasumi Sato quoted by Noland in *Avoiding the Apocalypse*, 104f; Chanlett-Avery, "North Korean Supporters in Japan," 4; and Manyin, "Japan-North Korea Relations," 14.

93. US Department of State, "International Narcotics Control Strategy Report 2003, Vol. 1: Southeast Asia"; Jay Solomon and Jason Dean, "Drug Money: Heroin Busts Point to Source of Funds for North Koreans," *The Wall Street Journal*, 23 April 2003, accessed via ProQuest Research Database, 21 November 2004.

94. Perl, "Drug Trafficking and North Korea," 6.

95. David E. Kaplan, "The Wiseguy Regime," *US News and World Report* 126, no. 6 (15 February 1999): 37–39; Solomon and Dean, "Drug Money"; Kim, "North Korea and Narcotics Trafficking," 7; "ROK Intelligence Service Website Describes DPRK Drug Production"; Green, "Dealing Drugs: North Korean Narcotics Trafficking"; Boyd, "North Korea: Hand in the Cookie Jar"; Perl, "Drug Trafficking and North Korea, 8; US Department of State, "International Narcotics Control Strategy Report 2003, Vol. 1"; "ROK Police Arrest 17 for Smuggling Alleged DPRK Methamphetamine," (text), Seoul *The Korea Times* (24 February 2004), FBIS Document ID KPP20040223000084, accessed 15 March 2005; Jin Ryu, "Turkey Expels Two NK Diplomats for Drug Smuggling," *The Korea Times*, 10 December 2004, www.times.hankooki.com/lpage/nation/200412/kt2004121017133111990.htm, accessed 6 April 2005.

96. Perl, "Drug Trafficking and North Korea," 6; Solomon and Dean, "Drug Money."

97. CIA, *The World Factbook Online 2004: North Korea*.

98. US Congress, *Drugs, Counterfeiting, and Weapons Proliferation: The NK Connection*, 36.

99. Triplett, *Rogue State*, 94.

100. Triplett, *Rogue State*, 94–95.

101. US Congress, *Drugs, Counterfeiting, and Weapons Proliferation: The NK Connection*, 5–26.

102. Tetsuya Suetsugu, "Risky Business Leading North Korea to Ruin," *The Daily Yomiuri*, 22 August 2003, accessed via LexisNexis Research Database, 15 January 2005.

103. Triplett, *Rogue State*, 94.

104. William Chapman, "N. Korea's Corps of Diplomatic 'Renegades'; Envoys Said to Traffic in Drugs and Weapons," *The Washington Post*, 13 November 1983, A28.

105. Solomon and Dean, "Drug Money."

106. Solomon and Dean, "Drug Money."

107. US Congress, *Final Report of the North Korean Advisory Group.*

108. Kim notes that although there were attempts to keep the production hidden from the public, the farms were an "open secret." Young Il Kim, "North Korea and Narcotics Trafficking: A View from the Inside," *North Korea Review*, Special Supplement to the *Jamestown Foundation China Brief*, no. 1 (27 February 2004): 6–7.

109. Kim, "North Korea and Narcotics Trafficking," 7.

110. Nick Green, "Dealing Drugs: North Korean Narcotics Trafficking," *Harvard International Review* 26, no. 1 (Spring 2004): 7.

111. Solomon and Dean, "Drug Money."

112. Kim, "North Korea and Narcotics Trafficking," 7.

113. Kaplan, "The Wiseguy Regime," 38.

114. Spaeth, "Kim's Rackets."

115. Green, "Dealing Drugs: North Korean Narcotics Trafficking," 7.

116. US Department of State, "International Narcotics Control Strategy Report 2003, Vol. 1."

117. US Department of State, "International Narcotics Control Strategy Report 2003, Vol. 1."

118. This might have been a re-emphasis or significant change from similar instructions in the 1970s. Kaplan, "The Wiseguy Regime," 39.

119. Mari Yamaguchi, "North Korea Plying Its Drugs in Japan," *Desert News*, 4 March 2003, www.mapinc.org/drugnews/v03/n356/a07.html, accessed via *The Media Awareness Project Website*, 29 January 2005.

120. US Department of State, "International Narcotics Control Strategy Report 2003, Vol. 1."

121. US Congress, *Drugs, Counterfeiting, and Weapons Proliferation: The NK Connection*, 5–26.

122. The Arirang Festival was a huge event billed as a "Grand Mass Artistic and Gymnastic Performance" and was intended to rival South Korea's co-hosting of the World Cup. Yamaguchi, "North Korea Plying Its Drugs in Japan" and Scott Fisher, "Arirang Festival," *1StopKorea Online*, www.1stopkorea.com/index.htm?nk-trip5.htm~

mainframe, accessed 29 January 2005.

123. Kim, "North Korea and Narcotics Trafficking," 7.

124. Solomon and Dean, "Drug Money."

125. US Congress, *Drugs, Counterfeiting, and Weapons Proliferation: The NK Connection*, 36.

126. William Bach testimony in US Congress, *Drugs, Counterfeiting, and Weapons Proliferation: The NK Connection*, 11.

127. US Congress, *Drugs, Counterfeiting, and Weapons Proliferation: The NK Connection*, 11; Perl, "Drug Trafficking and North Korea," 8.

128. "ROK Daily Reports DPRK Expanding Opium Farms, Selling Drugs Via China," (text), Seoul *Chosen Ilbo* (9 October 2004), FBIS Document ID KPP2004202000005410, accessed 22 March 2005.

129. "ROK Daily Reports DPRK Expanding Opium Farms."

130. US Department of State, "International Narcotics Control Strategy Report 2003, Vol. 1."

131. Kaplan, "The Wiseguy Regime," 38.

132. George W. Bush, President of the United States. "Presidential Determination No. 2004-47 on Major Drug Transit or Major Illicit Drug Producing Countries for FY05," 15 September 2004, *Weekly Compilation of Presidential Documents*, week ending 20 September 2004, 1998–2000.

133. United Nations, "World Drug Report 2004, Vol. 1," 71.

134. United Nations, "World Drug Report 2004, Vol. 2," 14.

135. US Department of State, Bureau for International Narcotics and Law Enforcement Affairs, "International Narcotics Control Strategy Report 2005, Vol. 1: Drug and Chemical Control," *US Department of State Website*, March 2005, www.state.gov/g/inl/rls/nrcrpt/2005/, accessed 20 July 2005.

136. US Department of State, "International Narcotics Control Strategy Report 2003, Vol. 1."

137. Perl, "Drug Trafficking and North Korea," 10.

138. While some estimates have drug production at nearly $500 million per year (see Kaplan, "The Far East Sopranos" and Solomon, "Money Trail"), a more realistic figure based on increased international attention and historic cash flows from drug operations makes $50–100 million a more plausible amount. Author's analysis and Perl, "Drug Trafficking and North Korea," 9.

139. Hiroko Kono, "Poppy Cultivation Ordered By Kim Family – Japan is Number One Buyer," (text), Tokyo *Yomiuri Shimbun* (20 May 2003), 6, FBIS Document ID JPP2003050000139, accessed 19 May 2005.

140. Green, "Dealing Drugs: North Korean Narcotics Trafficking," 7.

141. "The Superdollar Plot," on *Panorama*, BBC One, airdate 20 June 2004, transcript viewed online, www.news.bbc.co.uk/1/hi/programmes/panorama/3805581.stm, accessed 28 February 2004.

142. This is based on data from the US Secret Service on domestic counterfeit seizures added to extrapolations of estimated counterfeit US currency overseas. Ruth Judson and Richard Porter, "Estimating the World Wide Volume of Counterfeit US Currency: Data and Extrapolation," *Federal Reserve Online*, September 2003, www.federal reserve.gov/pubs/feds/2003/200352/200352pap.pdf, accessed 27 March 2005, 28.

143. The US Secret Service, organized under the Treasury Department, was initially established in 1865 to investigate and reduce the threat of counterfeit paper currency, which was estimated to be one-third to one-half of all money in circulation at the end of the US Civil War. *United States Secret Service Website*, www.secretservice.gov/, accessed 27 March 2005.

144. The ICAP was established as part of the US effort to redesign its currency in the mid-1990s. US Treasury Department, *The Use and Counterfeiting of US Currency Abroad, Part 2*, 45.

145. US Treasury Department, *The Use and Counterfeiting of US Currency Abroad, Part 2*, 45, 49. Intaglio-style presses are often used to make the very best counterfeit US currency and involve a solid etched chromium plate, which is initially covered with ink and then wiped clean. Printing sheets are then pressed into the plates and ink in the etched portion of the plates is transferred to the sheets creating a three-dimensional printing impression with a raised side and an indented side. "Intaglio Printing," *US Bureau of Engraving and Printing Website*, www.moneyfactory.com/document.cfm/18/109, accessed 27 March 2005.

146. US General Accounting Office, "Currency Paper Procurement: Meaningful Competition Unlikely Under Current Conditions," *GAO Online*, GAO/GGD-98-181 (August 1998), www.gao.gov/archive/1998/gg98181.pdf, accessed 27 March 2005, 4.

147. "Secrets of Making Money," on *NOVA*, PBS, airdate 22 October 1996, transcript viewed online, www.pbs.org/wgbh/nova/transcripts/2314secr.html, accessed 27 March 2005.

148. The added measures include embedded security threads that glow under ultraviolet light. "Secrets of Making Money."

149. US GAO, "Currency Paper Procurement," 4, 29. De La Rue Giori Corporation describes itself as "the world's largest commercial security printer and papermaker, involved in the production of over 150 national currencies." "Welcome to De La Rue," *De La Rue Giori Homepage*, www.delarue.com/, accessed 27 March 2005.

150. "Secrets of Making Money."

151. Judson and Porter, "Volume of Counterfeit US Currency," 6.

152. US Treasury Department, *The Use and Counterfeiting of US Currency Abroad, Part 2*, 45, 48.

153. Informal discussions with the US Secret Service in Judson and Porter, "Volume of Counterfeit US Currency," 6–7.

154. Judson and Porter, "Volume of Counterfeit US Currency," 24–25.

155. US Treasury Department, *The Use and Counterfeiting of US Currency Abroad, Part 2*, vii.

156. This total does not include currency that was seized prior to entering circulation. US Treasury Department, *The Use and Counterfeiting of US Currency Abroad, Part 2*, 50–51.

157. US Treasury Department, *The Use and Counterfeiting of US Currency Abroad, Part 2*, 50–51.

158. US Treasury Department, *The Use and Counterfeiting of US Currency Abroad, Part 2*, 77.

159. Andrew Hogg, "Getting Off on the Right Note," *The Banker* 917, no. 152 (July 2002): 116, accessed via InfoTrac Research Database, 12 March 2005.

160. Hogg, "Getting Off on the Right Note"; "The Superdollar Plot."

161. "Secrets of Making Money," PBS. Also see Kaplan, "The Wiseguy Regime," 39.

162. US Treasury Department, *The Use and Counterfeiting of United States Currency Abroad*, January 2000, (Washington, DC: US Government Printing Office, 2000), vi. Cited hereafter as US Treasury Department, *Counterfeit US Currency*.

163. US Treasury Department, *Counterfeit US Currency*, vi.

164. Iran also is considered a producer of counterfeit dollars and obtained six presses from the same company from 1973–1984. Banseok Seo, "North Korea Duped by Iranian Counterfeits," *Digital Chosonilbo*, 2 March 1999, enlish.chosun.com/w21data/html/news/199903/199903020369.html, accessed 27 March 2005; Kaplan, "The Wiseguy Regime," 39.

165. "DPRK Prints Super K Dollar Bills on Machine Provided by Former USSR KGB," *Tokyo Foresight* (in Japanese) 15 March–18 April 2003, quoted in Perl, "Drug Trafficking and North Korea," 10.

166. "Koreas: Defector says North producing counterfeit US dollars," *Yonhap News*, 12 January 2000, accessed via LexisNexis Research Database, 15 March 2005.

167. Triplett, *Rogue State*, 102; "North Korea Produces Bogus Dollars at Three Plants: Report," *Agence France Presse*, 28 June 1997, accessed via LexisNexis Research Database, 15 March 2005.

168. "North Korea Produces Bogus Dollars at Three Plants: Report."

169. Kang claimed to be related to Kim Il-sung's mother and the son-in-law of former North Korean Premier Kang Song San. Paul Alexander, "Defector Says Government making Heroin, Fake Dollars," *The Associated Press*, 22 June 1995, accessed via LexisNexis Research Database, 15 March 2005.

170. Japanese language newspaper reports from the *Sankei Shimbun* published on 28 June 1997 and 12 August 1997 quoted in Triplett, *Rogue State*, 102.

171. The NIS was called the Agency for National Security Planning (NSP) at the time of this report. "NK Prints $15 Mil. in Fake Dollars," *Korea Times Online*, 16 November 1998, www.hankooki.com, keyword search NK Prints, accessed 21 December 2005.

172. "The Superdollar Plot."

173. "Counterfeiting: Defector Says He Was Ordered To Get Fake US Dollars," *The Associated Press*, 8 June 1988, accessed via LexisNexis Research Database, 15 March 2005.

174. "Counterfeiting: Defector Says He Was Ordered To Get Fake US Dollars,"; Kaplan, "The Wiseguy Regime," 39.

175. One South Korean intelligence officer stated that "the North Koreans have identified the exact formula for making US Treasury paper," resulting in bills that were "better than the originals made at the US mint." Anthony LoBaido, "North Korea's financial dirty tricks: Stellar workmanship behind counterfeiting of US currency," *WorldNetDaily*, 14 August 1998, www.worldnetdaily.com/news/article.asp?ARTICLE_ID=16673, accessed 30 March 2005.

176. "What is a Superdollar?" *BBC News Online*, 19 June 2004, news.bbc.co.uk/1/hi/programmes/panorama/3819345.stm, accessed 31 March 2005.

177. Colin Joyce, "North Korean Forgers Set Their Sights on the Euro: Counterfeiters Produce Millions of Notes, Some Better Than Original," *The Sunday Telegraph*, 21 November 2004, accessed via LexisNexis Research Database, 15 March 2005.

178. "North Korea Prints $15 Million of Bogus Bills a Year," *The Korea Herald*, 17 November 1998, accessed via LexisNexis Research Database, 15 March 2005.

179. Harald Bruning, "Five North Koreans Arrested in Macao," *United Press International*, 29 June 1994, accessed via LexisNexis Research Database, 12 April 2005; Ron Moreau and Russell Watson, "Is it Real, or Super K? North Korean Suspected of Producing Counterfeit US currency," *Newsweek* 24, no. 127 (10 June 1996): 42; "Counterfeiting: 6 Arrested on Suspicion of Peddling Fake US Currency," *Kyodo News Service*, 16 June 1997, accessed via LexisNexis Research Database, 28 March 2005; Kaplan, "The Wiseguy Regime," 39; "NK Diplomats' Illegal Acts Get Bold," *The Korea Times*, 8 November 1998, accessed via LexisNexis Research Database, 28 March 2005; Ian MacWilliam, "US Embassy Keeping Silent on Bogus Bills," *The Moscow Times*, 25 January 1997, accessed via LexisNexis Research Database, 28 March 2005; The Russian-language newspaper Izvestiya commented that the diplomat attempted to exchange over $100,000 in bills for new US bills "for an appropriate fee." "North Korean Diplomat Expelled for Passing Fake Dollars," *Izvestiya*, 8 February 1997, accessed via LexisNexis Research Database, 28 March 2005; Nicholas D. Kristof, "Japan Holds 6 for Passing Counterfeit $100 Bills," *New York Times*, 18 June 1997, A6; "North Korea Prints $15 Million of Bogus Bills a Year"; Kaplan, "The Wiseguy Regime," 39; "The Superdollar Plot"; "$27m Counterfeit Gang Jailed," *BBC News Online*, July 2002, www.news.bbc.co.uk/1/low/england/2154474.stm, accessed 31 March 2005; Kaplan, "The Far East Sopranos," 34; Jin-bae Jeon, "Counterfeit $100 Notes Called Nearly Perfect," *JoongAng Daily Online*, 24 April 2003, joongangdaily.joins.com/, accessed 30 March 2005; "Taiwan Police Identify, Search for Suspected Counterfeiters of US Banknotes," *Central News Agency*, Taipei, 26 July 2004, accessed via LexisNexis Research Database, 17 March 2005; "Foreign Experts to Help Taiwan Identify Forged 100 US dollar bills," *Deutsche Presse-Agentur*, 27 July 2004, accessed via LexisNexis Research Database, 17 March 2005.

180. "The Superdollar Plot."

181. Kaplan, "The Far East Sopranos."

182. Analysts from both the US and South Korea generally agree on this figure. In 1998, The South Korean National Intelligence Service (NSP) estimated that the DPRK produced $15 million in counterfeit bills per year. "North Korea Prints $15 Million of Bogus Bills a Year"; Perl, "Drug Trafficking and North Korea," 10; US military officials in South Korea agreed with the $15–20 million per year figure, Asano Yoshiharu, "N. Korea Missile Exports Earned 580 Mil. Dollars in '01," *Yomiuri Shimbun*, 13 May 2003, accessed via LexisNexis Research Database, 15 March 2005.

183. Judson and Porter, "Volume of Counterfeit US Currency," 1–3, 34–35.

184. "North Korea Prints $15 Million of Bogus Bills a Year."

185. Hwashik Bong, "North Korea Accounts for 10 Percent of World's Counterfeit Notes," *JoongAng Daily Online*, 20 June 1999, www.joongangdaily.joins.com/, accessed 30 March 2005.

186. Sources include informal discussions with the US Secret Service in Judson and Porter, "Volume of Counterfeit US Currency," 6–7; "North Korea Prints $15 Million of Bogus Bills a Year"; Perl, "Drug Trafficking and North Korea," 10; and Asano Yoshiharu, "N. Korea Missile Exports Earned 580 Mil. Dollars in '01," *Yomiuri Shimbun*, 13 May 2003, accessed via LexisNexis Research Database, 15 March 2005.

187. "Super K Counterfeit Bills Meet Match With New Detector," *PR Newswire*, 15 March 2005, accessed via InfoTrac Research Database, 15 March 2005.

188. Asia policy analyst Balbwa Hwang suggested this in "The Superdollar Plot."

Chapter 4

Bureau 39: Kim's Money Machine

Having a TV in North Korea is like having a private airplane in the West.[1]
—Kim Kil Sun, former North Korean journalist

Controlling Kim Jong-il's money machine is no easy task. It requires the expertise and the organization of a business conglomerate, the connections and influence of the DPRK's overseas diplomats, and the backing of the North Korean government to orchestrate a vast network of operations. Within the North Korean government, an organization designated Bureau 39 has the function of managing banks and trading companies which earn foreign currency overseen by the Finance and Accounting Department of the Central Committee of the Korean Worker's Party (KWP). The organizational operations of Bureau 39 to manage Kim Jong-il's cash flows are the "nerve center of Pyongyang's legal and illegal ventures."[2] The following section will discuss this organization, its background and functions, and how its overall efforts facilitate support to the Kim regime.

Founding and Organization

Bureau 39 goes by several names to include Office 39, Department 39, Division 39, and Room No. 39, but all refer to the same group that is responsible for coordinating overall foreign currency fundraising efforts for the DPRK.[3] This organization is located in a corner of a six-story, rectangular concrete building within a heavily guarded Korean Worker's Party complex in the center of Pyongyang near the Russian embassy and a short distance from the Koryo Hotel, where many foreign visitors stay while visiting North Korea's capital.[4] When asked about Bureau 39's involvement in illicit activities, a North Korean diplomat in Hong Kong acknowledged the existence of but denied any involvement in illegal dealings and stated "I can say that this is a cynical campaign . . . and not true at all. . . . Historically, this [accusation] was used to defame our country."[5]

Origin and Purpose

Bureau 39 was established in 1974 soon after North Korea began efforts to "raise foreign currency to further the glorious revolution" as part of the KWP's Finance and Accounting Department.[6] Bureau 39 is the center for North Korea's foreign business interests, which ranges from legitimate sales of ginseng and rare mushrooms to narcotics trafficking, car smuggling, and counterfeit operations.[7] Additionally, this organization was intended to provide funds for Kim Jong-il's political career, which began in the 1970s when the "Great Leader"

Kim Il-sung designated the younger Kim as his successor.[8]

Defectors state that Kim Jong-il built Bureau 39 by consolidating and acquiring control of the "country's key natural resources, particularly the minerals that have fueled North Korea's economy since before the 1950–53 Korean War."[9] Kim chose his "closest confidantes" to run Bureau 39 operations and sought to learn from the business expertise of the West by sending his young designees to train in Europe on international business practices beginning in the 1970s.[10] Kim personally sent the son of North Korea's finance minister to Vienna in the mid-1980s to learn foreign-exchange trading and banking procedures and was later instrumental in the establishment of North Korea's Golden Star Bank in Vienna.[11]

Kim's Slush Funds

Bureau 39 has been in charge of amassing earnings from foreign business operations and consolidating these in the form of an external foreign exchange fund for Kim Jong-il. These "slush funds" were first created in the early 1970s when North Korea's Trade Representative Office in Singapore was instructed by Pyongyang to raise 20 million dollars for an overseas account for Kim Jong-il's use. Bureau 39 was in charge of raising these funds and, after it was later found that these funds were obtained illegally, the Singapore government issued an order for the arrest of Bureau 39's Vice Director, who fled by ship back to North Korea.[12]

Luxury Items for the Party

These funds are used at the discretion of Kim Jong-il to buy a variety of items to include gifts to reward loyal subordinates.[13] According to one source, Bureau 39 has two priorities: to obtain luxury items for both Kim's personal use and to secure party loyalty and to "procure overseas components and materials for North Korea's WMDs and missiles."[14] Bureau 39 funds are also used by Kim Jong-il to reward devotion to the party or recognize technological advances. A former North Korean journalist reported that after DPRK scientists at the Yongbyon nuclear facility made major technological advances in the early 1990s, Kim delivered television sets as gifts. The journalist commented that "having a TV in North Korea is like having a private airplane in the West."[15]

Another organization, Bureau 38, exists within the Finance and Accounting Department of the Central Party and is charged with the actual purchases of items for the personal use and distribution by Kim Jong-il.[16] Bureau 38 is "responsible for buying the daily necessities for Kim Jong-il and his family from foreign countries."[17]

Bureau 39 and the Daesong Group

The head of Bureau 39 is Kwon Yong-nok and he has been in charge of managing these types of funds since the 1980s. Currently in his 50s, Kwon is known to the outside world as KWP Central Committee Vice Director in Charge of Funds.[18] There are two divisions of Bureau 39: the overt operations are led by Daesong Group, which owns the Daesong Bank[19] and the now defunct Vienna's Golden Star Bank, and the other division is involved in both overt and secret operations to include "arms dealing and other illegal projects."[20] Daesong Bank was established in 1978 as "an external window for party organs," especially those organizations dealing with foreign trade and linked to Bureau 39.[21] North Korea does not disclose transactions from these banks to the public, demonstrating both the closed nature of North Korean society and the "limited role" of these institutions.[22]

The Palace Economy

The income managed by Bureau 39 contributes to the "Palace Economy" which provides for the living expenses of the Workers Party executives, for the "idolization" and continued worship of the Kim family, and for Kim Jong-il's personal use.[23] The Palace Economy is one of three "economies" that exist in North Korea. The other two are the "Military Economy" which is designated to maintain North Korea's military capabilities, and the "Central Economy."[24] The Central Economy is used to financially support Kim Jong-il and is "extorted to please the Party and the Military."[25] There is conflicting information over whether the Palace or Military Economy has the highest priority,[26] but both are financially supported, at least in part, by the activities of Bureau 39. Kim Jong-il's slush funds are managed under the auspices of the budget for the Palace Economy.[27]

As stated above, Bureau 39 manages both licit and illicit transactions for the DPRK. While both of these activities contribute to North Korea's bottom line, Bureau 39's "big cash" comes from illicit narcotics sales.[28] The following section will discuss the scope of Bureau 39 activities and provide some details on its most significant operations.

Operational Scope

Bureau 39 manages a host of moneymaking operations aimed at gaining foreign capital in support of the Kim regime. These include overseas banking and foreign trade organizations, direct dealings with foreign businesses, illicit criminal activity to include narcotics and counterfeit operations, and collection of "loyalty earnings" from DPRK citizens.[29]

Overseas Banking Organizations

To fulfill the need for a North Korean banking institution in Europe, North Korea established the Golden Star Bank in Vienna 1982 as a subsidiary of North Korea's Daesong Bank with the purpose "to engage in foreign exchange transactions and provide financial support for North Korean companies operating in Europe."[30] Bureau 39 funds are managed using several outlets associated with Daesong Bank, whose key functions are "remitting and approving the funds relating to the exportation and importation activities of Daesong General Trading Corporation and its affiliated marine products and shipping companies."[31] Daesong Bank is affiliated with North Korea's central bank, but remains formally outside its scope of control and Daesong General Trading Corporation is a key trade corporation component for contributions to the Kim's slush funds. Bureau 39 ultimately manages both.

Security services from Austria, South Korea, and the US have monitored North Korean banking practices in Europe for decades and have occasionally intervened. In fact, when the US froze North Korean bank accounts as part of its economic embargo in 1992, they froze $1.5 million of North Korean funds in a Bank of California branch in Austria. Seven years later, the balance had accrued to $2 million and the embargo was lifted – unfortunately for the DPRK, the Bank of California kept the money citing previous debts incurred by the Kim regime.[32]

Golden Star Bank

The details of the establishment and subsequent demise of the DPRK's Golden Star Bank provides insight into the operations of Bureau 39's subordinate organizations. In 1982, Daesong Bank established and controlled Golden Star Bank as the only North Korean bank in Europe.[33] Daesong Bank is controlled by senior North Korean communist party members, who supervised the Golden Star Bank branch that was tasked with providing "guarantees for foreign trade."[34] Beginning in 1997, Austrian security services began reporting that the DPRK's Golden Star Bank in Vienna was a front for various covert activities to include acquiring funds for Pyongyang's nuclear program.[35] During that same year, an Austrian Interior Ministry report noted that the Golden Star Bank was "named repeatedly in connection with money laundering and distributing counterfeit money and even involvement in the illegal trade of radioactive substances."[36]

Surveillance operations against Golden Star Bank enabled Austrian authorities to observe its dealings with front companies in both Slovakia and Hungary, and Austrian intelligence officials have linked the bank to distribution of counterfeit currency, money laundering, and radioactive material transactions.[37] By the end of 2001, Golden Star Bank's influence and operations had decreased significantly with assets totaling only around $20 million, according to an Austrian regulator.[38] In 2002, Austrian authorities intensified their monitoring of the

Golden Star Bank after a raid in Bratislava, 30 miles away from Vienna, that revealed invoices for millions of dollars linking North Korea to a missile technology deal with Egypt.[39]

In May 2003, an Austrian intelligence official stated that the Golden Star Bank was not involved in financial transactions any more, but had evolved to "a front for North Korean spies."[40] Austrian banking authorities had conducted a "special audit" of the bank in June 2003 and revealed involvement in money laundering and illegal weapons deals.[41] According to diplomatic sources in 2004, Golden Star Bank had virtually stopped all financial transactions partially due to Europe's increased focus on money laundering efforts.[42] Golden Star Bank was slated for closure in June 2004 by its North Korean overseers and for some time, the bank had not been able to do business with other institutions due to allegations of involvement with "financial irregularities."[43] As of May 2004, its assets were only about $18 million dollars and despite its closure as a financial institution, the bank was expected to continue to serve as a "liaison office" for other North Korean currency banks.[44]

Overseas Trade Organizations

The largest trade company under the direct management of Bureau 39 is Daesong General Trading Corporation. This organization "exports and imports all types of machinery and equipment to include gold and silver bars, chemical and textile products, mushrooms, fresh lilies, frozen swellfish, frozen octopus and ginseng" and runs satellite offices in key ports and railway stations.[45] One report described Daesong's overseas operations as "key 'passageways' for Kim Jong-il's slush funds."[46] After a failed 2002 agreement between Russia and Myanmar for the sale of a nuclear reactor, North Korea has stepped in to assist with the construction of the facility. This activity was accompanied by the arrival of Daesong Trade representatives in Myanmar.[47] There are over 20 overseas branches of the Daesong Trading Corporation, all controlled by Bureau 39.[48]

Chogwang Trading Company and Other Connections

One of the most notorious Daesong subordinates is Chogwang Trading Company, headquartered in Macao.[49] Macao police refer to the Chogwang Trading Company as "the command center that controls and regulates North Korean foreign currency-earning companies that have advanced into Macao. . . . It is an international crime organization, which disguised itself as a trading company."[50] This trading company, established in 1957, is one of at least 17 North Korean foreign currency earning companies operating in Macao. As of 2003, about 80 North Koreans were stationed there as employees of these companies and about 30 of these had diplomatic passports. Originally, this company was under the control of Bureau 35, which controls North Korean intelligence operations, but in 1992, Bureau 39 assumed responsibility for this organization. Since that time Chogwang has been involved in "foreign currency-earning projects [and] key duties are pursuing terror operations toward the south [Korea], managing Kim's 'slush funds' and earning foreign currency."[51]

The Macao police have historically referred to Chogwang as an "international crime organization."[52] The company has been cited as being heavily involved in methamphetamine[53] trafficking and Macao authorities began tracking its activities beginning in 1982.[54] Reporter Chong-ch'ang U visited to the company office in Macao and provided unique insight into the legitimacy of Chogwang operations:

> It was around 1000 (about 1100 Korea time) on Monday, 3 March, when I got there. The office door was open but the light was turned off. It was dark inside, and I could see no one. I stepped up to the door and peered inside. I saw a receptions area with a desk and a chair and a sofa set, and several partitioned booths behind the reception area. There were no telephones, fax machines, computers, or copiers commonly found in a trading company. I could intuitively sense from the office atmosphere that Chogwang Trading was a bogus company.[55]

Macao police also believe that Kim Hyon-hui, the bomber of Korean Air Flight 858, was an agent working for this office and noted that Macao has been used as a logistical and financial base for terrorist operations for decades.[56] Additionally, intelligence reports note that Bureau 39 used another Daesong subordinate, Zokwang Trading Company, as a venue for distribution of counterfeit dollars and for weapons procurement.[57]

Another connection of note involves Stanley Ho, the owner of most of Macao's casino businesses. Ho opened a casino in Pyongyang's Yanggakdo Hotel in 1999 by investing $29 million. When Ho went to Pyongyang to conclude the deal, he was accompanied by both the General Manager and President of Chogwang Trading Company.[58]

South Korea's Political Contributions

Some of the most controversial incidents involving Bureau 39 relate to the receipt of monies from South Korea in support of both political and economic ventures. In 1998, South Korea's newly elected President Kim Dae-Jung's embarked upon his "Sunshine Policy" of political and economic engagement with North Korea. This policy was "aimed at changing North Korea's policies over the long term by offering aid and cooperation without requiring short term policy changes in return."[59] One of the projects that South Korea approved as part of this policy was the development of North Korea's Mount Kumgang tourist area and cash payments of $942 million over six years from Hyundai Asan in support of this venture.[60] Analysts note that money paid to North Korea by the Hyundai organization for the Mount Kumgang project was "flowing into the Workers Party" and directed to Bureau 39 for Kim Jong-il's use.[61]

Probably the most significant episode involved the historic North-South Korea Summit in 2000. Prior to this meeting, press reports stated that Kim Jong-il demanded $1 billion from Hyundai Asan to meet with Kim Dae-jung; although the Hyundai CEO initially turned down this request, $500 million was agreed upon and was secretly transferred just prior to the summit in June 2000.[62] Awaiting payment, North Korea first unilaterally delayed talks until $200 million, of the $500 million promised, was received and postponed the meeting until 12 June, one day after the final payment was forwarded.[63] The mechanics of the deal attempted to mirror a standard business transaction, but were considered illegal when discovered by the Seoul government. Four separate creditor banks provided loans to Hyundai subsidiaries including the government-run Korea Development Bank and to finance the transfer of funds to North Korea.[64] On the eve of the 2000 Summit, this money reportedly went to representatives from Bureau 39.[65]

Bureau 39 and the Drug Trade

Illegal drug activity associated with North Korean diplomats stands in stark contrast to other nations: Pyongyang sponsors these actions as part of its official government functions. North Korean diplomats are charged with coordinating much of this activity, keeping a "minimum for living and continuous operations," and sending most of their income from illicit activity back to Pyongyang for management by Bureau 39.[66] One analyst commented, "North Korea may be the only country in the world that encourages such crimes as a government-imposed task."[67]

Bureau 39 oversees the "overall control of cultivation, production, transportation, and exportation" associated with North Korean narcotics trafficking efforts.[68] Additional evidence was provided by Hwang Chang-yop, the highest ranking North Korean defector to date and former member of Kim Jong-il's inner circle, who stated that Bureau 39 was established, in part, to "produce opium for [Kim Jong-il's] secret funds."[69] Bureau 39 controls domestic production and then transfers the drugs to trading companies and overseas missions for sales; money from these transactions is funneled into Kim Jong-il private slush fund used to "hand out favors, bankroll intelligence operations, and buy military hardware."[70]

Anthony Spaeth observed that, "drugs are the ultimate proof of loyalty. They cost little to produce, and make Kim the most money of all."[71] A former North Korean importer-exporter of legitimate items was approached in the late 1980s by individuals at Bureau 39 to engage in narcotics trafficking on the side and told to "consider the drug trading 'more important' than his regular job." The defector soon found himself dealing with the Japanese mafia, smuggling heroin hidden in boxes of dried squid, and skimming some of the proceeds for himself with the rest of the profits to going to Bureau 39. He commented that "if it goes to Bureau 39, it is the same as sending it to Kim Jong-il."[72]

North Korea's overseas companies and diplomats are also involved a variety of other illicit activities as well. These efforts include using state-owned companies to resell smuggled autos from Japan to China to gain hard currency.[73] There have been charges against North Korean diplomats stationed in Africa who have smuggled rhino horns and elephant ivory to raise cash. Additionally, the DPRK embassy staff in New Delhi were accused of the slaughter and black-market sales of beef in India, where killing cows is against the law.[74]

Loyalty Earnings and Other Fundraising Efforts

Bureau 39 has a domestic role as well and there are "annex offices" in each region of North Korea designated "No. 5 Management Offices" which direct projects aimed at earning and remitting "loyalty foreign currency" to Kim Jong-il via Bureau 39.[75] Defectors state that North Korean citizens are expected to make donations to Bureau 39 on important holidays honoring both the "Dear Leader" Kim Jong-il and "Great Leader" Kim Il-sung.[76] These "loyalty dona-tions" include the gathering of "mushrooms, clams, aralia shoots, and wild gin-ger roots, which Division 39 sells."[77] On an annual basis, approximately $100 million is raised from domestic sources as "loyalty payments" for Kim Jong-il's birthday on 16 February.[78] For example, Bureau 39 fundraising activities al-lowed North Korea to spend about $90 million on Kim Jong-il's 57th birthday in 1999, which was actually *less* that normal due to economic difficulties.[79]

Wild mushrooms, which are gathered and exported to other Asian nations, provide a source of legitimate income for Bureau 39. Mushroom exports, which have been about 1,200 tons per year, earn approximately $100 million annu-ally.[80] Gold is another domestic product that provides licit income. North Korea produces about 11 tons of gold annually from 17 goldmines under the manage-ment of Bureau 39, which supervises the production and exportation of gold bars, earning approximately $100 million per year from mining operations.[81]

Managing Kim's Funds

Bureau 39 continues to coordinate overseas fundraising efforts from North Korea's worldwide illicit and "gray area" activities. All companies earning for-eign currency reportedly remit 30 percent of their profits to Pyongyang.[82] In the past Kim Jong-il secret slush funds were kept in West German, Swiss and Aus-trian banks, but now are primarily in Swiss financial institutions, managed by the same individuals for over 20 years.[83] In 1984, rumors surfaced in North Ko-rea that Kim Jong-il's secret fund amounted over one billion dollars. In 1995, a North Korean defector who previously worked at the Central Committee's Fi-nance and Accounting Department stated that the fund amount was "two or three billion dollars."[84] Current analysis places this fund at approximately $4.3 billion in reserves for Kim's use.[85] A Korean-American lawyer commented that Kim Jong-il probably owns accounts under front companies established in countries where secret protection acts are in place.[86] The "Great Leader" Kim Il-sung also had similar reserves as Kim Jong-il's slush funds, but these were designated "presidential [chusok] bonds" and were for emergency funding in the event of a war amounting to approximately 3 percent of the national budget.[87]

The composition and details of these activities and support are displayed below:

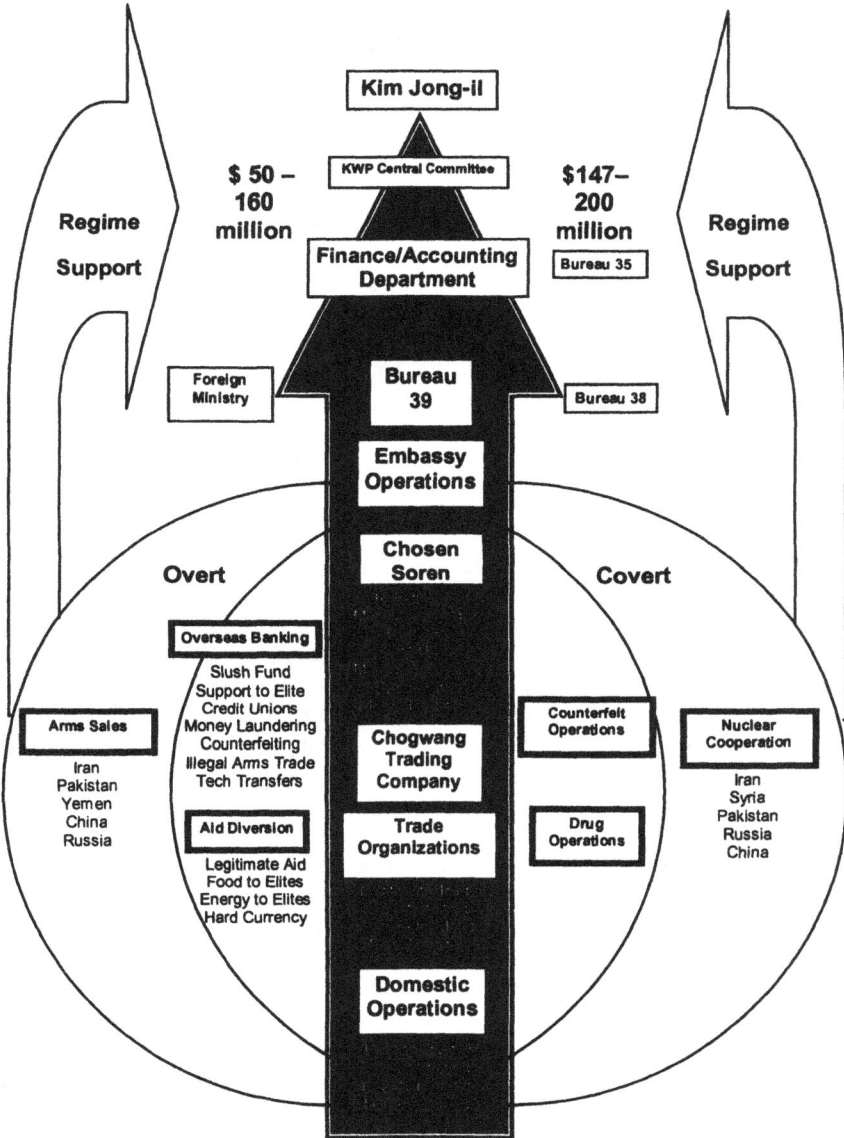

Figure 4. Hard Currency Flow Bureaucracy[88]

North Korea's practice of holding funds in Swiss accounts makes tracking financial activity virtually impossible. Banking is Switzerland's biggest "state project" and yields its largest profits and, based on the Bank Secrecy Act legislated in 1934, Switzerland neither discloses nor confirms a specific person's history of bank transactions. Violation of this act can result in imprisonment, fines, and lawsuits for contract violation and the obligation of keeping information a secret applies after an account is closed. For the amount of funds North Korea maintains in these types of accounts, interest rates do not exceed one percent and when certain funds seem to be suspicious, Swiss banks charge 10–15 percent in maintenance fees.[89]

Japanese and South Korean intelligence agencies state that Kim Jong-il puts approximately $65 million into his secret funds each year paid in the "form of letters of credit or cash paid in directly by the secret service."[90] During North Korea's financial crisis and famine in the 1990s, Kim's secret slush funds managed by Bureau 39 remained intact. Some defectors have stated that if international organizations had not provided North Korea with support during its economic crisis and famine, that the "slush funds" would have been used to buy food; but since the UN and others provided assistance, there was no need for Kim to tap his financial reserves.[91]

North Korea's Hard Currency Bureaucracy

Pyongyang's organizations designed to obtain overseas currency mirror the North Korean government and are not only satellite entities, but are part of the same organization. Kim Jong-il and the KWP ultimately control every aspect of government and society in North Korea and run their overseas fundraising activities in exactly the same manner. All activities are responsible for reporting to a higher authority within the North Korean government, which monitors these organizations with intense scrutiny. All of the activities mentioned in the previous chapters are inter-connected in some manner, both to Bureau 39 and to Pyongyang.

As shown in the previous figure, the overt operations contribute between $50 and $160 million annually to North Korea while the covert or illegal operations provide $147–$200 million. Connections appear between Bureau 39 and most of the administrative organizations conducting illicit activity in support of Kim Jong-il. Some of these Bureau 39 connections are well-documented, in the cases of overseas banking, trade organizations, and domestic operations. The relationship between Chosen Soren and Bureau 39 probably exists, as evidenced by the Chosen Soren's support of Taesong Corporation's alleged involvement in spy operations and technology transfers.[92] Ties between Bureau 38 (Kim's procurement operation) and aid diversion can be assumed but no evidence has been found to support this. Bureau 39 might also be involved in aid diversion, but substantial evidence for this suggestion has not been found.

Notes and references

1. Solomon, "In North Korea, Secret Cash Hoard Props Up Regime."

2. David J. Smith, "Reaching Into North Korea," in *North Korean Policy Elites*, ed. Kongdan Oh Hassig, *Institute for Defense Analysis*, IDA Paper P-3903, June 2004 (Alexandria, VA: Institute for Defense Analysis, 2004): V14.

3. North Korea's government uses bureaus as controlling departments for specific activities. For example Bureau 38 controls the purchase of items for Kim's personal use while Bureau 35 (also called Division 35) is in charge of intelligence operations. Yo'ngchin Han, "Loyal Foreign Currency Earning," (text), Seoul *The Daily NK* (6 April 2005), FBIS Document ID KPP20050408000022, accessed 18 May 2005. Sean Callebs and Larry Smith, "North and South Korea Skirmish at Border; Where Does Kim Jong-il Get His Money?" *CNN News*, transcript from *On the Money*, broadcast 9 July 2003, accessed via InfoTrac Onefile Research Database, 14 May 2005.

4. Spaeth, "Kim's Rackets"; Jay Solomon, "In North Korea, Secret Cash Hoard Props Up Regime," *The Wall Street Journal*, 14 July 2003, accessed via Lexis Nexis Research Database 14 May 2005.

5. Solomon, "In North Korea, Secret Cash Hoard Props Up Regime."

6. Spaeth, "Kim's Rackets."

7. Spaeth, "Kim's Rackets."

8. Solomon, "In North Korea, Secret Cash Hoard Props Up Regime"; Oh and Hassig, *North Korea Through the Looking Glass*, 87.

9. Solomon, "In North Korea, Secret Cash Hoard Props Up Regime."

10. Solomon, "In North Korea, Secret Cash Hoard Props Up Regime."

11. Golden Star was a North Korean bank set up in Vienna to support a variety of Bureau 39 activities. Choi later returned the DPRK to advise the Daesong Bank in Pyongyang. Solomon, "In North Korea, Secret Cash Hoard Props Up Regime."

12. Chong-ch'ang U, "Kim Chong-il's Slush Funds," (text), Seoul *Wolgan Choson* (01 November 2000), FBIS Document ID KPP20001019000046, accessed 19 May 2005. Cited hereafter as U, "Kim Chong-il's Slush Funds."

13. For example, Kim reportedly once used these monies to purchase a 60-foot yacht, possibly to reward a trusted subordinate. U, "Kim Chong-il's Slush Funds."

14. Niksch, "Korea-US Relations: Issues for Congress," 12; Solomon, "In North Korea, Secret Cash Hoard Props Up Regime."

15. Solomon, "In North Korea, Secret Cash Hoard Props Up Regime."

16. Han, "Loyal Foreign Currency Earning."

17. U, "Kim Chong-il's Slush Funds."

18. Chong-ch'ang U, "The World of Kim Chong-il's $4.3 Billion Slush Fund Seen Through $500 Million Cash Transfer to the North," (text), Seoul *Wolgan Choson*, (1 March 2003), FBIS Document ID KPP20040324000161, accessed 19 May 2005.

19. This is also known as Taesong Bank.

20. Michael Breen, *Kim Jong-il: North Korea's Dear Leader* (Singapore: John Wiley and Sons, 2004), 167.

21. Won-t'ae Sin, "North Korea's Banks," (text), Seoul *T'ongil Kyongje* (October 1997), FBIS Document ID FTS19971203000976, accessed 19 May 2005.

22. Sin, "North Korea's Banks."

23. Han, "Loyal Foreign Currency Earning."

24. Han, "Loyal Foreign Currency Earning"; Marcus Noland also discusses the significance of the relationship between the Military and Central "economies" that exist in the DPRK and notes that the military "maintains a completely integrated economic system . . . with separate administrative structures and foreign trade firms." Noland, *Avoiding the Apocalypse*, 71–73.

25. Han, "Loyal Foreign Currency Earning."

26. Yong-sin Yun and others, "Can There Be Any Way We Can Benefit? (Issues With Hyundai Mt. Kumgang Tour)," (text), Seoul *Wolgan Choson* (May 1999), FBIS Document ID FTS19990524000587, accessed 19 May 2005.

27. U, "Kim Chong-il's Slush Funds."

28. Smith, "Reaching Into North Korea," V14.

29. Noland, *Avoiding the Apocalypse*, 139; U, "Kim Chong-il's Slush Funds"; Kaplan, "The Wiseguy Regime," 38; Spaeth, "Kim's Rackets"; Chong-ch'ang U, "Organ of Southward Operations in Macao That Received the 'Slush Fund for North Korea Created by Kim Tae-chung and Hyundai,'" (text), Seoul *Wolgan Choson* (01 April 2003), FBIS Document ID KPP20040312000119, accessed 19 May 2005.

30. "North Korea's Only Bank in Europe Stops Business," *Kyodo News*, 28 July 2004, accessed via Infotrac Onefile Research Database, 17 April 2005.

31. U, "Kim Chong-il's Slush Funds."

32. U, "Kim Chong-il's Slush Funds."

33. "North Korea's Only Bank in Europe Stops Business."

34. "North Korean Outpost in Vienna," *Intelligence Online*, 31 October 2003, accessed via LexisNexis Research Database, 17 April 2005.

35. "North Korean Outpost in Vienna."

36. Solomon, "In North Korea, Secret Cash Hoard Props Up Regime."

37. "North Korean Outpost in Vienna."

38. Solomon, "In North Korea, Secret Cash Hoard Props Up Regime."

39. Jane Burgermeister, "North Korean Bank is 'Front for Arms Trade,'" *The Observer*, 27 July 2003, accessed via LexisNexis Research Database, 19 April 2005.

40. Solomon, "In North Korea, Secret Cash Hoard Props Up Regime."

41. "North Korea's Only Bank in Europe to Take Steps for Closure," *Yonhap News*, 5 May 2004, accessed via Infotrac Onefile Research Database, 10 May 2005.

42. "North Korea's Only Bank in Europe Stops Business."

43. "North Korea's Only Bank in Europe to Take Steps for Closure."

44. Kyung-hee Koo, "North Korea's Golden Star Bank to be Closed on June 30," 4 May 2004, *KOTRA Website,* www.crm.kotra.or.kr/main/info/nk/new2003, keyword search Golden Star Bank, accessed 22 May 2005.

45. U, "Kim Chong-il's Slush Funds."

46. U, "Kim Chong-il's Slush Funds."

47. Bertil Lintner and Shawn W. Crispin. "For US, a New North Korean Problem," *The Wall Street Journal,* 18 November 2003, accessed via ProQuest Research Database 10 May 2005.

48. Yun and others, "Can There Be Any Way We Can Benefit?"

49 Originally colonized by the Portuguese in the 16th century, Macao became a Chinese "Special Economic Region" in 1999. Central Intelligence Agency, *CIA World Factbook 2004: Macao,* www.cia.gov/cia/publications/factbook/geos/mc.html, accessed 27 May 2005.

50. U, "Organ of Southward Operations in Macao That Received the Slush Fund for North Korea."

51. U, "Organ of Southward Operations in Macao That Received the Slush Fund for North Korea."

52. U, "Organ of Southward Operations in Macao That Received the Slush Fund for North Korea."

53. Methamphetamines are also called philopon in many Asian countries.

54. U, "Organ of Southward Operations in Macao That Received the Slush Fund for North Korea."

55. U, "Organ of Southward Operations in Macao That Received the Slush Fund for North Korea."

56. U, "Organ of Southward Operations in Macao That Received the Slush Fund for North Korea."

57. Solomon, "In North Korea, Secret Cash Hoard Props Up Regime."

58. U, "Organ of Southward Operations in Macao That Received the Slush Fund for North Korea."

59. This policy sought to make positive progress in North-South relations; his predecessor relied on reciprocal actions from North Korea in engagement policies, which had not proved successful in advancing inter-Korean relations. Oh and Hassig, *North Korea Through the Looking Glass,* 199–200.

60. Hyundai Asan is part of South Korea's Hyundai conglomerate and one of the most significant on-peninsula investors in joint North-South Korean business ventures. Niksch, "Korea-US Relations: Issues for Congress," 12.

61. Yun and others, "Can There Be Any Way We Can Benefit?"

62. This included $200 million from Hyundai Merchant Marine, $150 million from Hyundai Engineering and Construction, $100 million from Hyundai Electronics, and $50

million in luxury goods provided by Hyundai Asan. Niksch, "Korea-US Relations: Issues for Congress," 11.

63. Chong-ch'ang U, "The World of Kim Chong-il's $4.3 Billion Slush Fund Seen Through $500 Million Cash Transfer to the North," (text), Seoul *Wolgan Choson*, (1 March 2003), FBIS Document ID KPP20040324000161, accessed 19 May 2005.

64. South Korea's Financial Supervisory Service reported that the Korea Development Bank, Korea Exchange, Woori Bank and Cho Hung Bank provided loans worth a total of $763 million to two Hyundai subsidiaries, Hyundai Engineering and Construction and Hyundai Merchant Marine. These loans were partially the result of pressure from South Korean President Kim Dae-jung's staff on the Korea Development Bank to extend the loans to Hyundai. "Loan to Hyundai Units Used for Secret Transfer," *Digital Chosonilbo*, 16 February 2003, english.chosun.com/w21data/html/news/200302/200302 160019.html, accessed 26 June 2005; "Six Key Figures in NK Payoff Scandal Convicted," *Korea Times*, 27 September 2003, accessed via LexisNexis Research Database, 26 June 2005.

65. Eberstadt, "The Persistence of North Korea."

66. Ji-ho Kim, "Cash-Strapped N.K. Resorts to International Crimes," *The Korea Herald*, 12 October 1999, accessed via LexisNexis Research Database, 19 April 2005.

67. Kim, "Cash-Strapped N.K. Resorts to International Crimes."

68. Hiroko Kono, "Poppy Cultivation Ordered By Kim Family – Japan is Number One Buyer," (text), Tokyo *Yomiuri Shimbun* (20 May 2003), FBIS Document ID JPP2003050000139, accessed 19 May 2005.

69. Chong-hun Yi, "Black Deal of South Korean Organized Criminals-Japanese Yakuza-North Korean Methamphetamine," (text), Seoul *News Plus* (9 June 1999), FBIS Document ID FTS19990213000908, accessed 20 May 2005.

70. Kaplan, "The Wiseguy Regime," 38.

71. Spaeth, "Kim's Rackets."

72. Spaeth, "Kim's Rackets."

73. In Japan, autos quickly become obsolete due to environmental regulations and these foreign vehicles are in high demand in China. Spaeth, "Kim's Rackets."

74. Kevin Sullivan and Mary Jordan, "Famine, Nuclear Threat Raise Stakes in Debate Over N. Korea," *Washington Post Foreign Service*, 13 March 1999, www.washingtonpost.com/wp-rv/inatl/longterm/korea/stories/famine031399.htm, accessed 27 May 2005.

75. In honor of the "Dear Leader," the citizens of North Korea provide these payments or "donations" through the No. 5 Management Offices to Bureau 39. U, "Kim Chong-il's Slush Funds."

76. Solomon, "In North Korea, Secret Cash Hoard Props Up Regime."

77. Breen comments that even prisoners and the elderly in North Korea are involved in these efforts. Breen, *Kim Jong-il: North Korea's Dear Leader*, 168–169; Spaeth, "Kim's Rackets."

78. U, "The World of Kim Chong-il's $4.3 Billion Slush Fund Seen Through $500 Million Cash Transfer to the North."

79. In the past over $100 million has been spent on this event; this included an estimated $45 million for special foods and gifts for people, $43.8 million for clothes, boarding fees, and transportation expenses for those mobilized to participate in 20 separate commemorative programs, $3 million to invite Pro-Pyongyang foreigners to the festivities, and $1.5 million to purchase gifts by overseas missions for Kim Jong-il. Yun and others, "Can There Be Any Way We Can Benefit?"

80. U, "Kim Chong-il's Slush Funds."

81. U, "Organ of Southward Operations in Macao That Received the Slush Fund for North Korea"; Han, "Loyal Foreign Currency Earning"; U, "Kim Chong-il's Slush Funds."

82. U, "The World of Kim Chong-il's $4.3 Billion Slush Fund Seen Through $500 Million Cash Transfer to the North."

83. U, "Kim Chong-il's Slush Funds"; U, "The World of Kim Chong-il's $4.3 Billion Slush Fund Seen Through $500 Million Cash Transfer to the North."

84. U, "Kim Chong-il's Slush Funds."

85. U, "The World of Kim Chong-il's $4.3 Billion Slush Fund Seen Through $500 Million Cash Transfer to the North."

86. These include the Cayman Islands, Channel Islands, Austria, and Luxemburg. Twenty of these types of nations exist throughout the world. U, "The World of Kim Chong-il's $4.3 Billion Slush Fund Seen Through $500 Million Cash Transfer to the North."

87. U, "Kim Chong-il's Slush Funds."

88. Triplett, *Rogue State*, 196; Kongdan Oh Hassig and others, *North Korean Policy Elites*, Institute for Defense Analysis, IDA Paper P-3903, June 2004 (Alexandria, VA: Institute for Defense Analysis, 2004), I-6 and Figure I-2; and author's analysis.

89. U, "The World of Kim Chong-il's $4.3 Billion Slush Fund Seen Through $500 Million Cash Transfer to the North."

90. "North Korean Outpost in Vienna."

91. U, "Kim Chong-il's Slush Funds."

92. See section on the Chosen Soren for more information on these activities. Chang, "Excerpts From Book by North Korean Operative in Japan"; "Chongron Affiliate Ordered Jet Mill."

Chapter 5

North Korea's Regime Support System

> If you cut off Bureau 39, you can kill Kim Jong-il. Kim can't exist as leader of North Korea without it.
>
> *—North Korean defector, quoted by*
> *Anthony Spaeth in "Kim's Rackets"*

A key component of Kim Jong-il's approach to maintain his regime has been "creative financing." Spurred by financial difficulties dating back to the 1970s and 1980s, these methods of raising hard currency have included both legitimate and illicit moneymaking schemes initiated, supported, and managed by the North Korean government. State-sponsored illegal activities, to include drug trafficking, counterfeiting, weapons proliferation, aid diversion, bank fraud, and slush funds have provided Kim Jong-il a "safety net" of financial reserves.

In 1999, South Korea's Unification Ministry estimated that North Korea made approximately $100 million or 12 percent of its foreign income from illicit activities.[1] Additionally, a US Congressional Research Service report stated that the money provided to North Korea by Hyundai Corporation for the development of Mount Kumgang and other economic projects accounted for 30 percent of North Korea's foreign currency earnings between 1999 and 2000.[2] The money raised by these activities and managed by Bureau 39 is critical to the survival of the regime and the cessation of its operations would effectively "shut down Kim Jong-il."[3]

North Korea has been running a trade deficit for years (see Chapter 2) and according to the CIA, this figure stood at approximately $900 million in 2003.[4] Due to its credit rating and economic difficulties, Pyongyang has few legitimate options to fund this deficit, making overt and covert fundraising an essential component for regime support. These provide hard currency cash flows to fund between 22–30 percent, approximately $197–$270 million, of the deficit.

The following figure provides an estimate of the annual funding gap and how covert and overt fundraising help to mitigate this deficit on an annual basis:

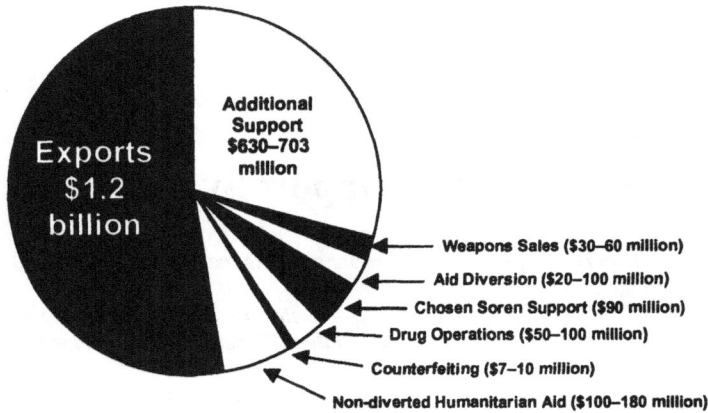

Annual Exports	$ 1,200 million
Annual Imports	$ 2,100
Trade Gap	$ < 900 >
Overt Operations	
Weapons Sales	$ 30–60
Humanitarian Aid	$ 20–100
Covert Operations	
Chosen Soren Support	$ 90
Drug Operations	$ 50–100
Counterfeiting	$ 7–10
Total Hard Currency Earnings	$ 197–270 million

Note: "Additional Support" includes a variety of annual donations through the WFP and aid outside the scope of UN control to include support from South Korea, China, Japan, and a host of other nations. Additionally, energy assistance from China and bartering transactions for goods and services are also included in these totals.

Figure 5. Funding the Trade Deficit[5]

With these efforts providing a crucial funding source for the regime, this situation provides a significant area of leverage for the United States. Pyongyang's ability to maintain this level of hard currency cash flow and reserves allowed it to conduct hardnosed negotiations and demand concessions without reciprocal actions. On the other hand, if these sources of income and reserves are depleted and the future of the regime is threatened, negotiations might take a significantly different path.

Research Summary

North Korea's problems, which have caused its pursuit of alternate funding sources necessary, are rooted in its history and interaction with the rest of the world. These have been complicated by its current form of government, which evolved from 50 years of Japanese occupation and the chaos of civil war on the peninsula. The occupation by the Japanese had a devastating effect on its culture and the Allies' victory during World War II saved Korea from the fate of complete cultural assimilation. Yet this victory was short-lived and overcome by the outbreak of the Cold War, which quickly divided the Korean nation into two hostile camps. The hasty division and subsequent occupation by the US and USSR, which stood at opposite poles of the political spectrum, only served to allow the two superpowers to manipulate the peninsula for their own purposes.

In 1950, war partitioned Korea into a communist state in the North with ties to the USSR and China and a semi-democracy in the South under significant influence of the United States.[6] North Korea became a model communist state after the war and under the tutelage of the "Great Leader" Kim Il-sung, initially following the examples of both the USSR and China. The DPRK soon found its own way and by using the concept of self-sufficiency or *juche*, Kim developed a uniquely Korean communist state. This philosophy was used to justify the actions undertaken by Pyongyang throughout the years and was the ideological impetus for the types of criminal and underhanded actions that have brought North Korea into the international spotlight.

Economic Crisis and Overt Activities

When North Korea's economy began to show signs of strain in the 1970s and Pyongyang began to default on its credit obligations, the Kim government continued to plod on without significant internal changes. In the 1980s, the loss of significant Soviet and Chinese aid resulted in North Korea's "tightening its belt" and limited market reforms, but again saw no significant systematic changes. The Soviet Union's demand for hard currency for oil in 1990 followed by similar demands by China resulted in devastating effects on North Korea's agricultural sector.[7] The loss of Chinese support was particularly significant due to both the historic Sino-Korean relationship and North Korea's ever-decreasing "circle of friends" throughout the world. Adaptation did come in the form of significant increases in alternate methods of raising hard currency and in Pyongyang's reliance on these, justified by *juche*, to compensate for the gap between income and expenses. As a result, North Korea relies on two key overt activities to raise funds, to include weapons sales and humanitarian aid diversion.

Weapons sales are often considered potentially the most dangerous of North Korea's fundraising activities, but do stand as an excellent example of Pyongyang's entrepreneurial spirit. North Korea has found a niche on the world marketplace as a supplier of low-cost ballistic missiles. Middle Eastern nations seem to be the biggest buyers of these systems and considering their extensive use during the Iran-Iraq War,[8] North Korea's missiles have been in high demand over the past few decades. The hard currency aspect of these interstate activities is difficult to quantify but funds generated by these efforts are a necessary component of the North Korea's missile and nuclear programs. The current North Korean nuclear relationship with Iran is of critical concern to the United States and monitoring hard currency transactions between these nations may provide a more accurate status of North Korean proliferation efforts.

How to adequately provide humanitarian aid to North Korea remains one of the most divisive international issues. The World Food Program and a host of NGOs contend that despite the problems with aid monitoring, food is getting to the North Koreans who need it most. Others argue that aid only sustains a totalitarian regime and food ultimately allows the elites to maintain their standard of living at the expense of the poorest of North Koreans. The severity of North Korea's famine and the resulting effects has left a generation physically and emotionally scarred with overall impacts that will be felt for years to come.[9] While an unintended outcome of these aid efforts has been insights into this extremely closed communist nation, the fact that North Korea has remained intact and a threat to the region can be partially attributed to the humanitarian assistance proved through international aid.

Covert Activities Ensure North Korea's Future

For the DPRK, the pursuit of covert activities to maintain the regime's economy and military became a necessary means of ensuring its future. The elder Kim and his successor, the "Dear Leader" Kim Jong-il, kept the impoverished nation afloat through the worst of circumstances. These fundraising efforts, which began in the 1960s and 1970s, consist of a variety of activities that range from pure criminal activity to "gray area" transactions to financially support the regime. Most of these activities have been associated either directly or indirectly with Bureau 39, which oversees foreign hard currency raised by both licit and illicit means.

The support provided by the Chosen Soren group includes both legal financial transfers and illegal activities facilitated by Koreans in Japan. Once a key component of Pyongyang's overseas fundraising operations, this organization's impact has been vastly muted compared to previous decades. In the mid-1980s, as North Korea's economy began its descent into disarray, the Chosen Soren stepped forward and became a significant source of income for Pyongyang. As time went on, North Korea's actions became more desperate, membership in the group decreased, the Japanese government became more watchful, and a string of business failures all contributed to a less prominent role for the organization. As a group, the Chosen Soren will probably be around for a while. But as a significant supporter of Pyongyang, the group's role has been reduced although it does remain a yen-based hard currency source for North Korea. Many of its activities, pachinko gambling operations for example, have thus far been left intact by the Japanese government. While not always criminal, many of Chosen Soren's covert activities do not comply with local regulations or tax laws and can be interdicted if Japanese authorities choose to enforce existing laws.

While North Korea's efforts in illegal drug production and smuggling might seem small compared to other major narcotics trafficking nations, Pyongyang has found a regional market. Through the production and trafficking of both opium and methamphetamines, North Korea has established itself as a key supplier in the region. Its efforts are state-sponsored and enjoy both diplomatic and military protection, which make law enforcement efforts against the DPRK itself much more difficult. These actions bring in a significant amount of currency for North Korea and will most likely continue to be a problem in Asia for the foreseeable future.

Counterfeit operations have also provided North Korea with a method of literally making money, but one that is vulnerable to the technical expertise of the US Treasury Department and other nations' currency organizations. Due to efforts such as the redesign of US currency and the technological requirements of keeping up with ever-increasing security measures, North Korea's counterfeiting efforts will remain on the periphery of its criminal efforts and of little consequence on a global scale. Because these operations affect third parties outside of North Korea, counterfeiting activities and can be tracked and exposed.

Controlling the Chaos

Examining the overarching coordination operations of Bureau 39 provides insight into the extent of layered operations involved in Pyongyang's fundraising efforts. North Korea's state-sponsorship of illegal and legal activity to earn money for Kim Jong-il's regime provides unique advantages to these currency fundraising efforts themselves. By hiding behind diplomatic immunity, North Koreans have been able to take risks and conduct operations that others engaged in similar enterprises would not attempt. The large amount of currency reserves facilitated by Bureau 39 has provided a means of security for Kim Jong-il that allows for risky political and military behavior. Bureau 39 and its associated hub of activity can be seen as a vulnerable and exploitable aspect of North Korea's overall fundraising efforts.

Threats to the United States

North Korea has been a threat to the international order and a regional wildcard since its inception and establishment over 60 years ago. Kim Jong-il's government has effectively obtained vast amounts of foreign aid through a combination of both international pleas for humanitarian relief and hostile behavior towards the US and its allies. Repeatedly, the DPRK has demonstrated that its provocative actions are a means to drive negotiations. The US Congress' North Korean Advisory Group observed that "North Korea has found that concessions from the United States are easier to win if the North Korean leadership presents a threatening, irrational, and unpredictable image to the outside world."[10]

Given its deft ability to be unpredictable and engage in aggressive and controversial activity, the fundamental question remains: Are North Korea's fundraising activities a direct threat to the United States, as identified in Congressional testimony?[11] Most US government sources tend to support mainstream thought on North Korea's illicit activities: Kim Jong-il's pursuit of alternate means to fund his government are a direct threat to the safety and security of the United States. Yet while these activities are disconcerting to other nations in the region, the low level of actual threat these actions pose is surprising. With the exception of weapons proliferation, *North Korea's fundraising efforts pose a very limited threat to the US.*

When considering these actions and the actual threats posed to the US, the most significant activity remains weapons proliferation activities. North Korea's efforts to sell military hardware and technology across the world do pose a risk to the security of the United States. North Korean weapons technology proliferation to US adversaries could provide capabilities that threaten the continental United States, deployed military forces, or citizens residing overseas.[12] North Korea's efforts in nuclear technology remain the most alarming and US responses have included intense diplomatic negotiations, the halt of oil shipments, and cessation of work on North Korea's light water nuclear reactor.[13] US reaction to conventional arms transfers to include ballistic missiles has been limited to trade sanctions on a few North Korean businesses,[14] increased scrutiny of DPRK transportation activities through the Missile Technology Control Regime (MTCR),[15] and implementation of the Proliferation Security Initiative (PSI) in 2003.[16] Most US efforts against North Korean fundraising activities have been focused in this area due to both the dangerous nature of the weapons and political concerns to include the ongoing nuclear crisis.[17]

The most important aspect of these efforts is the support they provide to the Kim Jong-il regime. Yet in some instances, there have been responses initiated by the US to North Korean overseas activities despite the determination that these types of criminal behavior pose a limited direct threat to the United States. North Korea is not identified by the US as a "major illicit drug producing country,"[18] but as discussed in Chapter 3, DPRK drug activities do pose a regional threat to Asian nations. US responses to North Korea's drug efforts have included identification of North Korean trafficking efforts by President George W. Bush[19] and enhanced law enforcement and maritime cooperation to enforce existing international anti-drug laws.[20]

The overall threat posed to the United States and its economy from North Korea's efforts to produce bogus US currency is comparatively low. The overall number of overseas counterfeit notes is relatively small, estimated at one to two bills for every 10,000 notes in circulation.[21] Despite this fact, North Korea did reportedly account for approximately 10 percent of all forged US bills in 1999.[22] The most significant US response to global counterfeit activity has been the re-vamp of its currency design, beginning with the $100 bill in 1996.[23] This redesign was followed by the issue of newly designed $20 notes in 2003 and $50 notes in 2004.[24]

The Chosen Soren poses almost no threat to the US due to the regional focus of this organization. Chosen Soren activities are limited to direct financial support to North Korea, but do include some indirect technology assistance to the DPRK and its military industry.[25] There have been no significant US public responses to Chosen Soren activities due to the nature of the organization and its operational span, which is primarily in Japan and North Korea. But any US efforts to stem the flow of technology transfers, arms acquisitions, and drug trafficking would likely have an indirect effect on Chosen Soren activities. The US government relies primarily on its regional allies to include Japan and South Korea to monitor and respond to Chosen Soren incidents.

As an organization, Bureau 39 has not conducted any significant direct activities against US interests or on US territory. Nevertheless, through its dealings in support of a variety of North Korean illicit fundraising activities, it does pose an indirect threat to US interests.[26] While the US has not responded directly to Bureau 39 activities, Asian and European governments have conducted surveillance and operations to hamper this organization, resulting in closure of some of North Korea's overseas banks and curtailment of other questionable activities.[27]

These fundraising efforts ensure Kim Jong-il has adequate funds to continue governing North Korea and the synergistic effect of these activities and possible end result poses the most notable threat to the United States. If US policymakers intend to curb these activities *without* causing the downfall of the Kim regime, then continued cooperation with allies in Asia and enforcement of existing international criminal laws remains the best option for policymakers. If the overall plan for Pyongyang is to *spur a regime change*, then eliminating these sources of income could play a considerable role in an effort to pressure Kim Jong-il to retire.

Recommended Actions

At the international level, dealing with North Korea and its unconventional behavior remains a daunting task. Assuming standard methods of negotiation will allow for progress often is both a waste of time and detrimental to the overall objective of engaging North Korea.[28] In deciding how to deal with the DPRK, the US must tread lightly, do its homework, and understand that North Korea will always attempt to turn any situation to its advantage.

Kim Jong-il will continue to conduct these types of fundraising activities as long as he remains the leader of this communist state. Thus the US and its allies must understand that these types of actions will continue to occur as North Korea attempts to support and maintain its current government. Most of these activities will continue despite international efforts, as most of North Korea's criminal actions are protected or overlooked by its own government and other nations in the region. As Kenneth Strong observed, "Unlike non-state criminal organizations, Pyongyang is able to employ sovereignty as a shield."[29]

Discreet Diplomacy and Intelligence Sharing

The US should maintain focus on the criminal aspect of North Korean hard currency acquisition activities and violation of local laws throughout the world. However, in dealing with North Korea's "bad behavior," current US policy remains limited in scope due to both the risks involved and the overall small return for its efforts.[30] The United States role should be engagement with the allied governments and information sharing with intelligence and law enforcement officials. In determining who should be doing what in regards to North Korea, we first have to define appropriate roles for the US and key players to include South Korea, China, Japan, the Association of Southeast Asian Nations (ASEAN), the Commonwealth countries, and the European Union.[31] Each can play a significant role in curtailing these fundraising activities and maintaining the stability of the region by engaging North Korea in a variety of ways, ranging from sympathy to hard line realism.

Roles for the US and Other Key Players

Curtailment efforts to stem narcotics activities should include US efforts with China, Japan, and South Korea to strengthen border and port inspections of North Korean vessels and individuals associated with drug trafficking. Continued endeavors by the US Treasury and Secret Service to monitor the distribution of fake dollars and prosecution of those involved will ensure the US remains "one step ahead" of North Korea's productions efforts. Tying humanitarian aid to access, as is currently being done with food aid through the WFP, should be expanded to include all types of humanitarian aid. Sea and air port inspections of North Korean shipments associated with arms transfers as well as global cooperation on initiatives like the MTCR and PSI will pressure North Korean weapons marketing activities. Finally, cooperating with its allies to monitor Bureau 39 activities, threatening action before the UN Security Council, appealing to Interpol, and using its own organizations to monitor North Korea's financial transactions that contribute to Bureau 39 are additional options available to the United States. Continued efforts in these areas remain the best way for the US and its allies to monitor and interdict these fundraising activities.

The US Plays the Bad Cop

The US role can be termed the *Bad Cop* who attempts to deal with North Korea in a pragmatic manner and is unsympathetic to North Korea's poverty and isolation.[32] Efforts to bring North Korea before the UN Security Council, threats of economic sanctions, continued military presence and exercises aimed at reacting to a crisis on the Korean peninsula, and unwillingness to compromise have all characterized US actions in dealing with North Korea. While these activities are aimed at keeping peace in the region, they also serve to monitor and deter North Korean activity in the region and around the world.

South Korea as Sympathetic Peer

South Korea receives an incredible amount of criticism for its role in dealing with North Korea as a *Sympathetic Peer*. The ROK's stance towards the North has consisted of a *dual track* policy, which has included both diplomatic negotiations to stem North Korea's threatening activities while concurrently providing both humanitarian assistance and fostering economic cooperation.

South Korea can lessen North Korea's dependence on these types of fundraising activities by providing continued economic opportunity to the cash-strapped DPRK. Through continued joint commercial ventures such as the Kaesong Industrial Complex in North Korea, efforts to connect the Trans-Siberian Railroad through the DPRK, and increased inter-Korean trade, South Korea can help its sibling attempt to move towards economic stability. While a financially strong North Korea is not a possibility in the near future, less dependence on "questionable" funding sources could be a viable result of DPRK economic progress. At the same time, South Korea does provide leverage opportunities by both its enforcement of existing laws concerning North Korea's fundraising efforts and linkage of aid to decreases or cessation of Pyongyang's illicit dealings.

China as a Close Relative

China remains North Korea's staunchest ally, but chooses to play the role of a *Close Relative* by providing significant support when North Korea is in need and, conversely, by taking the occasional hard-line stance when it deems necessary.[33] By increased trade, continued economic assistance, and the willingness to discipline its younger relative when necessary, Beijing also can help reduce North Korea's dependence on these types of fundraising activities, especially North Korea's drug smuggling activities, which have surfaced throughout China, to include Hong Kong and Macao. Additionally, enforcement of access for aid and inspections by Chinese government officials would be optimal, but hard implement since China has been willing to provide aid without being overly concerned with accountability. Being its closest communist neighbor, China's power over North Korea, if used correctly, could push this desperate economic failure towards legitimate participation in the international economy.

Japan as the Suspicious Neighbor

Japan does hold sway over two key sources of fundraising support for Pyongyang: the Chosen Soren and drug trafficking markets. Japan does retain the ability to take more aggressive actions to shut these sources of income down, if necessary, but has chosen to allow them to continue. In this respect, Japan as the unpredictable *Suspicious Neighbor* can afford to run the political gamut of appeasement to punishment when dealing with the DPRK. Japan does have the advantage of not having the constraints facing United States, South Korea, or China, which all have become diplomatically solidified in their regional roles. Japan's already strained relations with all of Asia actually work to its advantage in allowing it to pursue policy options independent of these restrictions.

ASEAN as the Neutral Broker

Given the peculiar nature of North Korea's culture and government, a neutral player is essential to balancing the hard and soft lines taken by these nations to decrease the threats posed by these fundraising activities. In this sense, ASEAN fits nicely into the overall scheme of engagement for North Korea as the *Neutral Broker*. Pyongyang has shown a willingness to work within the ASEAN framework and began attending annual member meetings beginning in 2000, which included historic talks between the US and North Korea on a variety of issues.[34] Over the past few years, ASEAN meetings have provided an alternate venue for the key players in the region to conduct "sidebar" discussions on current issues. Continuing to foster these types of discussions provides an opportunity for formal and informal diplomatic contact with North Korea in an Asia-centered forum. In playing the neutral part, ASEAN avoids the formal trappings associated with United Nations dialogues and provides a non-threatening atmosphere for regional discussions of illegal and questionable activities in the region.

Commonwealth Countries, the EU, and International Organizations

Other nations and international organizations also can affect North Korea fundraising efforts as part of an overall strategy to keep peace in the region. By enforcing existing laws, monitoring North Korea's illicit and questionable activities within their borders or interest areas, and by sharing this information, these organizations can help play an active role in observing and interdicting Pyongyang's actions. US efforts to build consensus among these organizations are crucial to any viable policies intended to affect these North Korean activities.

Curtailing DPRK Fundraising Activities

Actions aimed at restricting North Korea's illicit activities using national and international law enforcement efforts will serve to curtail but not eliminate Pyongyang's actions. North Korea's state protection of its illicit activities makes most efforts, even if successful, ultimately futile considering the DPRK's capability to redirect and revamp its illicit efforts when profits are in danger to ensure continued support of the Kim regime. A total block of these activities is unrealistic, but there are some actions that the US and its allies can take to affect a reduction in criminal activity and acquire political leverage over North Korea. The following paragraphs discuss these issues and provide some limited policy options for the US to curtail Pyongyang's fundraising efforts.

Weapons Sales and International Aid

Weapons sales remain extremely difficult to interrupt. The hard currency generated by weapons sales is difficult to track and almost impossible to affect due to the often legitimate nature of these transactions. As the recent 2002 Yemen Scud incident illustrated,[35] North Korea still is able to sell and transport arms across the world.

Additionally, while humanitarian aid-monitoring efforts might ensure more donated supplies reach intended recipients, the ultimate effect of any aid is more support to the current North Korean regime. As a result, while aid-monitoring efforts are certainly the correct moral and legal actions to take, in the end, they are ultimately futile due to the previously discussed "fungible" nature of this type of support.

Drug Trafficking, Counterfeiting, and the Chosen Soren

Interdiction of drug operations, counterfeiting, and weapons proliferation can be done with little risk through enforcement of national and international laws. Also, there is almost no risk in attempting to curtail many of North Korea's overseas operations, especially ones that are the result of links between diplomatic and commercial cover. For example, drug trafficking has been habitually associated with diplomatic missions and efforts to expel diplomats and close embassies suspected of drug operations would affect these activities. Additionally, a comprehensive enforcement program specifically targeted at North Korea drug operations in Japan, China, and Taiwan would curtail the markets for illegal narcotics.

Interdicting counterfeiting operations overseas is a difficult proposition, but continued scrutiny by US and international law enforcement agencies of all US bills handled by North Korean-related enterprises is essential. Penalties for North Korean entities using counterfeit currency must be tough and should include embargoes, detention of responsible individuals, and revocation of business licenses in countries in which they are found to have passed counterfeit notes.

Japan is the only country that can effectively deal with the Chosen Soren and shutting down this organization, freezing its assets and deporting its key leadership (to North Korea or a third country) would effectively result in the demise of this group. Other overseas means of support that are vulnerable to influence and interdiction include the Daesong General Trading Company and Kim Jong-il's slush funds held in Swiss banks. An international consensus to boycott Daesong and freeze its funds would effectively marginalize the company. Additionally, by seizing Kim Jong-il's overseas funds, North Korea's overseas reserves would not remain a source of "rainy day" funding. Neither of these tasks would be easy and the latter would require linkage of North Korean activities to criminal enterprises in the eyes of the Swiss judiciary.

Importance of Diplomacy and Intelligence Sharing

The most effective method of dealing with North Korea's fundraising activities is through diplomacy and intelligence sharing. Elimination of these sources of funds for North Korea could only be justified by an international consensus that Kim Jong-il poses a threat to stability within the region and the benefits of leadership change outweigh the costs of these actions. North Korea has publicly stated it considers any form of economic sanctions would be "tantamount to a declaration of war."[36] As a result, policymakers pursuing any attempts to eliminate North Korea's hard currency flows from these sources must consider the possibility of a severe reaction from North Korea.

Areas for Further Research

This research has uncovered a host of questions that need to be answered prior to implementation of policies to curtail or interdict North Korea's quest for hard currency. The following sections provide brief discussions of these issues and recommendations for subsequent research into the issues surrounding overt and covert fundraising activities.

Weapons and Technology Sales

Weapons proliferation remains one of the most visible actions North Korea engages in and is of significant interest to the intelligence community. While proliferation monitoring is imperfect, it does command the attention of both the US press and government agencies. North Korea's less visible efforts, to include small arms sales and training agreements with a variety of third-world nations,[37] might offer more insight into its overseas operations. A thorough investigation of these transactions and associated weapons supply and training operations can help understand Pyongyang's overall efforts to provide military support to other nations in exchange for foreign capital.

Humanitarian Aid Diversion

The controversy surrounding aid diversion continues to pit the humanitarian factions against those who see the continued existence of North Korea as a threat to peace in the region. Aid diversion will continue to remain the most difficult of North Korea's fundraising activities to prove and efforts at finding the truth will continue to be filtered through the lens of defector reporting and anecdotal evidence. While more research on the levels and incidence of aid diversion is needed, without credible first-hand reporting, determining the actual impacts of diversion will remain difficult, if not impossible. But valuable information is gathered by UN organizations and NGOs operating in North Korea and their transactions with the DPRK government, its corporations, and local businessmen can provide credible information into how currency flows within its borders. Details on the differences between amounts paid and estimates of actual costs incurred are difficult to determine, but also could provide insight on how much money North Korea skims from transactions relating to international organizations operating within the DPRK.

Drug Trafficking

More research and investigation into the details of North Korea's drug trafficking efforts is essential for law enforcement operations. Identification of the relationships with the Russian Mafia and Japanese Yakuza, which have allegedly been formed, would help with curtailment of these activities. Additionally, the connection between North Korean drug runners and both Chinese and South Korean counterparts is also possibly extensive, but requires more examination and research to determine the scope and vulnerabilities. Finally, the operations surrounding current DPRK embassy efforts in support of drug smuggling, such as the use of diplomatic pouches, connections with local organized crime, distribution networks, and identification of the sellers of drugs would provide additional needed intelligence information for both law enforcement and policy officials.

Counterfeiting Efforts

Although counterfeiting activities seem to be declining, identification and interdiction of primary avenues of money transfers (via diplomatic or other couriers, or laundering and electronic transfer through banks) is crucial for successful policy initiatives. Additionally, North Korea retains the ability to produce high quality reproductions of a variety of documents for espionage purposes.[38] This capability most likely supports much of the illegal fundraising activities mentioned previously, but no one really knows the extent of these efforts. Other areas that bear more scrutiny are the actual "first use" of counterfeit money, how it initially enters the system, and what organizations or individuals are involved. Determining the individual players would assist local and national law enforcement agencies in tracing and interdicting the supply of counterfeit bills.

Chosen Soren Activities

While the declining influence of the Chosen Soren has been well-documented, other organizations sympathetic to North Korea's plight also provide similar support. North Korean sympathizers in China, South Korea, and other nations throughout Asia play a significant role in providing humanitarian and other types of aid to the DPRK. While their activities are generally known, the linkage between regime survival and these groups has not been considered in detail. Examining these means of support as essential to the regime might help provide a more comprehensive understanding of other sources of support for North Korea's government. Additionally, the type of funds provided by supporters and transactions with North Korea usually is reported in dollar equivalents. Most likely, the support from overseas Koreans is sent in Japanese yen and then converted at some point into dollars, euros, or exchanged for goods. A more extensive look at the movement of yen to North Korea and how this is disposed of would provide invaluable data on the systems Pyongyang has established to handle currency transactions.

Bureau 39

The actions of Bureau 39 in coordinating North Korea's foreign currency efforts can be studied through its dealings with other international business interests and organizations. Information on Bureau 39 activities does exist, but details on the investments, movement of funds, accounts, and expenditures are difficult, if not impossible, to obtain. While these accounts are supposedly protected under Swiss banking rules, the involvement of North Korea in illicit activities has most likely resulted in this information being released to agencies that investigate these types of behavior. A detailed examination of how and where Kim Jong-il keeps his funds overseas would provide a more complete picture of North Korea's foreign reserves.

North Korea's International Dealings

Finally, as mentioned previously, there are still significant financial dealings that occur between North Korea and a host of nations throughout the world. By monitoring Pyongyang's business partners, which include countries like China, Russia, Iran, and Syria, more insight on the financial dealings involving North Korea can be gained. Establishing methods of determining how much money North Korea spends and where they spend it will allow analysts and policymakers to determine trends, areas of emphasis, and vulnerabilities in Pyongyang's currency system.

Final Thoughts

North Korea's efforts have caused much angst in the region and among US leaders who consider the Kim regime's continued belligerent activities as a threat to Asian and worldwide stability. Most nations judge North Korea's actions by their own standards and fail to fully understand that Kim Jong-il not only plays by his own rules, but also in a completely different "game" than the rest of the world. Kongdan Oh appropriately observed that "understanding North Korea is difficult not only because of its secretive nature, but also because it is so very different in culture and politics from Western Capitalist societies."[39]

North Korea bases its decisions on an entirely different mindset and political culture than the West. By considering this difference, researchers can begin to fathom the complicated nature of North Korea's government and society and its need to engage in illicit and questionable activities.[40] The pitfalls of trying to understand Pyongyang's actions and predict its future activity include the problems associated with "mirror imaging" and a failure to fully understand the inherent determination of the North Korean leadership to remain in power. If analysts examine North Korea's actions through the lens of *leadership support and regime survival*, then these illicit and "gray area" activities are understandable as a long-term policy option for the North Korean regime. The Kim regime has shown a willingness to engage in practically any activity to support its hold on power over North Korea and examining these issues in that context provides valuable insight into what might seem like incomprehensible and irresponsible nation-state behavior.

Some observers see North Korea's actions in terms of black and white, moral or immoral, legal or illegal: unfortunately, this view utilizes an inadequate process of analyzing Pyongyang's hard currency fundraising activities. Examining Pyongyang's actions in terms of national self-interest and regime survival is a much better framework to utilize in exploring this closed society and its government. The best way for policymakers to deal with these activities can only occur through an objective examination of the facts and observations, rather than value judgments based on Western political and societal norms. Keeping this concept in mind helps understand that North Korea will most likely continue to engage in overt and clandestine fundraising measures in the foreseeable future. Despite international displeasure with these activities, North Korea will engage in these types of actions as long as needed to retain control over its people and ensure the future of its nation.

Notes and references

1. Kim, "Cash-Strapped N.K. Resorts to International Crimes."

2. Niksch, "Korea-US Relations," 11.

3. Comments of North Korean defector Kim Dok Hong who worked with Bureau 39 trade companies. Solomon, "In North Korea, Secret Cash Hoard Props Up Regime."

4. Imports for 2003 stood at $2.1 billion while exports were $1.2 billion with a $900 million dollar trade deficit. CIA, *The World Factbook Online 2004: North Korea.*

5 Noland, *Avoiding Apocalypse*, 118; "NK Earns $100 Million Annually from Missile Exports"; and "Scud missile sales 'earned North Korea 60 million dollars in 2002'"; Noland and Haggard, "The North Korean Human Rights Act of 2004: Issues and Implementation"; Manyin, "Foreign Assistance to North Korea," 8, 9, 26; Johnston, "The North Korea Abduction Issue and Its Effect"; "12.7 billion yen sent to North Korea over 3-year period"; Eberstadt, "Financial Transfers from Japan to North Korea," 524; Kasumi Sato quoted by Noland in *Avoiding the Apocalypse*, 104; Chanlett-Avery, "North Korean Supporters in Japan," 4; Manyin, "Japan-North Korea Relations," 14; Author's analysis and Perl, "Drug Trafficking and North Korea," 9; Judson and Porter, "Volume of Counterfeit US Currency," 6–7; "North Korea Prints $15 Million of Bogus Bills a Year"; Perl, "Drug Trafficking and North Korea," 10; Asano Yoshiharu, "N. Korea Missile Exports Earned 580 Mil. Dollars in '01," *Yomiuri Shimbun*, 13 May 2003, accessed via LexisNexis Research Database, 15 March 2005; and CIA, *The World Factbook Online 2004: North Korea.*

6. After a series of military rulers dating back to 1961, the South Korean presidential election in 1987 was a turning point for its pursuit of democracy. That year, direct presidential elections were held and former military general Roh Tae-woo was confirmed as president; five years later, the election of civilian Kim Young-sam heralded the end of military control over the presidency and beginning of democracy in practice for the South.

7. *North Korea: A Country Study*, 154.

8. Bermudez, *A History of Ballistic Missile Development in the DPRK*, 12.

9. Fiona Terry, "The Deadly Secrets of North Korea," *Doctors Without Borders Website*, August 2001, www.doctorswithoutborders.org/publications/other/deadly_2001.shtml, accessed 29 April 2005.

10. US Congress, *Final Report of the North Korean Advisory Group*.

11. US Congress, *Drugs, Counterfeiting, and Weapons Proliferation: The NK Connection*, 1–2.

12. Niksch, "Korea: US-Korean Relations – Issues for Congress," 8.

13. Niksch, "North Korea's Nuclear Weapons Program," 1.

14. Dianne E. Rennack, "North Korea: Economic Sanctions," *CRS Report for Congress* RL31696, 24 January 2003 (Washington, DC: Congressional Research Service, Library of Congress, 2003), 8–9.

15. Cohen, *Proliferation: Threat and Response*, 72.

16. Feickert, "Missile Survey: Ballistic and Cruise Missiles of Foreign Countries," 26.

17. Most responses from the US have been focused on weapons proliferation and enforcement of current maritime and international laws. There has been a deliberate reluctance to crack down on many of these activities to ensure policy options exist during the ongoing nuclear crisis with North Korea. See Perl, "Drug Trafficking and North Korea," 1–2.

18. US Department of State, "International Narcotics Control Strategy Report 2003, Vol. 1," 4–5.

19. Designating North Korea as a "state sponsor" of narcotics trafficking carries a heavy toll according to US law: the cessation of all aid, to include food and medical assistance. As a result, US officials have been reluctant to push for this designation because it might show an "over prioritizing" of drug issues (over the nuclear issue) and may limit US options in dealing with the DPRK. Bush, "Presidential Determination No. 2004-47," 1998–2000; Perl, "Drug Trafficking and North Korea," 1–2.

20. See Andrew Hollis' statement in US Congress, *Drugs, Counterfeiting, and Weapons Proliferation: The NK Connection*, 4–5.

21. US Treasury Department, *The Use and Counterfeiting of United States Currency Abroad, Part 2*, March 2003 (Washington, DC: US Government Printing Office, 2003), vii.

22. Bong, "North Korea Accounts for 10 Percent of World's Counterfeit Notes."

23. US Treasury Department, *Counterfeit US Currency, 2000*, x.

24. US Federal Reserve, "US Unveils New $50 Note With Background Colors," *Federal Reserve Board Website*, Joint Press Release, 26 April 2004, www.federalreserve.gov/boarddocs/press/Other/2004/20040426/default. htm, accessed 7 June 2005.

25. US Congress, *Drugs, Counterfeiting, and Weapons Proliferation: The NK Connection*, 30.

26. Smith, "Reaching Into North Korea," V14.

27. U, "Organ of Southward Operations in Macao That Received the Slush Fund for North Korea."

28. Richard Saccone, *To the Brink and Back: Negotiating with North Korea* (Seoul: Hollym, 2003), 29–58.

29. Strong, *North Korea: The Transnational Criminal State*, 3.

30. The US continues to have a difficult time in effectively engaging North Korea, as evidenced by the political failures during negotiations surrounding the second North Korean nuclear crisis, which began in 2002. Kongdan Oh provided a valuable description and critique of US attempts to bring North Korea back into multi-lateral negotiations in "Ratcheting Down the Rhetoric," *Time Asia Online*, 7 February 2005, www.time.come/time/asia/magazine/article/0,13673,501050214-1025220,00.html, accessed 8 February 2005.

31. Russia could also be included in this list and has been influential to some extent in the region. But its current ability to change North Korean behavior is judged as minimal and its influence over North Korea has never approached the levels of the former Soviet Union in the 1960s or of China today.

32. When engaging North Korea, the optimal role for the US is similar to cliché roles seen in the movies as the "heavy" or the "tough guy" who enforces the law according to his own rules.

33. In late 2003, China shut off its oil supply to North Korea "for a few days" in response to Pyongyang's indications that it would announce itself as a nuclear state. This action did temporarily cause North Korea to return to negotiations in early 2004 and is an example of the influence China can exercise over the DPRK. Bradley K. Martin, *Under the Loving Care of the Fatherly Leader: North Korea and the Kim Dynasty* (New York: Thomas Dunne Books, 2004), 660.

34. US Secretary of State Madeline Albright met with North Korean foreign Minister Paek Namsun on the sidelines of the ASEAN conference, the first high-level meeting in 50 years between these two nations. Anna Kuchment and Malcolm Beith, "A New Script? Korean foreign minister receives favorable treatment at ASEAN meeting," *Newsweek International*, 7 August 2000, accessed via InfoTrac Onefile Research Database, 26 June 2005.

35. Sanger and Shanker, "Reluctant US Gives Assent for Missiles to Go to Yemen," 1.

36. Kanako Takahara, "Public wants sanctions–but at what price?" *Japan Times Online*, 24 December 2004, www.japantimes.co.jp/cgi-bin/getarticle.pl5?

nn20041224a1.htm, accessed 14 June 2005.

37. Lintner and Crispin, "Dangerous Bedfellows," 22–23; *North Korea: A Country Study*, 260–261.

38. Alexander, "Defector Says Government making Heroin, Fake Dollars."

39. Kongdan Oh Hassig, *North Korean Policy Elites*, IDA Paper P-3903, June 2004 (Alexandria, VA: Institute for Defense Analysis, 2004), ES-1.

40. More detailed information can be found in Saccone, *To the Brink and Back: Negotiating with North Korea*, 27–58.

Appendix A

North Korea's Famine[1]

1987	PDS daily grain rations (from 600–800 grams per day) cut by 10 percent.[2]
1990–1991	Russia and China significantly reduce subsidized oil exports to North Korea.
1992	Kim Il-sung introduces "two-meal a day" campaign to deal with diminishing food supplies.
	PDS distribution begins to become intermittent in the northeastern areas of North Korea.
1994	Korean Central News Agency (KCNA) broadcasts admit the existence of food shortages.[3]
July	Kim Il-sung dies; Kim Jong-il becomes de-facto successor.
	Regime shuts down PDS in northeastern DPRK.
October	North Korea signs Agreed Framework in return for international assistance.
	North Korean authorities decide to "triage" the four northeastern provinces (North Hamgyong, South Hamgyong, Rangang, and Kangwon) to ensure adequate food is available to the western Provinces.[4]
	The PDS stops distributing food in the northeast exception for four times throughout the year during national holidays.[5]
1995	
August	Massive flooding throughout North Korea.
September	North Korea appeals to the World Food Program for food aid.
	Pyongyang reduces grain rations for rural families.[6]
Fall	Military coup discovered in northeastern provinces.

Significant movements of people seeking food begin to occur.

1996

April   North Korea agrees to join US, South Korea, and China in four party peace talks.

DPRK central government decentralizes authority for dealing with the famine from the national level down to the country administrators.

Pyongyang residents, party cadre and workers from critical industries continue to get food distributions while the general population fends for itself.

July   Additional floods occur in North Korea.

1997

Spring   UN Development Program sends a delegation to Pyongyang to assist with agricultural reform; North Korea declines to make changes.[7]

Drought occurs throughout North Korea.

Unconfirmed reports surface that Kim Jong-il imposes martial law.

September   Regime creates detention camps (designated "927") in each county for internally displaced persons caught traveling without permits.

1998

January   MSF leaves North Korea citing denial of access.[8]

Pyongyang announces that each individual family was responsible for feeding itself rather that relying on either the PDS or county administrators for food.

Spring   Food prices in private markets decrease due to influx of international aid.

Summer   Pyongyang tightens travel regulations to reestablish order after period of population displacement due to lack of food.

1999 Food production in North Korea increases due to better weather and fertilizer aid.[9]

December World Concern (US NGO) halts relief shipments due to aid diversion.[10]

2000

March Action Against Hunger (French NGO) leaves North Korea due to DPRK government interference.[11]

CARE (US NGO) leaves North Korea citing aid accountability issues.[12]

June Historic North-South Korean Summit; The South's Sunshine Policy begins.[13]

2002

June Pyongyang announces an increase of daily food distribution from the PDS from 250 to 350 grams per person.[14]

July North Korea announces economic initiatives to include "microeconomic policy changes, macroeconomic policy changes, special economic zones, and aid seeking." Analysts see this as an attempt to "kick-start the economy."[15]

Notes and references

1. Sources for this timeline are from Natsios, "The Politics of Famine in North Korea," 5–10 unless otherwise annotated.

2. Marcus Noland, "Famine and Reform in North Korea, Working Paper 03-5," *Institute for International Economics Website*, July 2003, www.iie.com/publications/wp/2003/03-5.pdf, accessed 30 April 2005.

3. Noland, "Famine and Reform in North Korea."

4. Natsios argues this was done because the northeastern areas were "politically and militarily less important to the survival of the central government than the western provinces." Natsios, "The Politics of Famine in North Korea," 5.

5. Jasper Becker, *Hungry Ghosts: Mao's Secret Famine* (New York: Owl Books, 1998), 323.

6. Natsios, *The Great North Korean Famine*, 5.

7. Natsios, *The Great North Korean Famine*, 139.

8. Noland, "Famine and Reform in North Korea," 11.

9. FAO/WFP report, cited in Noland, *Avoiding the Apocalypse*, 193.

10. Noland, "Famine and Reform in North Korea," 11.

11. Noland, "Famine and Reform in North Korea," 11.

12. Noland, "Famine and Reform in North Korea," 11.

13. Natsios, *The Great North Korean Famine*, 140.

14. Suk, *North Korea at a Crossroads*, 138.

15. Noland, "Famine and Reform in North Korea," 19.

Appendix B

The DPRK Missile Program

1962–1963   North Korea receives a battalion of SA-2 surface to air missiles from the Soviet Union.[1]

1965   Kim Il-sung establishes the National Defense University in Hamgyong to develop missile technology and "nurture those personnel who will develop mid- and long-range missiles."[2]

1965   USSR and DPRK sign military technology exchange agreement.[3]

1968   USSR delivers FROG-5 surface-to-surface missiles to the DPRK.[4]

1971   China replaces the USSR as primary source for DPRK missile technology.[5]

1972   USSR allegedly supplies 20 Scud-B missiles to North Korea in exchange for access to the *USS Pueblo*, a captured US surveillance vessel.[6]

1975   North Korea establishes "multi-faceted ballistic missile program" and begins efforts to produce surface to surface missiles.[7]

1979–1981   Egypt provides Scud missiles to North Korea.[8]

1983   Pyongyang and Tehran sign missile cooperation treaty.[9]

1984   North Korea test launches its first domestically produced Hwasong-5 (Scud-B).[10]

1985–1987   Iran and the DPRK conduct negotiations leading to a $500 million arms package in which North Korea provides 90–100 Hwasong-5 missiles and a production facility in Iran.[11]

1987–1988   Pyongyang begins Hwasong-6 (Scud-C) missile program.[12]

1989   The UAE purchases 25 Hwasong-5s for $160 million.[13]

1990   North Korea conducts its first of five Hwasong-6 launches.[14]

1991   Pyongyang begins to ship Hwasong missiles to Iran.[15]

1991–1995   Syria obtains 60 Hwasong-6 missiles and 12 mobile launchers from North Korea.[16]

1993   Pyongyang test launches one No Dong-1 missile.[17]

1998–1999   Vietnam obtains a "small number" of Hwasong-6 missiles from the DPRK.[18]

1998   Pyongyang attempts to launch a satellite into orbit using a Taepo Dong-1 with possible technical assistance from Iran; launch arcs over Japan causing increased tensions in the region.[19]

1999   Pending Taepo Dong-2 test aborted; North Korea declares test moratorium in exchange for US lifting of economic sanctions.[20]

2000   North Korea sells 12 No Dong rocket motors to Iran.[21]

2001   Iran received another missile technology shipment from DPRK.[22]

2002   North Korea sells $60 million in Scud missiles to Iraq, Iran, Syria, Yemen and Pakistan.[23]

2002   North Korean shipment of Scuds to Yemen seized and released by Spanish and US authorities.[24]

2002   Iraq reportedly made a $10 million down payment on delivery of a single No Dong missile. North Korea failed to deliver the system, citing pressure from the US, and failed to provide a refund.[25]

2003   Reports surfaced that the DPRK was developing nuclear technology capable of adapting nuclear warheads to fit onto NoDong missiles.[26]

2003   Ballistic Missile Test Flight Moratorium (signed by North Korea in 1999) expires.[27]

2004   Libya announces cessation of missile trade with North Korea in exchange for lifting US trade sanctions.[28]

Notes and references

1. This was part of a long-term agreement between the DPRK and USSR to modernize North Korea's military. These were deployed in the Pyongyang area. Bermudez, *History of DPRK Missile Development*, 1.

2. US Congress, *North Korean Missile Proliferation*, 11.

3. Bermudez, *History of DPRK Missile Development*, 4–5.

4. Yun, "Long-range Missiles," 123.

5. Yun, "Long-range Missiles," 123.

6. Information from an interview of a North Korean defector by Daniel A. Pinkston in "North Korea's Ballistic Missile Exports."

7. Bermudez, *History of DPRK Missile Development*, 4.

8. Bermudez, *History of DPRK Missile Development*, 10; Yun, "Long-range Missiles," 124.

9. Yun, "Long-range Missiles," 125.

10. Yun, "Long-range Missiles," 125.

11. Bermudez, *History of DPRK Missile Development*, 12.

12. Bermudez, *History of DPRK Missile Development*, 14–15.

13. Bermudez, *History of DPRK Missile Development*, 12.

14. Bermudez, *History of DPRK Missile Development*, 17.

15. Bermudez, *History of DPRK Missile Development*, 18.

16. Bermudez, *History of DPRK Missile Development*, 18.

17. Bermudez, *History of DPRK Missile Development*, 17.

18. Karniol, "Vietnam Stocking up 'SCUDs.'"

19. Initially, analysts disagreed on whether this was a missile test or, as North Korea claimed, a failed satellite launch. Most now conceded this was a failed attempt to launch a vehicle into space. Nanto, "North Korea Chronology of Provocations," 17; "North Korea Fires Missile."

20. Yun, "Long-range Missiles," 129; Niksch, "North Korea's Nuclear Weapons Program," 9.

21. Bill Gertz, "North Korea Sends Missile Parts, Technology to Iran," *The Washington Times*, 18 April 2001, accessed via LexisNexis Research Database, 15 March 2005.

22. Gertz, "North Korea Sends Missile Parts."

23. "North Korea has Delivered 400 Ballistic Missiles to the Mideast," *World Tribune Online*, 216.26.163.62/2003/ea_nkorea_10_27.html, accessed 11 April 2005; Kralev, "Pakistan Purchases N. Korean Missiles," 1.

24. Jay Solomon, "A Global Journal Report: Some Speak of Pyongyang Blockade – Bush Administration Hawks Consider Ways to Stop Exporting of Arms, Drugs," *The*

Wall Street Journal, 5 May 2003, accessed via ProQuest Research Database, 14 March 2005; Sanger and Shanker, "Reluctant US Gives Assent for Missiles to Go to Yemen," 1.

25. Kempe and Cloud, "Baghdad Records Show Hussein Sought Missiles."

26. David E. Sanger, "CIA Said to Find Nuclear Advances By North Koreans," *The New York Times*, 1 July 2003, A1.

27. Feickert, "Missile Survey: Ballistic and Cruise Missiles of Foreign Countries," 13.

28. Judith Miller, "Libya Halts Military Trade With North Korea, Syria, and Iran," *The New York Times*, 14 May 2004, accessed via LexisNexis Research Database, 15 March 2005.

Appendix C

Arms Exports[1]

	Arms Exports (millions of dollars)	Total Exports (millions of dollars)	Arms Exports/Total Exports
1971	0	335	0.0%
1972	0	400	0.0%
1973	0	500	0.0%
1974	0	720	0.0%
1975	10	785	1.3%
1976	80	605	13.2%
1977	20	*	*
1978	90	967	9.3%
1979	80	1320	6.8%
1980	190	*	*
1981	575	1410	40.8%
1982	650	*	*
1983	300	*	*
1984	575	1600	35.9%
1985	350	1380	25.4%
1986	250	1700	14.7%
1987	400	*	*
1988	700	2400	29.2%
1989	420	1950	21.0%
1990	210	2020	10.4%
1991	220	1025	17.6%
1992	170	1300	7.7%
1993	180	1220	9.0%
1994	70	858	8.2%
1995	60	736	8.2%
1996	110	727	15.1%
1997	90	905	10.0%
1998	100	559	17.9%
1999	140	515	27.2%
2000	50–100	556	9–18.0%
2001	50–100	650	7.7–15.3%
2002	50–100	736	6.8–13.6%
2003	50–100	777	6.4–12.9%

* Information not available

Notes and references

1. US Arms Control and Disarmament Agency, *World Military Expenditures and Arms Transfers 1971–1980* (Washington, DC: US Government Printing Office, 1983), 97; US Arms Control and Disarmament Agency, *World Military Expenditures and Arms Transfers 1985* (Washington, DC: US Government Printing Office, 1985), 111; US Arms Control and Disarmament Agency, *World Military Expenditures and Arms Transfers 1995* (Washington, DC: US Government Printing Office, 1996), 131; US Arms Control and Disarmament Agency, *World Military Expenditures and Arms Transfers 1999–2000* (Washington, DC: US Government Printing Office, 2002), 132.; Noland, *Avoiding Apocalypse*, 118; export data from 1994–2003 from Cho, "North Korea's 2003 Foreign Trade."

Appendix D

Fundraising and US Responses

Activity	Threat to US	US Responses
Drug Production and Trafficking	**Low** Not identified by the US as a "major illicit drug producing country,"[1]; DPRK drug activities do pose a regional threat to East Asian nations.	Responses have been limited to public identification of trafficking by US by President George W. Bush[2] and enhanced maritime cooperation to enforce existing international anti-drug laws.[3]
Counterfeit Operations	**Low** The overall number of overseas counterfeit notes is relatively small: 1–2 for every 10,000 notes in circulation.[4] North Korean counterfeiting efforts accounted for approximately 10 percent of all forged US bills in 1999.[5]	Most significant US response has been the redesign of currency, beginning with the $100 bill in 1996.[6] This redesign was followed by the issue of new $20 notes in 2003 and $50 notes in 2004.[7]
Aid Diversion	**Low** While the diversion of food and other aid sent to North Korea has no direct effect on the US, reports of misuse does spur calls for increased oversight of distribution operations.	US responses to reports of aid diversion and other North Korean provocative activities has been a significant decrease in humanitarian aid.[8] Despite WFP efforts to increase monitoring activities over the past few years, many areas are still declared "off-limits" by DPRK authorities.[9]

Activity	Threat to US	US Responses
Weapons Proliferation	**Medium** Proliferation of weapons technology to US adversaries could provide capabilities threatening the continental United States, deployed military forces or citizens residing overseas. North Korea has been repeatedly described as a "dangerous proliferators of missiles."[10]	The halt of oil shipments and cessation of work on North Korea's light water have been the US responses to the DPRK nuclear program.[11] US reaction to conventional arms transfers has been limited to trade sanctions on a few North Korean businesses,[12] increased scrutiny of DPRK transportation activities through the Missile Technology Control Regime (MTCR),[13] and implementation of the Proliferation Security Initiative (PSI) in 2003.[14]
Chosen Soren	**Low** Chosen Soren activities are limited to direct financial support to North Korea, but do include some indirect technology assistance.[15]	There have been no significant US responses to Chosen Soren activities due to the nature of the organization and its operational scope—primarily in Japan and North Korea. The US relies on Japan and South Korea to monitor and respond to Chosen Soren incidents.

Notes and references

1. International Narcotics Control Strategy Report, March 2005, 4–5.

2. Designating North Korea as a "state sponsor" of narcotics trafficking carries a heavy toll according to US law: the cessation of all aid, to include food and medical assistance. As a result, US officials have been reluctant to push for this designation because it might show an "over prioritizing" of drug issues (over the nuclear issue) and may limit US options in dealing with the DPRK. *Presidential Determination*, September 2004; Perl, "Drug Trafficking and North Korea," 5 December 2003, 1–2.

3. See Andrew Hollis' statement in *Drugs, Counterfeiting and Weapons Proliferation: The NK Connection*, 4–5.

4. US Treasury, "Counterfeit US Currency, 2003," vii.

5. Bong, "North Korea Accounts for 10 Percent of World's Counterfeit Notes."

6. US Treasury, "Counterfeit US Currency," x.

7. US Federal Reserve, "US Unveils New $50 Note With Background Colors."

8. Manyin and Jun, "US Assistance to North Korea," 17; "USAID Press Release 2002-051," *USAID Website*, 7 June 2002, www.usaid.gov/press/releases/2002/pr020607. html, accessed 30 April 2005.

9. Manyin and Jun, "US Assistance to North Korea," 12; WFP, "World Hunger – Korea (DPR)."

10. Niksch, "Korea: US-Korean Relations – Issues for Congress," 8.

11. Niksch, "North Korea's Nuclear Weapons Program," 1.

12. Rennack, "North Korea: Economic Sanctions," 8–9.

13. Cohen, *Proliferation: Threat and Response*, 10.

14. Feickert, "Missile Survey: Ballistic and Cruise Missiles of Foreign Countries," 26.

15. US Congress, *Drugs, Counterfeiting, and Weapons Proliferation: The NK Connection*, 30.

Bibliography

"Abductees' families protest return of N. Korean ferry." *The Asahi Shimbum Online*, 19 May 2005. www.asahi.com/english/Herald-asahi/TKY200505190088.html. Accessed 26 June 2005.

Alexander, Paul. "Defector Says Government making Heroin, Fake Dollars." *The Associated Press*, 22 June 1995. Accessed via LexisNexis Research Database, 15 March 2005.

"Asia: Through a glass, darkly; North Korea." *The Economist* 370, no. 8366 (13 March 2004): 64.

Association of Southeast Asian Nations (ASEAN) Website. www.aseansec.org/home.htm. Accessed 27 June 2005.

Banbury, Tony. "Food Programme Press Conference on the DPRK." *The Nautilus Institute's NAPSNet Daily Report*, 31 March 2005. www.nautilus.org/napsnet/sr/2005/0528A_Banbury.html. Accessed 29 April 2005.

Bank of Korea Online. www.bok.or.kr/index.jsp. Keyword search, "North Korea." Accessed 6 February 2005.

"Bar Suspicious Vessels from Port." *Daily Yomiuri*, 5 September 2003. Accessed via InfoTrac Onefile Research Database, 15 March 2005.

Becker, Jasper. *Hungry Ghosts : Mao's Secret Famine.* New York: Owl Books, 1998.

Bermudez, Joseph S. Jr. *A History of Ballistic Missile Development in the DPRK*, Center for Nonproliferation Studies Occasional Papers: #2. Monterey, CA: Center for Nonproliferation Studies, Monterey Institute of International Studies, November 1999.

_____. "North Korea's Long Range Missiles." in *Jane's Ballistic Missile Proliferation*, 2000, 5.

Bong, Hwashik. "North Korea Accounts for 10 Percent of World's Counterfeit Notes." *JoongAng Daily Online*, 20 June 1999. joongangdaily.joins.com/. Accessed 30 March 2005.

"Book Describes Korean Group's Illegal Money Transfers from Japan to DPRK." (text). Tokyo *Waga Chosen Soren no Tsumi to Batsu* (30 April 2002). FBIS Document ID JPP20030403000048. Accessed 12 January 2005.

Boyd, Alan. "North Korea: Hand in the Cookie Jar." *Asia Times Online*, 29 April 2003. www.atimes.com/atimes/Korea/ED29Dg01.html. Accessed 29 January 2005.

Breen, Michael. *Kim Jong-il: North Korea's Dear Leader.* Singapore: John Wiley and Sons, 2004.

Brooke, James. "Japan Frees North Korean Ferry After Holding It For Day In Port." *New York Times*, 27 August 2003, A4.

Bruning, Harald. "Five North Koreans Arrested in Macao." *United Press International*, 29 June 1994. Accessed via LexisNexis Research Database, 12 April 2005.

Burgermeister, Jane. "North Korean Bank is 'Front for Arms Trade.'" *The Observer*, 27 July 2003. Accessed via LexisNexis Research Database, 19 April 2005.

Bush, George W., President of the United States. "Presidential Determination No. 2004-47 on Major Drug Transit or Major Illicit Drug Producing Countries for FY05," 15

September 2004. *Weekly Compilation of Presidential Documents*, week ending 20 September 2004, 1998–2000.

Buzo, Adrian. *The Making of Modern Korea: A History (Asia's Transformations)*. New York: Routledge, 2002.

Callebs, Sean and Larry Smith. "North and South Korea Skirmish at Border; Where Does Kim Jong-il Get His Money?" *CNN News*, transcript from *On the Money*, broadcast 9 July 2003. Accessed via InfoTrac Onefile Research Database, 14 May 2005.

Center for Nonproliferation Studies. *Nuclear Threat Initiative Online*, 1 November 2000. www.nti.org/e_research/profiles/NK/Missile/65.html. Accessed 15 May 2005.

Central Intelligence Agency. "International Crime Threat Assessment." CIA Electronic Reading Room, December 2000. www.foia.cia.gov/search.asp. Keyword search, "International Crime Threat Assessment." Accessed 28 February 2005.

_____. "Korea Peninsula Map." *University of Texas Libraries Online*, 1993. www.lib.utexas.edu/maps/middle_east_and_asia/korean_peninsula.gif. Accessed 20 January 2005.

_____. *CIA World Factbook 2004: Macao.* www.cia.gov/cia/ publications/factbook/geos/mc.html. Accessed 27 May 2005.

_____. *The World Factbook Online 2004: North Korea.* www.cia.gov/cia/ publications/factbook/geos/kn.html. Accessed 28 February 2005.

_____. "Unclassified Report to Congress on the Acquisition of Technology Relating to Weapons of Mass Destruction and Advanced Conventional Munitions, 1 January Through 30 June 2002," *CIA Website.* www.odci.gov/cia/reports/721_reports/jan_ jun2002.html. Accessed 1 March 2005.

Cha, Victor. "Responding to Provocations." *The Japan Times*, 24 April 2003. www.japantimes.co.jp/cgi-bin/geted.pl5?eo20030424a1.htm. Accessed 21 May 2005.

Chanlett-Avery, Emma. "North Korean Supporters in Japan: Issues for US Policy." *CRS Report for Congress* RL32137. Washington, DC: Congressional Research Service, Library of Congress, 7 November 2003.

Chang, Christine Y. "A Field Survey Report of North Korean Refugees in China." *The Commission to Help North Korean Refugees*, 1999. www.cnkr.org/. Accessed 30 April 2005.

Chapman, William. "N. Korea's Corps of Diplomatic 'Renegades'; Envoys Said to Traffic in Drugs and Weapons." *The Washington Post*, 13 November 1983, A28.

Chin, Hee-gwan. "Divided by Fate: The Integration of Overseas Koreans in Japan." *East Asian Review* 13, no. 2 (Summer 2001): 59.

Cho, M.A. "North Korea's 2003 Foreign Trade." *KOTRA Website*, 13 August 2004. www.crm.kotra.or.kr/main/info/nk/new2003/. Accessed 22 March 2005.

"Chogin Tokyo 'Hid Chongryon Ties' Credit Union Allegedly Granted New Loans to Help Problem Debtors." *Daily Yomiuri*, 20 November 2001. Accessed via InfoTrac Onefile Research Database, 26 March 2005.

"Chogin-Chongryon Ties Said Tight." *Daily Yomiuri*, 30 November 2001. Accessed via InfoTrac Onefile Research Database, 26 March 2005.

"Chogins Funneled Money to Group." *Asahi Shimbun*, 8 January 2002. Accessed via LexisNexis Research Database, 15 May 2005.

"Chongron Affiliate Ordered Jet Mill." *The Yomiuri Shimbun*, 15 June 2003. Accessed via InfoTrac OneFile, 15 April 2005.

"Chosen Soren: Chongryun Schools to Ax Kim Portraits." *Asahi Shimbun*, 10 September 2002. Accessed via LexisNexis Research Database, 17 April 2005.

"Chosen Soren: N. Korean Ship Calls at Niigata as Abduction Issue Stirs Anger." *Asahi News Service*, 26 November 2002. Accessed via LexisNexis Research Database, 15 May 2005.

"Chosen Soren: North Korean Ferry Back in Niigata Port." *International Herald Tribune*, 27 April 2004. Accessed via LexisNexis Research Database, 15 May 2005.

"Chosen Soren: One Way Ticket: Many Korean Residents Who Went to North Korea." *International Herald Tribune*, 10 March 2004. Accessed via LexisNexis Research Database, 15 May 2005.

Chung Dae-kyun. "Japan's Korean Community In Transition," *Japan Echo* 30, no. 2, (April 2003): 30–33.

Chung, Joseph. "North Korea's Economic Development and Capabilities." *Asian Perspective* 11, no. 1 (Spring–Summer 1987): 45–74.

Cohen, Warren I. *East Asia at the Center*, New York: Columbia University Press, 2000.

Cohen, Hon. William S., Secretary of Defense. *Proliferation: Threat and Response*. January 2001, Office of the Secretary of Defense. Washington, DC: US Government Printing Office, 2001.

Congressional Research Service. "What is the Congressional Research Service?" *CRS Website*. www.loc.gov/crsinfo/whatscrs.html. Accessed 28 February 2005.

Cornell, Erik. *North Korea Under Communism: Report of an Envoy to Paradise*. New York: RoutledgeCurzon, 2002.

"Counterfeiting: Defector Says He Was Ordered To Get Fake US Dollars." *The Associated Press*, 8 June 1988. Accessed via LexisNexis Research Database, 15 March 2005.

"Counterfeiting: 6 Arrested on Suspicion of Peddling Fake US Currency." *Kyodo News Service*, 16 June 1997. Accessed via LexisNexis Research Database, 28 March 2005.

Creamer, Dewayne J., Captain, USAF. *The Rise and Fall of Chosen Soren: Its Effect on Japan's Relations on the Korean Peninsula*, Master's Thesis chaired by Edward A. Olsen. Monterey, CA: Naval Postgraduate School, 2003.

"Credit Unions in Japan Suspected of Illegal Remittances to N. Korea." *Agence France Presse*, 29 August 1999. Accessed via LexisNexis Research Database, 25 March 2005.

"Credit Unions Suspected of Sending Money to N. Korea." *Kyodo News Service*, 28 August 1999. Accessed via LexisNexis Research Database, 25 March 2005.

Crossette, Barbara. "US Study Finds Lack of Control in U.N. Food Aid to North Korea." *New York Times*, 12 October 1999, A8.

Cumings, Bruce. *Korea's Place in the Sun: A Modern History*. New York: W.W. Norton and Company, 1997.

_____. *North Korea: Another Country*. New York: The New Press, 2004.

_____. *Origins of the Korean War, Vol. 1: Liberation and the Emergence of Separate Regimes, 1945–1947*. Princeton, NJ: Princeton University Press, 1981.

_____. *Origins of the Korean War Vol. 2: The Roaring of the Cataract, 1947–1950*, Princeton, NJ: Princeton University Press, 1990.

Daoudi, M.S. and M.S. Dajani. *Economic Sanctions: Ideals and Experience*. London: Routledge & Kegan Paul Books, 1983.

"Deadbeat Debtor." *Financial Times*, 29 April 1995, Accessed via LexisNexis Research Database, 19 April 2005.

"Defector on DPRK Missiles, Drug Smuggling." (text), Tokyo *Kitachose to iu Akuma* (10 September 2002). FBIS Document ID KPP20040628000114. Accessed 6 April 2005.

Doxey, Margaret P. *International Sanctions in Contemporary Perspective.* New York: St. Martin's Press, 1996.

Eberstadt, Nicolas. "Financial Transfers from Japan to North Korea: Estimating the Unreported Flows." *Asian Survey* 36, No. 5 (May 1996): 523–542.

_____. *Policy and Economic Performance in Divided Korea, 1945–1995.* Doctoral Dissertation. Cambridge, MA: Harvard University, 1995.

_____. *The End of North Korea.* Washington, DC: American Enterprise Institute Press, 1999.

_____. "The Persistence of North Korea." *Policy Review Online* (Oct 2004). www.policyreivew.org/oct04/eberstadt.html. Accessed 15 March 2005.

Eckert, Carter, J. and others. *Korea Old and New: A History.* Cambridge, MA: Harvard University Press, 1990.

Efron, Sonni. "N. Korea Working on Missile Accuracy," *Los Angeles Times*, 12 September 2003, A3.

Elliot, Kimberly Ann. "Economic Leverage and the North Korean Nuclear Crisis," Number PB03-3, *International Economics Policy Briefs*, April 2003, Washington, DC: Institute for International Economics, 2003.

"Egypt Gives US 'Satisfactory Replies' on Missile Deal with North Korea." *Financial Times*, 15 July 2001. Accessed via LexisNexis Research Database, 15 May 2005.

Faiola, Anthony. "Revolution is Brewing at N. Korean Schools in Japan." *The Washington Post*, 10 October 2003, A1.

Fehrenbach, T.R. *This Kind of War: A Study in Unpreparedness.* New York: The Macmillan Company, 1963.

Feickert, Andrew. "Missile Survey: Ballistic and Cruise Missiles of Foreign Countries." *CRS Report for Congress* RL30427. Washington, DC: Congressional Research Service, Library of Congress, 5 March 2004.

_____. "North Korean Ballistic Missile Threat to the United States." *CRS Report for Congress* RL21473. Washington, DC: Congressional Research Service, Library of Congress, 25 March 2003.

Feickert, Andrew and K. Alan Kronstadt. "Missile Proliferation and the Strategic Balance in South Asia." *CRS Report for Congress* RL32115. Washington, DC: Congressional Research Service, Library of Congress, 17 October 2003.

Fisher, Scott. "Arirang Festival." *1StopKorea Online.* www.1stopkorea.com/index.htm ?nk-trip5.htm~mainframe. Accessed 29 January 2005.

Flake, L. Gordon. "Testimony Before the Subcommittee on Asia and the Pacific, House Committee on International Relations." *US House of Representatives Committee on International Relations Website*, 28 April 2004. wwwc.house.gov/international_ relations/108/fla042804.htm. Accessed 30 April 2005.

"Food Program Official Suspects 'Diversion' of Food Aid in North Korea." *Yonhap News*, 28 February 2002. Accessed via InfoTrac OneFile Research Database, 10 February 2005.

Foreign Experts to Help Taiwan Identify Forged 100 US dollar bills." *Deutsche Presse-*

Agentur, 27 July 2004. Accessed via LexisNexis Research Database, 17 March 2005.

"Former Korean University Professor Tells of Bogus Monetary Transfers to North Korea." (text). Tokyo *Shukan Posuto* (2 December 2002), FBIS Document ID. Accessed 12 January 2005.

Foster-Carter, Aidan. "Symbolic Links, Real Gaps." *Comparative Connections East Asia Online Journal, North Korea—South Korea Relations*, 2nd Quarter (2003). www.csis.org/pacfor/cc/0302Qnk_sk.html. Accessed 23 February 2005.

"Four Lenders to Take over Chogin Banking Operations." *The Japan Times*, 21 March 2002. www.japantimes.co.jp/cgi-bin/getarticle.pl5?nb20020321a7.htm. Accessed 1 July 2005.

Furukawa, Katsu. "Japan's View of the Korea Crisis." *Center for Nonproliferation Studies Website*. www.cns.miis.edu/research/korea/jpndprk.htm. Accessed 14 June 2005.

"GDP of North Korea." *Bank of Korea Online*. www.bok.or.kr/index.jsp. Keyword search, "North Korea." Accessed 6 February 2005.

Gertz, Bill. "Cuba, North Korea getting cozy, US fears." *The Washington Times*, 29 November 1991. Accessed via LexisNexis Research Database, 25 April 2005.

————. "North Korea Sends Missile Parts, Technology to Iran." *The Washington Times*, 18 April 2001. Accessed via LexisNexis Research Database, 15 March 2005.

Green, Nick. "Dealing Drugs: North Korean Narcotics Trafficking." *Harvard International Review* 26, no. 1 (Spring 2004): 7–8.

Grimmett, Richard F. "Conventional Arms Transfers to Developing Nations." *CRS Report for Congress* RL32547. Library of Congress, Washington, DC: Government Printing Office, 2003.

Han, Yo'ng-chin. "Loyal Foreign Currency Earning." (text). Seoul *The Daily NK* (6 April 2005), FBIS Document ID KPP20050408000022. Accessed 18 May 2005.

"Hana Credit Union on Notice." *Daily Yomiuri* editorial, 19 December 2002. Accessed via InfoTrac OneFile Research Database 12 April 2005.

Halloran, Richard. "Iran Is Said To Get North Korean Arms." *The New York Times*, 19 December 1982. Accessed via LexisNexis Research Database, 25 April 2005.

Hicks, George. *Japan's Hidden Apartheid: The Korean Minority and the Japanese*. Brookfield, VT: Ashgate, 1997.

Hogg, Andrew. "Getting Off on the Right Note." *The Banker* 917, no. 152 (July 2002): 116. Accessed via InfoTrac Research Database, 12 March 2005.

Honda, Masakazu. "Under Fire: Chongrun is Dragged Kicking and Screaming." *Asahi News Service*, 27 September 2002. Accessed via LexisNexis Research Database, 15 May 2005.

"Intaglio Printing." *US Bureau of Engraving and Printing Website*. www.moneyfactory.com/document.cfm/18/109. Accessed 27 March 2005.

"Japan to Suspend North Korea Food Aid 'Immediately.'" *Yonhap News*, 13 December 2004. Accessed via LexisNexis Research Database, 26 January 2005.

"Japanese Protesters Meet North Korean Ferry Docking at Niigata Port." *BBC Monitoring Asia Pacific*, 20 October 2004. Accessed via LexisNexis Research Database, 25 March 2005.

Jeon, Jin-bae. "Counterfeit $100 Notes Called Nearly Perfect." *JoongAng Daily Online*, 24 April 2003. joongangdaily.joins.com/. Accessed 30 March 2005.

Jones, Gary L. "Nuclear Nonproliferation: Heavy Fuel Oil Delivered to North Korea

Under the Agreed Framework." Testimony before the House of Representatives Committee on International Relations. *US General Accounting Office Website*, 27 October 1999. www.gao.gov/archive/2000/rc00020t. pdf. Accessed 30 April 2005.

Johnston, Eric. "Chongryun Tax Breaks Face Hard Scrutiny." *The Japan Times*, 26 July 2003. Accessed via LexisNexis Research Database, 17 April 2005.

Jordan, Mary and Kevin Sullivan. "Pinball Wizards Fuel North Korea—Japan's Passion Aids Communist State; Pachinko Players Underwrite North Korea." *The Washington Post*, 7 June 1996, A25.

Joyce, Colin. "North Korean Forgers Set Their Sights on the Euro: Counterfeiters Produce Millions of Notes, Some Better Than Original." *The Sunday Telegraph*, 21 November 2004. Accessed via LexisNexis Research Database, 15 March 2005.

Judge, Michael. "North Korea's Dr. Evil." *The Wall Street Journal*, 15 October 2002, A20.

Judson, Ruth and Richard Porter. "Estimating the World Wide Volume of Counterfeit US Currency: Data and Extrapolation." *Federal Reserve Online*, September 2003. www.federalreserve.gov/pubs/feds/2003/200352/200352pap.pdf. Accessed 27 March 2005.

Kang, Chol-Hwan. *The Aquariums of Pyongyang*. New York: Basic Books, 2001.

Kaplan, David E. "The Far East Sopranos; What a Racket." *US News and World Report* 3, no. 134 (27 January 2003): 34.

_____. "The Wiseguy Regime." *US News and World Report* 126, no. 6 (15 February 1999): 38.

Karniol, Robert. "Vietnam Stocking up 'SCUDs.'" *Jane's Defence Weekly*, 14 April 1999, 63.

KCNA. *Korean News: News from Korean Central News Agency of DPRK*. www.kcna.co.jp/index-e.htm. Accessed 25 February 2005.

Kempe, Fredrick and David S. Cloud. "Baghdad Records Show Hussein Sought Missiles, Other Aid Abroad." *The Wall Street Journal*, 3 November 2003, A1.

Kim, Ji-ho. "Cash-Strapped N.K. Resorts to International Crimes." *The Korea Herald*, 12 October 1999. Accessed via LexisNexis Research Database, 19 April 2005.

Kim, S.J. "In Japan: Educational Plight of Residents Reviewed." *The Korean Republic*, 15 April 1961, 2.

Kim, Sam-o. "South Korea: Situation Normalising." *Far East Economic Review* 71, no. 13 (27 Mar 1971): 64.

Kim, Il-Young and Lakhvinder Singh. "The North Korean Nuclear Program and External Connections." *The Korean Journal of Defense Analysis* 16, no.1 (Spring 2004): 81+.

Kim, Young Il. "North Korea and Narcotics Trafficking: A View from the Inside." *North Korea Review*, Special Supplement to the Jamestown Foundation China Brief 1, no. 1 (27 February 2004): 6.

Kirk, Don. "Despite 'Reforms,' Food Crisis Hits N. Korea." *The Christian Science Monitor*, 28 January 2005. www.csmonitor.com/2005/0128/p06s02-woap.htm. Accessed 29 April 2005.

Kissinger, Henry. *Diplomacy*. New York: Touchstone, 1994.

Korean Overseas Trade Association (KOTRA). *KOTRA Website*. www.crm.kotra.or.kor/main. Accessed 18 March 2005.

"Koreas: Defector says North producing counterfeit US dollars." *Yonhap News*, 12 January 2000. Accessed via LexisNexis Research Database, 15 March 2005.

Kono, Hiroko. "Poppy Cultivation Ordered By Kim Family – Japan is Number One Buyer." (text). Tokyo *Yomiuri Shimbun* (20 May 2003). FBIS Document ID JPP2003050000139. Accessed 19 May 2005.

Koo, Kyung-hee. "North Korea's Golden Star Bank to be Closed on June 30." 4 May 2004, *KOTRA Website.* www.crm.kotra.or.kr/main/info/nk/new2003. Keyword search, "Golden Star Bank." Accessed 22 May 2005.

Kralev, Nicholas. "Pakistan Purchases N.Korean Missiles." *Washington Times*, 31 March 2003.

Kristof, Nicholas D. "Japan Holds 6 for Passing Counterfeit $100 Bills." *New York Times*, 18 June 1997, A6.

Kuchment, Anna and Malcolm Beith. "A New Script? Korean foreign minister receives favorable treatment at ASEAN meeting." *Newsweek International*, 7 August 2000. Accessed via InfoTrac Onefile Research Database, 26 June 2005.

Kurose, Yoshinari. "North Korea reportedly sold arms to group linked to al-Qaida." *The Yomiuri Shimbun,* 4 January 2005. Accessed via LexisNexis Research Database, 25 April 2005.

Lee, Alice K. *Koreans in Japan: Their Influence on Korean-Japanese Relations*, Master's Thesis chaired by Claude A. Buss, Monterey, CA: Naval Postgraduate School, 1979.

Lintner, Bertil. "It's Hard to Help Kim Jong Il," *Far Eastern Economic Review* 166, no. 12 (27 March 2003): 20–22.

Lintner, Bertil, and Shawn W. Crispin. "Dangerous Bedfellows: Evidence of a blossoming military relationship between Rangoon and Pyongyang," *Far Eastern Economic Review* 166, no. 46 (20 November 2003): 22–23.

_____. "For US, a New North Korean Problem." *The Wall Street Journal*, 18 November 2003. Accessed via ProQuest Research Database 10 May 2005.

"Loan to Hyundai Units Used for Secret Transfer." *Digital Chosonilbo*, 16 February 2003. www.english.chosun.com/w21data/html/news/200302/200302160019.html. Accessed 26 June 2005.

LoBaido, Anthony. "North Korea's Financial Dirty Tricks: Stellar Workmanship Behind Counterfeiting of US Currency." *WorldNetDaily*, 14 August 1998. www.worldnetdaily.com/news/article.asp?ARTICLE_ID=16673. Accessed 30 March 2005.

Macdonald, Donald S. *The Koreans: Contemporary Politics and Society.* 3rd ed. Boulder, CO: Westview Press, 1996.

MacWilliam, Ian. "US Embassy Keeping Silent on Bogus Bills." *The Moscow Times*, 25 January 1997. Accessed via LexisNexis Research Database, 28 March 2005.

Maier, Charles S. *Dissolution: The Crisis of Communism and the End of East Germany.* Princeton, NJ: Princeton University Press, 1999.

"Mangyongbong-92 Expected to Enter Niigata Port on May 18." *Jiji Press*, 11 May 2005. Accessed via LexisNexis Research Database, 15 May 2005.

Manyin, Mark E. "Foreign Assistance to North Korea." *CRS Report for Congress* RL31785. Washington, DC: Congressional Research Service, Library of Congress, 26 March 2005.

_____. "Japan-North Korea Relations: Selected Issues." *CRS Report for Congress* RL32161. Washington, DC: Congressional Research Service, Library of Congress, 26 November 2003.

_____. "US Assistance to North Korea: Fact Sheet," *CRS Report for Congress*

RS21834. Washington, DC: Congressional Research Service, Library of Congress, 11 February 2005.

Manyin, Mark E. and Ryun Jun. "US Assistance to North Korea." *CRS Report for Congress* RL31785. Washington, DC: Congressional Research Service, Library of Congress, 17 March 2003.

Martin, Bradley K. *Under the Loving Care of the Fatherly Leader: North Korea and the Kim Dynasty.* New York: Thomas Dunne Books, 2004.

"METI Busts N. Korea Trader." *Daily Yomiuri*, 14 June 2003. Accessed via InfoTrac Onefile, 15 April 2005.

Miller, Judith. "Libya Halts Military Trade With North Korea, Syria, and Iran." *The New York Times*, 14 May 2004. Accessed via LexisNexis Research Database, 15 March 2005, A4.

Mitchell, Richard H. *The Korean Minority in Japan.* Berkeley, CA: University of California Press, 1967.

"More Koreans Go North." *The New York Times*, 12 December 1960, 9.

Moreau, Ron, and Russell Watson. "Is it Real, or Super K? North Korean Suspected of Producing Counterfeit US Currency." *Newsweek* 24, no. 127 (10 June 1996): 42.

Morris, James T. "The State of the World Report on Hunger from Africa to North Korea." Testimony during a Hearing before the Committee on Foreign Relations, US House of Representatives, *US Senate Committee on Foreign Relations Website.* www.foreign.senate.gov/testimony/2003/MorrisTestimony030225.pdf. Accessed 30 April 2005.

"N. Korean Ferry Arrives at Niigata, Inspectors Go On Board." *Kyodo News Service*, 13 July 2004. Accessed via LexisNexis Research Database, 25 March 2005.

"N. Korean Ship Gives Up Entering Japanese Port." *Yonhap News*, 20 April 2005. Accessed via Infotrac Onefile Research Database, 1 May 2005.

"N. Korean Ship to Japan Equipped with Military Sonar." *Kyodo News Service*, 6 June 2003. Accessed via LexisNexis Research Database, 15 May 2005.

"N. Korean Ship to Make Port Call in Japanese Port Next Week." *Yonhap News*, 11 May 2005. Accessed via Infotrac Onefile Research Database, 15 May 2005.

"N. Korean Spy Got Orders on Aid Ship." *Asahi News Service*, 30 January 2003. Accessed via LexisNexis Research Database, 15 May 2005.

Nanto, Nick. "North Korea: Chronology of Provocations, 1950–2003." *CRS Report for Congress* RL30427. Washington, DC: Congressional Research Service, Library of Congress, 2003.

Natsios, Andrew S. *The Great North Korean Famine: Famine, Politics, and Foreign Policy.* Washington, DC: United Stated Institute of Peace, 2001.

_____. "The Politics of Famine in North Korea." *United States Institute of Peace*, Special Report 51, 2 August 1999. www.usip.org/pubs/specialreports/sr990802.html. Accessed 30 April 2005.

Niksch, Larry A. "Korea: US-Korea Relations – Issues for Congress." *CRS Report for Congress* IB98045. Washington, DC: Congressional Research Service, Library of Congress, 27 August 2003.

_____. "North Korea's Nuclear Weapons Program." *CRS Report for Congress* IB91141, Washington, DC: Congressional Research Service, Library of Congress, 28 September 2004.

"NK Earns $100 Million Annually from Missile Exports." *The Korea Times*, 1 April

1999. Accessed via LexisNexis Research Database, 15 May 2005.

"NK Diplomats' Illegal Acts Get Bold." *The Korea Times*, 8 November 1998. Accessed via LexisNexis Research Database, 28 March 2005.

"NK Prints $15 Mil. in Fake Dollars," *Korea Times Online*, 16 November 1998, www.hankooki.com. Keyword search, "NK Prints." Accessed 21 December 2005.

"No Diversion of Food Aid to N.K.'s Military: S. Korean Officials." (text). Seoul *Yonhap News*, 9 October 2003. FBIS Document ID KPP20031009000107. Accessed 5 January 2005.

Noland, Marcus. *Avoiding the Apocalypse: The Future of the Two Koreas*. Washington, DC: Institute for International Economics, 2000.

————. "Famine and Reform in North Korea: Working Paper 03-5." *Institute for International Economics Website*, July 2003. www.iie.com/publications/wp/2003/03-5.pdf. Accessed 30 April 2005.

————. "North Korea's External Economic Relations." Working Paper, *Institute for International Economics*, February, 2001. www.iie.com/publications/papers/noland0201-1.htm#23. Accessed 30 April 2005.

North Korea: A Country Study. Ed. Andre Matles Savada, Federal Research Division, Library of Congress. Washington, DC: Library of Congress, 1994.

"North Korea armed Islamic group in Philippines." *World Tribune Online*, 5 January 2005. www.worldtribune.com/worldtribune/05/breaking2453376.1868055556.html. Accessed 2 March 2005.

"North Korea Country Profile 2005." *Economist Intelligence Unit Online*. www.db.eiu.com/report_dl.asp?mode=pdf&eiu_issue_id=618020461. Accessed 22 February 2005.

"North Korea: Country Report 2005–2006." *Economist Intelligence Unit Online*. www.db.eiu.com/report_dl.asp?mode=pdf&eiu_issue_id=118001811. Accessed 10 February 2005.

"North Korea Ferry Returns to Japan," *CNN Online*, 18 May 2005. www.cnn.com/2005/WORLD/asiapcf/05/17/japan.nkorea.ferry.reut/index.html. Accessed 18 May 2005.

"North Korea Fires Missile Across Northern Japan Into Pacific." *Korea Times*, 1 September 1998. Accessed via LexisNexis Research Database, 15 April 2005.

"North Korea has Delivered 400 Ballistic Missiles to the Mideast." *World Tribune Online*. 216.26.163.62/2003/ea_nkorea_10_27.html. Accessed 11 April 2005.

"North Korea Prints $15 Million of Bogus Bills a Year." *The Korea Herald*, 17 November 1998. Accessed via LexisNexis Research Database, 15 March 2005.

"North Korea Produces Bogus Dollars at Three Plants: Report." *Agence France Presse*, 28 June 1997. Accessed via LexisNexis Research Database, 15 March 2005.

"North Korea Profile: Missile Overview." *Nuclear Threat Initiative Online*. www.nti.org/e_research/profiles/NK/Missile/index.html. Accessed 12 March 2005.

"North Korean Diplomat Expelled for Passing Fake Dollars." *Izvestiya*, 8 February 1997. Accessed via LexisNexis Research Database, 28 March 2005.

"North Korean Ferry Calls Off Japan Port Call Due to Insurance Problem." *BBC Monitoring International Reports*, 6 January 2005. Accessed via LexisNexis Research Database, 15 May 2005.

"North Korean Outpost in Vienna." *Intelligence Online*, 31 October 2003. Accessed via LexisNexis Research Database, 17 April 2005.

"North Korean Ships Warned as Japan Starts Checks on Foreign Vessels." *Kyodo News*

Service, 1 March 2005. Accessed via Infotrac Onefile Research Database, 12 March 2005.

"North Korea's Ballistic Missile Exports." *Center for Nonproliferation Studies Nuclear Threat Initiative Online.* www.nti.org/e_research/profiles/NK/Missile/66_1279.html. Accessed 1 March 2005.

"North Korea's Only Bank in Europe Stops Business." *Kyodo News*, 28 July 2004. Accessed via Infotrac Onefile Research Database, 17 April 2005.

"North Korea's Only Bank in Europe to Take Steps for Closure." *Yonhap*, 5 May 2004. Accessed via Infotrac Onefile Research Database, 10 May 2005.

"North Korea's Taepo Dong I Missile Priced at $6 Million." *Korea Times*, 29 October 1999. Accessed via LexisNexis Research Database, 16 May 2005.

North Korea's Weapons Programmes: A Net Assessment. International Institute for Strategic Studies. Ed. Gary Samore. New York: Palgrave Macmillan, 2004.

Oberdorfer, Don. "An Assassin Comes 'Home' to Korea." *The Washington Post*, 3 September 1974, A11.

———. *The Two Koreas: A Contemporary History.* Indianapolis: Basic Books, 1997.

Oh Hassig, Kongdan and others. *North Korean Policy Elites.* IDA Paper P-3903, June 2004, Alexandria, VA: Institute for Defense Analysis, 2004.

Oh, Kongdan. "Ratcheting Down the Rhetoric." *Time Asia Online*, 7 February 2005. www.time.come/time/asia/magazine/article/0,13673,501050214-1025220,00.html. Accessed 8 February 2005.

Oh, Kongdan and Ralph C. Hassig. *North Korea: Through the Looking Glass.* Washington, DC: Brookings Institute Press, 2000.

Ono, Kazuichiro. "The Problem of Japanese Emigration." *Kyoto University Economic Review*, 28 (April 1958): 40–54.

Paved with Good Intentions: The NGO Experience in North Korea. Eds. L. Gordon Flake and Scott Snyder. Westport, CT: Praeger Publishers, 2003.

Perl, Raphael F. "Drug Trafficking and North Korea: Issues for US Policy." *CRS Report for Congress* RL32167. Washington, DC: Congressional Research Service, Library of Congress, 5 December 2003.

"Policy Raid Chongron HQ Over Alleged Embezzlement." *Kyodo News International— Japan Weekly Monitor*, 3 December 2001. Accessed via InfoTrac OneFile Research Database, 20 April 2005.

Pollack, Jonathan D. "China and a Changing North Korea: Issues, Uncertainties, and Implications." Paper presented at *Conference on North Korea's Engagement-Perspectives, Outlook, and Implications*, National Intelligence Council, 23 February 2001. www.odci.gov/nic/confreports_northkorea.html. Accessed 14 July 2005.

Reese, David. *The Prospects for North Korea's Survival.* Adelphi Paper 323. International Institute for Strategic Studies. New York: Oxford University Press, 1998.

Reforming Asian Socialism: The Growth of Market Institutions. Eds. John McMillan and Barry Naughton. Ann Arbor, MI: University of Michigan Press, 1996, 317–336.

Rennack, Dianne E. "North Korea: Economic Sanctions." *CRS Report for Congress* RL31696, 24 January 2003. Washington, DC: Congressional Research Service, Library of Congress.

Righter, Rosemary. "Is North Korea crazy enough to court annihilation?" *The Times (London)*, 7 August 2004. Accessed via LexisNexis Research Database, 19 March 2005.

"ROK Daily Reports DPRK Expanding Opium Farms, Selling Drugs Via China." (text). Seoul *Chosen Ilbo* (9 October 2004). FBIS Document ID KPP2004202000005410. Accessed 22 March 2005.

"ROK Intelligence Service Website Describes DPRK Drug Production." (text). Seoul *National Intelligence Service* (20 April 04). FBIS Document ID KPP20040420000034. Accessed 1 November 2004.

ROK Police Arrest 17 for Smuggling Alleged DPRK Methamphetamine." (text). Seoul *The Korea Times* (24 February 2004). FBIS Document ID KPP20040223000084. Accessed 15 March 2005.

Rodgers, Donald M. *Taiwan and North Korea: Division, Legitimacy, Competition, and Nation-State Identity.* Doctoral Dissertation. Athens, GA: University of Georgia, 2000.

Ryang, Sonia. *North Koreans in Japan: Language, Ideology and Identity.* Boulder, CO: Westview Press, 1997.

Ryu, Jin. "Turkey Expels Two NK Diplomats for Drug Smuggling." *The Korea Times*, 10 December 2004. times.hankooki.com/lpage/nation/200412/kt2004121017133111990.htm. Accessed 6 April 2005.

Saccone, Richard. *To the Brink and Back: Negotiating with North Korea.* Seoul: Hollym, 2003.

"Sailing Across a Sea of Trouble." *Japan Inc*, October 2003, 6.

Sanger, David E. "CIA Said to Find Nuclear Advances By North Koreans." *The New York Times*, 1 July 2003, A1.

Sanger, David, and Thom Shanker. "Reluctant US Gives Assent for Missiles to Go to Yemen." *The New York Times*, 12 December 2002, A1.

Schloms, Michael. *North Korea and the Timeless Dilemma of Aid: A Study of Humanitarian Action in Famines.* Piscataway, NJ: Transaction Publishers, 2004.

"SCOPE: Japanese Women Make Trip on N. Korean Ferry." *Kyodo News Service*, 21 September 2004. Accessed via LexisNexis Research Database, 25 March 2005.

"Scud missile sales 'earned North Korea 60 million dollars in 2002.'" *Deutsche Presse-Agentur*, 23 October 2003. Accessed via LexisNexis Research Database, 28 March 2005.

"Secrets of Making Money." On *NOVA*. PBS, airdate 22 October 1996. Transcript viewed online. www.pbs.org/wgbh/nova/transcripts/2314secr.html. Accessed 27 March 2005.

Siegel, Ronald H. "The Missile Programs of North Korea, Iraq, and Iran," *Institute for Defense & Disarmament Studies Working Paper 3*, September 2001. www.nautilus.org/VietnamFOIA/archives/DPRKbriefingbook/missiles/IDDS-SeigelReport.html. Accessed 21 December 2005.

"Seishin Sold Jet Mills to China, India." *Daily Yomiuri*, 14 June 2003. Accessed via InfoTrac Onefile Research Database, 15 April 2005.

Seo, Banseok. "North Korea Duped by Iranian Counterfeits" *Digital Chosonilbo*, 2 March 1999. www.english.chosun.com/w21data/html/news/199903/199903020369.html. Accessed 27 March 2005.

Seong, Chaiki. "A Decade of Economic Crisis in North Korea: Impacts on the Military." *Korea Institute for Defense Analyses.* KIDA Paper No. 3 (October 2003). www.kida.re.kr/eng/publications/publications02.htm. Accessed 14 March 2005.

Shin, Jae Hoon. "Koreans Abroad: Shaky Finances." *Far Eastern Economic Review* 160, no. 49 (4 December 1997): 29.

Siegel, Ronald H. *The Missile Programs of North Korea, Iraq, and Iran.* Working Paper 3, Institute for Defense & Disarmament Studies, September 2001. www.idds.org/iddswkp3.html. Accessed 15 May 2005.

Sin, Won-t'ae. "North Korea's Banks." (text). Seoul *T'ongil Kyongje* (October 1997). FBIS Document ID FTS19971203000976. Accessed 19 May 2005.

"Six Key Figures in NK Payoff Scandal Convicted." *Korea Times*, 27 September 2003. Accessed via LexisNexis Research Database, 26 June 2005.

Smith, Anthony. "Asia Pacific Security: Dilemmas of Dominance, Challenges to Community." *East-West Center Senior Policy Seminar 2003.* www.eastwestcenter.org/stored/pdfs/SeniorPolicySeminar2003.pdf. Accessed 4 February 2004.

Smith, Charles. "Cash Lifeline: Koreans in Japan Subsidise Pyongyang." *Far Eastern Economic Review* 156, no. 36 (9 September 1993): 23.

Sokolski, Henry. "Axis of Proliferators." *The Wall Street Journal*, 19 August 2003. Accessed via Proquest Research Database, 15 March 2005.

Solomon, Jay. "A Global Journal Report: Some Speak of Pyongyang Blockade – Bush Administration Hawks Consider Ways to Stop Exporting of Arms, Drugs." *The Wall Street Journal*, 5 May 2003. Accessed via ProQuest Research Database, 2 April 2005.

_____. "In North Korea, Secret Cash Hoard Props Up Regime." *The Wall Street Journal*, 14 July 2003. Accessed via Lexis Nexis Research Database, 14 May 2005.

_____. "Money Trail." *The Wall Street Journal*, 14 July 2003. Accessed via ProQuest Research Database, 2 April 2005.

Solomon, Jay and Jason Dean. "Drug Money: Heroin Busts Point to Source of Funds for North Koreans." *The Wall Street Journal*, 23 April 2003. Accessed via ProQuest Research Database, 21 November 2004.

Sources of Korean Tradition, Volume I. Eds. Yongho Choe, and others. New York: Columbia University Press, 1997.

Sources of Korean Tradition, Volume II. Eds. Yongho Choe and others. New York: Columbia University Press, 2000.

South Korean Ministry of Unification, *Ministry of Unification Website.* www.unikorea.go.kr/en/northkorea. Accessed 18 March 2005.

Spaeth, Anthony. "Kim's Rackets." *Time Asia Magazine*, 2 June 2003. www.time.com/time/nation/article/0,8599,455850,00.html. Accessed 22 May 2005.

Squassoni, Sharon A. "Weapons of Mass Destruction: Trade Between North Korea and Pakistan." *CRS Report for Congress* RL31900. Washington, DC: Congressional Research Service, Library of Congress, 7 May 2003.

Stuek, William. *Rethinking the Korean War: A New Diplomatic and Strategic History.* Princeton, NJ: Princeton University Press, 2002.

Strong, Kenneth A., Lieutenant Commander, USN. *North Korea: The Transnational Criminal State.* Research Report chaired by Paul R. Kan. Maxwell Air Force Base, AL: Air Command and Staff College Air University. April 2003.

Struck, Doug. "Murder Shines a Light on the Lives of Koreans in Japan." *The Washington Post,* 1 June 2000, A21.

_____. "N. Korea's Closed Society Keeps Trade Routes Open; Flow of Money, Goods Frustrates US Drive to Tighten Isolation." *The Washington Post*, 3 February 2003. Accessed via accessed via LexisNexis Research Database, 25 March 2005.

Suetsugu, Tetsuya. "Risky Business Leading North Korea to Ruin." *The Daily Yomiuri*, 22 August 2003. Accessed via LexisNexis Research Database, 15 January 2005.

Suk, Hi Kim. *North Korea at a Crossroads*. Jefferson, NC: McFarland Publishers, 2003.

Suk, Sarah. "WFP Chief Confident Food for N. Korea Reaching Intended Recipients." (text). Tokyo *Kyodo World Service*, 26 October 2004. Document ID JPP20041026000087. Accessed 5 January 2005.

Sullivan, Kevin, and Mary Jordan. "Famine, Nuclear Threat Raise Stakes in Debate Over N. Korea." *Washington Post Foreign Service*, 13 March 1999. www.washingtonpost. com/wp-srv/inatl/longterm/korea/stories/famine031399.htm. Accessed 27 May 2005.

Sung, Chul Yang. *The North and South Korean Political Systems: A Comparative Analysis*. Elizabeth, NJ: Hollym International, 1999.

"Super K Counterfeit Bills Meet Match With New Detector." *PR Newswire*, 15 March 2005. Accessed via InfoTrac Research Database, 15 March 2005.

Swearingen, Roger and Paul Langer. *Red Flag in Japan: International Communism in Action, 1919–1951*. Cambridge, MA: Harvard University Press, 1952.

"Taiwan Police Identify, Search for Suspected Counterfeiters of US Banknotes." *Central News Agency*, Taipei, 26 July 2004. Accessed via LexisNexis Research Database, 17 March 2005.

Takahara, Kanako. "Public wants sanctions—but at what price?" *Japan Times Online*, 24 December 2004. www.japantimes.co.jp/cgi-bin/getarticle.pl5?nn20041224a1.htm. Accessed 14 June 2005.

Terry, Fiona. "The Deadly Secrets of North Korea." *Doctors Without Borders Website*, August 2001. www.doctorswithoutborders.org/publications/other/deadly_2001. shtml. Accessed 29 April 2005.

"Thai Senate raises suspicions on rice exports to North." *Joongang Daily Online*, 22 May 2002. joongangdaily.joins.com/200205/22/200205221602254659900902 09021.html. Accessed 30 April 2005.

The International Institute of the Juche Idea Website. www.cnet-ta.ne.jp/juche/defaulte. htm. Accessed 28 April 2005.

The Military Balance: 2003–2004. Ed. Christopher Langton, International Institute for Strategic Studies, London: Oxford University Press, 2003.

"The Superdollar Plot." On *Panorama*. BBC One, airdate 20 June 2004. Transcript viewed online, news.bbc.co.uk/1/hi/programmes/panorama/3805581.stm. Accessed 28 February 2004.

"Tokyo Seizes 3 Chongryn Facilities." *International Herald Tribune*, 10 September 2003. Accessed via LexisNexis Research Database, 17 April 2005.

Torchia, Christopher. "North Korea's Missiles: A Source of Cash, Prestige and Bargaining Power." *The Associated Press*, 21 February 2002. Accessed via LexisNexis Research Database, 15 March 2005.

Triplett, William C. III. *Rogue State: How a Nuclear North Korea Threatens America*. Washington, DC: Regnery Publishing, 2004.

Trumbull, Robert. "Festivity Marks Koreans' Sailing." *The New York Times*, 15 December 1959, 14.

U, Chong-ch'ang. "Kim Chong-il's Slush Funds." (text). Seoul *Wolgan Choson* (01 November 2000). FBIS Document ID KPP20001019000046. Accessed 19 May 2005.

_____. "Organ of Southward Operations in Macao That Received the 'Slush Fund for North Korea Created by Kim Tae-chung and Hyundai.'" (text). Seoul *Wolgan Cho-*

son (01 April 2003). FBIS Document ID KPP20040312000119. Accessed 19 May 2005.

————. "The World of Kim Chong-il's $4.3 Billion Slush Fund Seen Through $500 Million Cash Transfer to the North." (text). Seoul *Wolgan Choson*, (01 March 2003). FBIS Document ID KPP20040324000161. Accessed 19 May 2005.

United Nations. "International Food Aid Information System (INTERFAIS)." *World Food Program Website*. www.wfp.org/interfais/. Accessed 21 February 2005.

————. "World Drug Report 2004, Volume 1: Executive Summary." *United Nations Office on Drugs and Crime Website*. www.unodc.org/unodc/world_drug_report. html. Accessed 28 February 2005.

————. "World Drug Report 2004, Volume 2: Statistics." *United Nations Office on Drugs and Crime Website*. www.unodc.org/unodc/world_drug_report.html. Accessed 28 February 2005.

United States Secret Service Website. www.secretservice.gov/. Accessed 27 March 2005.

US Arms Control and Disarmament Agency. *World Military Expenditures and Arms Transfers 1971–1980*. Washington, DC: US Government Printing Office, 1983.

————. *World Military Expenditures and Arms Transfers 1985*. Washington, DC: US Government Printing Office, 1985.

————. *World Military Expenditures and Arms Transfers 1995*. Washington, DC: US Government Printing Office, 1996.

————. *World Military Expenditures and Arms Transfers 1999–2000*. Washington, DC: US Government Printing Office, 2002.

US Army. "The Korean War, 1950–1953." *American Military History Online*. www.army.mil/cmh-pg/books/AMH/AMH-25.htm. Accessed 22 January, 2005.

US Congress, House. *Final Report of the North Korean Advisory Group*, 29 October 1999. *Federation of American Scientists Website*. www.fas.org/nuke/guide/dprk/nkag-report.htm. Accessed 28 February 2005.

US Congress, House, Committee on International Relations. *US Policy Toward North Korea II: Misuse of US Aid to North Korea*, 106th Cong., 1st sess., 27 October 1999. H. Rept. 106-01. Washington, DC: US Government Printing Office, 2003.

US Congress, House, International Relations Subcommittee on East Asia and the Pacific, "North Korea: The Humanitarian Situation and Refugees," *Doctors Without Borders Website*, 2 May 2002, www.doctorswithoutborders.org/publications/speeches/2002/sd_nkorea.shtml. Accessed 29 April 2005.

US Congress, House, Committee on International Relations Subcommittee on East Asia and the Pacific, "North Korea: The Humanitarian Situation and Refugees," *Doctors Without Borders Website*, 2 May 2002, www.doctorswithoutborders.org/publications/speeches/2002/sd_nkorea.shtml. Accessed 29 April 2005.

US Congress, House, Subcommittee on East Asia and the Pacific of the Committee on International Relations. *North Korea: Humanitarian and Human Rights Concerns*. 107th Cong., 2nd sess., 2 May 2002, H. Rept. 107–95. Washington, DC: US Government Printing Office, 2002.

US Congress, Senate, Financial Management, The Budget, and International Security Subcommittee of the Committee on Governmental Affairs. *Drugs, Counterfeiting, and Weapons Proliferation: The North Korean Connection*. 108th Cong., 1st sess., 20 May 2003, S. Hrg. 108-157. Washington, DC: US Government Printing Office, 2003.

US Congress, Senate, International Security, Proliferation and Federal Services Sub-committee of the Committee on Governmental Affairs. *CIA National Intelligence Estimate of Foreign Missile Developments and the Ballistic Missile Threat Through 2015*. 107th Cong., 2nd sess., 11 March 2002, S. Hrg. 107-467. Washington, DC: US Government Printing Office, 2003.

_____. *North Korean Missile Proliferation*. 105th Cong., 1st sess., 21 October 1997, S. Hrg. 105-241. Washington, DC: US Government Printing Office, 2003.

US Congress, Senate, Subcommittee on East Asian and Pacific Affairs of the Committee on Foreign Relations. *Life Inside North Korea*. 108th Cong., 1st sess., 5 June 2003, S. Hrg. 108-131. Washington, DC: US Government Printing Office, 2003.

US Department of State, Bureau for International Narcotics and Law Enforcement Affairs. "International Narcotics Control Strategy Report 2003, Vol. 1: Southeast Asia." *US Department of State Website*, March 2004. www.state.gov/g/inl/rls/nrcrpt/2003/vol1/html/29837.htm. Accessed 28 February 2005.

US Department of State, Bureau for International Narcotics and Law Enforcement Affairs. "International Narcotics Control Strategy Report 2005, Vol. 1: Drug and Chemical Control." *US Department of State Website*, March 2005. www.state.gov/g/inl/rls/nrcrpt/2005/. Accessed 20 July 2005.

US General Accounting Office. *Counterfeit US Currency Abroad: Issues and US Deterrence Efforts*. GAO/GGD96-11, 26 Feb 1996. Washington, DC: General Accounting Office, 1996.

_____. "Currency Paper Procurement: Meaningful Competition Unlikely Under Current Conditions." *GAO Online*, GAO/GGD-98-181, August 1998. www.gao.gov/archive/1998/gg98181.pdf. Accessed 27 March 2005.

_____. *Foreign Assistance: North Korea Restricts Food Aid Monitoring*, GAO/NSIAD-00-35, October 1999. Washington, DC: General Accounting Office, 1999.

_____. "Foreign Assistance: North Korea Restricts Food Aid Monitoring." Report to the Chairman, Committee on International Relations, House of Representatives. *GAO Archive*, GAO/NSIAD-00-35, October 1999. www.gao.gov/archive/2000/ns00035.pdf. Accessed 15 March 2005.

US Office of the National Counterintelligence Executive. "North Korea: Channeling Foreign Information Technology to Leverage IT Development." *Archives*, December 2003. www.ncix.gov/archives/docs/north_korea_and_foreign_it.pdf. Accessed 18 May 2005.

"US Official Worried North Korea May Be Receiving Missile Test Data From Iran." *Financial Times Information*, 27 May 2004. Accessed via LexisNexis Research Database, 13 March 2005.

"US Ties N Korea to Nuclear Deal." *BBC News Online*, 5 February 2005. www.news.bbc.co.uk/1/hi/world/asia-pacific/4228713.stm. Accessed 10 February 2005.

US Treasury Department. *The Use and Counterfeiting of United States Currency Abroad*. Washington, DC: US Government Printing Office, 2000.

_____. *The Use and Counterfeiting of United States Currency Abroad, Part 2*. Washington, DC: US Government Printing Office, 2003.

"US Unveils New $50 Note With Background Colors." *Federal Reserve Board Website*, Joint Press Release, 26 April 2004. www.federalreserve.gov/boarddocs/press/

Other/2004/20040426/default.htm. Accessed 7 June 2005.

"USAID Press Release 2002-051." *USAID Website*, 7 June 2002. www.usaid.gov/press/releases/2002/pr020607.html. Accessed 30 April 2005.

Wagner, Edward W. *The Korean Minority in Japan, 1904–1950.* New York: International Secretariat, Institute of Pacific Relations, 1951.

Weiner, Eric. "Tokyo Diarist: Pinball Wizards." *The New Republic*, 7 & 14 July 2003, 38.

"Welcome to De La Rue." *De La Rue Giori Homepage.* www.delarue.com/. Accessed 27 March 2005.

"What is a Superdollar?" *BBC News Online*, 19 June 2004. news.bbc.co.uk/1/hi/programmes/panorama/3819345.stm. Accessed 31 March 2005.

Woo, Seongji. *The Politics of Asymmetrical Triangles: Cooperation and Conflict in Northeast Asia.* Doctoral Thesis. Bloomington, IN: Indiana University, May 2001.

World Food Program. "World Hunger—Korea (DPR)." *United Nations Website.* www.wfp.org/country_brief/indexcountry.asp?country=408#. Accessed 30 April 2005.

Yamaguchi, Mari. "North Korea Plying Its Drugs in Japan." *Desert News,* 4 March 2003. www.mapinc.org/drugnews/v03/n356/a07.html. Accessed via *Media Awareness Project Website,* 29 January 2005.

Yi, Chong-hun. "Black Deal of South Korean Organized Criminals-Japanese Yakuza-North Korean Methamphetamine." (text). Seoul *News Plus* (9 June 1999). FBIS Document ID FTS19990213000908. Accessed 20 May 2005.

Yoshiharu, Asano. "N. Korea Missile Exports Earned 580 Mil. Dollars in '01." *Yomiuri Shimbun,* 13 May 2003. Accessed via LexisNexis Research Database, 15 March 2005.

Yun, Duk-Min. "Long-range Missiles." in *North Korea's Weapons of Mass Destruction: Problems and Prospects.* Ed. Kim Kyoung Soo, Elizabeth, NJ: Hollym, 2004, 121–148.

Yun, Yong-sin and others. "Can There Be Any Way We Can Benefit? (Issues With Hyundai Mt. Kumgang Tour)." (text). Seoul *Wolgan Choson* (May 1999). FBIS Document ID FTS19990524000587. Accessed 19 May 2005.

Ziegler, Jean. Special Rapporteur on the Right to Food. "The Right to Food." *United Nations Economic and Social Council Commission on Human Rights,* E/CN.4/2001/53, 7 February 2001.

"$2.2 Billion Flows Into NK Since 1996: Report." *Korea Times*, 16 November 2004. Accessed via LexisNexis Research Database, 1 April 2005.

"12.7 billion yen sent to North Korea over 3-year period." *Yomuiri Shimbun*, 28 June 2003. Accessed via LexisNexis Research Database, 25 March 2005.

"$27m Counterfeit Gang Jailed." *BBC News Online*, July 2002. news. www.bbc.co.uk/1/low/england/2154474.stm. Accessed 31 March 2005.

Index

About the Author

Major Robert Daniel Wallace is a career military intelligence officer with over 18 years in the US Army, having participated in Operation Desert Shield/Desert Storm, three tours in South Korea, and variety of other intelligence-related assignments. He holds a BA in business/economics from Bethany College (Lindsborg, KS), an MA in political science from Kansas State University, and a MS in Strategic Intelligence from the Joint Military Intelligence College at the Defense Intelligence Agency in Washington, DC. Major Wallace currently lives and works in Seoul.

www.ingramcontent.com/pod-product-compliance
Lightning Source LLC
Chambersburg PA
CBHW020355270326
41926CB00007B/441